Ordnance Survey
THE COMPLETE
Road Atlas
IRELAND

I	DISTANCE CHART - CONVERSION TABLES
II	ROUTE PLANNER
III	MOTORING INFORMATION, REPUBLIC OF IRELAND
IV	MOTORING INFORMATION, NORTHERN IRELAND
V	TRAVEL INFORMATION
VI	LEGEND TO NATIONAL MAPS

1-70 NATIONAL MAPS

TOWN MAPS

71	DUBLIN	80	LIMERICK	86	DOWNPATRICK DUNDALK	92	PORTRUSH ROSSLARE HBR
73	BELFAST	81	WATERFORD	87	ENNISKILLEN KILLARNEY	93	SLIGO TRALEE
75	CORK	82	ARMAGH ATHLONE	88	LARNE LETTERKENNY	94	WESTPORT WEXFORD
77	LONDONDERRY	83	BALLYMENA BANGOR	89	LISBURN MULLINGAR		
78	GALWAY	84	CASHEL COLERAINE	90	NEWCASTLE NEWRY		
79	KILKENNY	85	CRAIGAVON-LURGAN CRAIGAVON-PORTADOWN	91	NEWTOWNARDS OMAGH.		

95	TOURIST OFFICES
97	GOLF INFORMATION
99	GAZETTEER

INDEX TO MAP PAGES - INSIDE FRONT COVER

Published in 1998 by
Ordnance Survey of Ireland,
Phoenix Park, Dublin 8.

© Ordnance Survey of Ireland.

Northern Ireland information supplied by
Ordnance Survey of Northern Ireland, Crown Copyright 1998

Printed by Ordnance Survey of Ireland, Phoenix Park, Dublin 8.

Distance Chart

Distances: Kilometres in black **(146)**, Miles in blue *(153)*

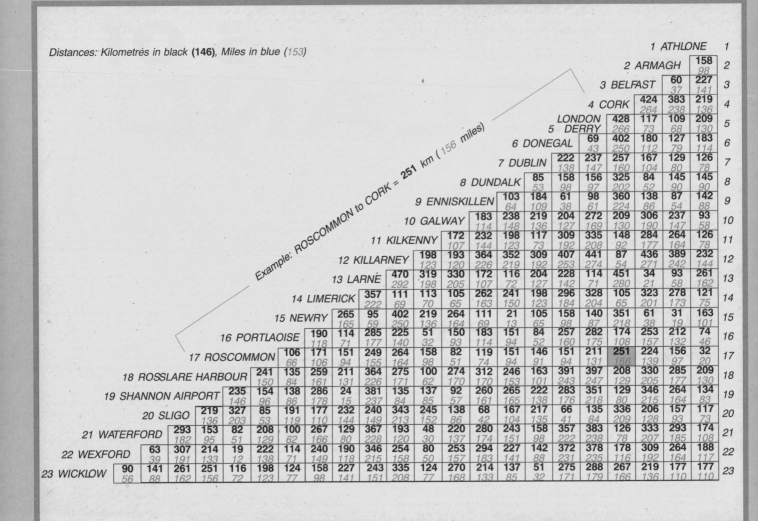

Example: ROSCOMMON to CORK = **251** km (*156* miles)

Conversion Tables

DISTANCES AND SPEED

1 Mile = 1.609344 Kms

1 Kilometre = 0.621371 Miles

1 Yard = 91.4 Cms

1 Foot = 30.5 Cms

1 Inch = 2.5 Cms

WEIGHTS

1 Pound = 0.45 Kilogrammes

1 Kilogramme = 2.20 Pounds

VOLUMES

0.5 Pint = 0.28 Litre

1 Pint = .57 Litre

1 Litre = 0.22 Gallon

PRESSURE

Pounds per sq. inch
to
kgs. per sq. cm.

ppi	kpc
26	1.83
28	1.96
30	2.10
32	2.24
36	2.52
40	2.80

TEMPERATURE

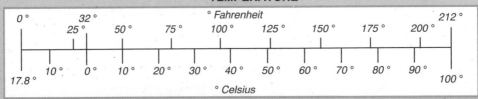

ROUTE PLANNER

MOTORING INFORMATION
REPUBLIC OF IRELAND

DRIVING IS ON THE LEFT THROUGHOUT IRELAND.
SEAT BELTS must be worn by drivers and passengers.
CRASH HELMETS must be worn by motorcyclists and pillion passengers.

WARNING SIGNS

The following are examples of the principal signs.

TWO-WAY TRAFFIC

Dangerous Corner or Bend Ahead — Series of Dangerous Corners or Bends Ahead — Slippery Stretch of Road Ahead — Sharp Rise Ahead — Sharp Depression Ahead — Series of Bumps or Hollows Ahead

Junction Ahead With Road or Roads of Equal Importance. — Steep Ascent Ahead — Steep Descent Ahead — Road Narrows Dangerously — Roundabout Ahead

Junction Ahead With Roads of Less Importance. (minor roads shown by thin arms) — Unprotected Quay, Canal or River — Road Works Ahead — Children Sign (School etc.) — Traffic Lights Ahead

With Roads of Equal Importance — Junctions Ahead With Roads of Less Importance — Advanced Warning of a Major Road Ahead — 12' 6" Low Bridge Ahead — Level Crossing Ahead guarded by gates. — Level Crossing Ahead Unguarded. — End of Dual Carriageway.

EMERGENCIES

☎ **999 / 112**

Police
Ambulance
Fire Brigade
Life Boat
Coastal Rescue

REGULATORY SIGNS

These signs implement road regulations and show the course to follow etc.

 STOP

Traffic must proceed in the direction of the arrow.

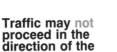

Keep to Left Carriageway

Traffic may not proceed in the direction of the arrow.

Parking

 Parking Permitted

  Clearway Stopping or Parking Prohibited (except Buses and Taxis)

  Parking Prohibited

  TAXI RANK Parking for taxis only.

Give Way

 YIELD RIGHT OF WAY

SPEED LIMITS

MOTORWAY 70 mph/112 kph.

NATIONAL LIMIT 60 mph/96 kph

OTHER LIMITS MAY APPLY IN TOWNS, BUILT-UP AREAS AND SOME ROADS AS INDICATED.

30   40   End of Speed Limit

INFORMATION SIGNS

These signs will give information regarding direction, distance, place etc.
Amenities of particular interest to tourists are displayed in white on a brown background.

↑ Loch Garman N11 WEXFORD
← Bré BRAY

 ↑ N11 / N7
← N81

◄ 2 Bré BRAY
N4 →
← N11

Cearnóg Mhuirfean Merrion Square 2

 Motorway ahead
NO L-drivers, Vehicles under 50 c.c., Slow vehicles (under 30 mph) Invalid-carriages, Pedal-cycles, Pedestrians, Animals
Motorway ahead

 M50 Entry to Motorway

 Motorway Regulations no longer apply

500m Approaching end of Motorway

← An Nás NAAS

 4 km   2 km

 ℹ Eolas do Thurasóirí TOURIST INFORMATION

 ◄ Slí na Bóinne BOYNE DRIVE

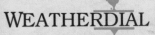

CONTROL ZONES

Cities and towns in Northern Ireland may have special parking and security restrictions in some areas - Control Zones - details of which are posted locally.

Control Zone — NO VEHICLE TO BE LEFT UNATTENDED at any time

WARNING SIGNS

 Traffic merges from right

 Cross roads

 Side road

 T junction

 Staggered junction

 GIVE WAY 50 yds — Distance to "Give Way" line ahead

 School — Children going to or from school

 Road narrows on both sides

 Dual carriageway ends

 REDUCE SPEED NOW — Plate below some signs

 Sharp deviation of route to left (or right if chevrons reversed)

 Double bend first to left (may be reversed)

 Slippery road

 Two-way traffic straight ahead

 Two-way traffic crosses one-way road

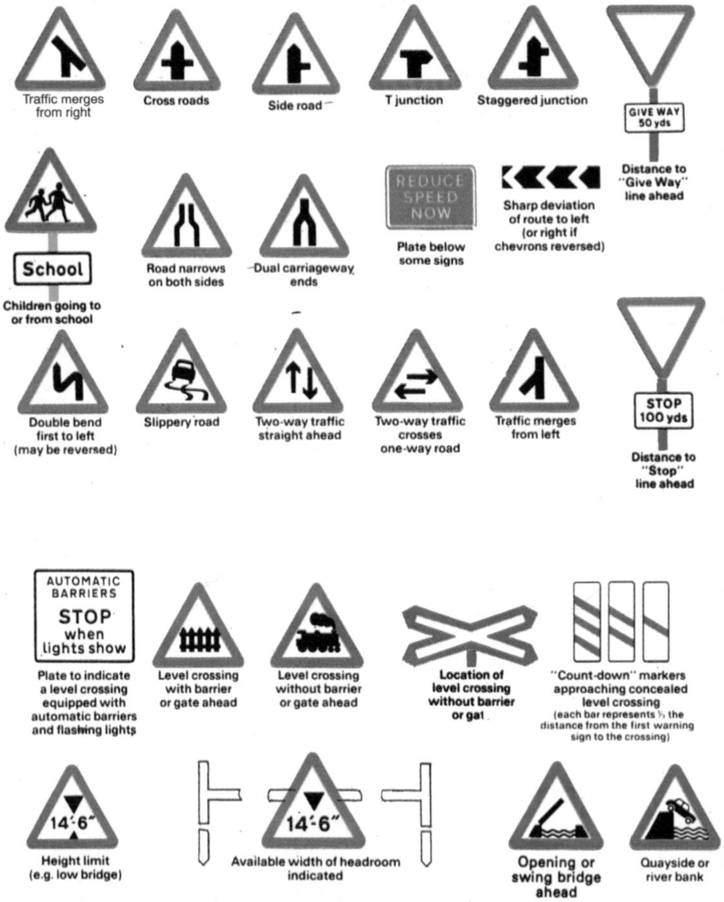

Traffic merges from left

 STOP 100 yds — Distance to "Stop" line ahead

 AUTOMATIC BARRIERS STOP when lights show — Plate to indicate a level crossing equipped with automatic barriers and flashing lights

 Level crossing with barrier or gate ahead

 Level crossing without barrier or gate ahead

Location of level crossing without barrier or gate

"Count-down" markers approaching concealed level crossing (each bar represents ⅓ the distance from the first warning sign to the crossing)

 14'6" — Height limit (e.g. low bridge)

 14'6" — Available width of headroom indicated

 Opening or swing bridge ahead

 Quayside or river bank

These signs are mostly circular and those with red circles are mostly prohibitive

 40 Maximum speed

 National speed limit applies

 STOP — Stop and Give Way

 GIVE WAY — Give way to traffic on major road

 STOP CHILDREN — School crossing patrol

STOP POLICE

No entry for vehicular traffic

 No right turn

 No left turn

 No U turns

No overtaking

No vehicles

No stopping (Clearway)

 Give priority to vehicles from opposite direction

 URBAN CLEARWAY — No stopping during times shown except for up to 2 mins. to set down or pick up passengers

Signs with blue circles but no red border are mostly compulsory

Ahead only

 Turn left ahead (right if symbol reversed)

 Turn left (right if symbol reversed)

Keep left (right if symbol reversed)

Vehicles may pass either side to reach same destination

Route to be used by pedal cyclists only

30 Minimum speed

End of minimum speed

Mini-roundabout (roundabout circulation — give way to vehicles from the immediate right)

One-way traffic (Note compare circular "Ahead only" sign)

DIRECTION SIGNS

Signs on motorways — *Blue backgrounds*

 M1 — Start of motorway

 Belfast M2 / Ballyclare Larne Templepatrick A 57 — On approaches to junctions (junction number on black background)

 M2 Belfast 14 (Larne 17) — Route confirmatory sign after junction

 End of motorway

 Belfast M1 — At the junction

 Carrickfergus Greencastle / Belfast M2 — Downward pointing arrows mean "Get in lane"

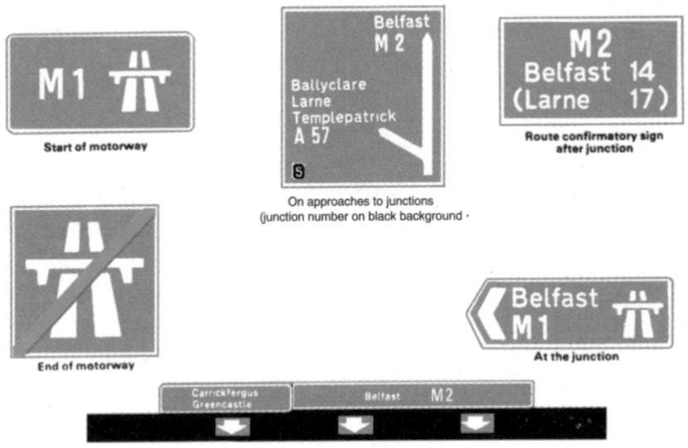

DIRECTION SIGNS

Signs on primary routes
Green backgrounds

 A 1 — Belfast 24, Dromore 7, Lisburn 16 — Route confirmatory sign after junction

 (A 46) Route confirmatory sign after junction

 R — Ring Road

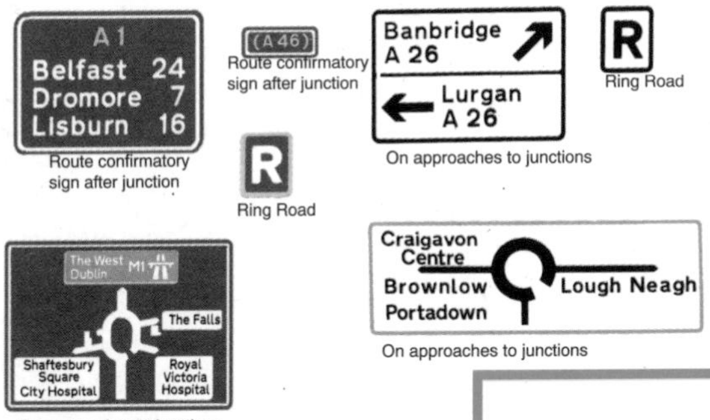

Signs on non-primary routes
Black borders

 Banbridge A 26 / Lurgan A 26 — On approaches to junctions

 R — Ring Road

 The West Dublin M1 / The Falls / Shaftesbury Square City Hospital / Royal Victoria Hospital — On approaches to junctions (The blue panel indicates that the motorway commences from the junction ahead. The motorway shown in brackets can also be reached by proceeding in that direction.)

Craigavon Centre / Brownlow / Portadown / Lough Neagh — On approaches to junctions

ROAD INFORMATIOM

AA ROAD WATCH   0336 401 118
Calls charged at 36p per minute cheap rate
48p per minute at other times.

MOTORING ORGANIZATIONS
GENERAL ENQUIRIES
AA   (01232) 328924
RAC   (01232) 232640

WEATHER INFORMATION

WEATHERCALL   0891 500 427

MARINECALL   0891 500 465
calls charged at 36p per minute cheap rate
48p per minute at other times.

INFORMATION SIGNS

 ONE WAY — One-way street

 Priority over vehicles from opposite direction

 No through road

 H Hospital — Hospital ahead

 P — Parking place; plate may indicate any restrictions on use

 Forton Services — Direction to service area with fuel, parking, cafeteria and restaurant facilities

 "Count-down" markers at exit from motorway (each bar represents 100 yards to the exit) Green-backed markers may be used on primary routes

Other direction signs

 Appropriate traffic lanes at junction ahead

 Mount Stewart

 300yds

 Zoo

 300yds

TRAVEL INFORMATION REPUBLIC OF IRELAND

BUS

Bus Atha Cliath - Dublin Bus	(01) 8734222
Bus Eireann - Irish Bus	(01) 8366111
ATHLONE	(0902) 73322
BALLINA	(096) 71800
BALLYSHANNON	(072) 51101
CAVAN	(049) 31353
CORK	(021) 508188
DROGHEDA	(041) 35023
DUBLIN	(01) 8366111
DUNDALK	(042) 34075
ENNIS	(065) 24177
GALWAY	(091) 562000
KILLARNEY	(064) 34777
LETTERKENNY	(074) 21309
LIMERICK	(061) 313333
LONGFORD	(043) 45208
MONAGHAN	(047) 82377
ROSSLARE HARBOUR	(053) 33114
SLIGO	(071) 60066
STRANORLAR	(074) 31089
TRALEE	(066) 23566
WATERFORD	(051) 790000

RAIL

IARNROD EIREANN	(01) 8366222

IRISH RAIL (including DART surburban rail).

AIR

Arrivals and departures enquiries (same day only)

DUBLIN AIRPORT	(01) 705 6705
CORK AIRPORT	
(0715- 2300 hours)	(021) 313131
(2300- 0700 hours)	(021) 313288
SHANNON AIRPORT	(061) 471444
	(061) 471666
CONNAUGHT INT. AIRPORT	(094) 67222
DONEGAL AIRPORT	(075) 48284/232
KERRY AIRPORT	(066) 64350
SLIGO AIRPORT	(071) 68280
WATERFORD AIRPORT	(051) 75589

SEA

STENA SEALINK		
	DUBLIN	(01) 2047777
	DUN LAOGHAIRE	(01) 2047700
	ROSSLARE	(053) 33115
	CORK	(021) 272965
	LIMERICK	(061) 316259
IRISH FERRIES		
	DUBLIN	(01) 6610511
	ROSSLARE	(053) 33158
	CORK	(021) 551995
BRITTANY FERRIES, CORK		(021) 277801
SWANSEA / CORK FERRIES		(021) 271166
ISLE OF MAN STEAM PACKET COMPANY		
		(01) 8741231

TRAVEL INFORMATION NORTHERN IRELAND

AIR

BELFAST INTERNATIONAL	(018494) 422888
BELFAST CITY	(01232) 457745
CITY OF DERRY	(01504) 810784
ENNISKILLEN AIRPORT	(01365) 322771

RAIL

NORTHERN IRELAND RAILWAYS	
	(01232) 899400

SEA

STENA LINE	(0990) 204204
P&O EUROPEAN FERRIES	(0990) 980777
SEACAT	(0345) 523523
NORSE IRISH FERRIES	(01232) 779090
ISLE OF MAN STEAM PACKET COMPANY	
	(0345) 523523
BELFAST FREIGHT FERRIES	(01232) 770112
ARGYLL and ANTRIM STEAM PACKET COMPANY	
	(0345) 523523

BUS

ULSTERBUS HOTLINE	(01232) 333000

OUTSIDE HOTLINE HOURS	
MON. - FRI.	0730 - 2030 hours
SATURDAY	0900 - 1800 hours
SUNDAY	0900 - 1930 hours

EUROPA BUS CENTRE	(01232) 320574
LAGANSIDE BUS CENTRE	(01232) 232356
CITYBUS	(01232) 246485

Eolas Turasóireachta Tourist Information
Information Touristique Touristeninformationen

Láithreán carbhán (idirthurais)
Caravan site (transit)
Terrain de camping (pour caravanes)
Campingplatz für Wohnwagen

 Ionad eolais turasóireachta
(ar oscailt ar feadh na bliana)
Tourist Information (regular opening)
Information Touristique
(ouverture régulière)
Touristeninformation
(regelmäßig geöffnet)
Northern Ireland

Láithreán campála
Camping site
Terrain de camping
Campingplatz

Ionad eolais turasóireachta
(ar oscailt le linn an tséasúir)
Tourist Information centre
(restricted opening)
Information Touristique
(ouverture limitée)
Touristeninformation
(beschränkte Öffnungszeiten)
Northern Ireland

Brú An Óige / Neamhspleách
Hostel An Óige / Independent
Auberge An Óige / Indépendant
Herberge An Óige / Unabhängig

Tearmann Dúlra
Nature Reserve
Réserve naturelle
Naturschutzgebiet

Ionad páirceála
Parking
Parking
Parkplatz

A T
An Taisce
National Trust
Société-pour la conservation
des sites et des monuments
Denkmale oder Landschaft unter
staatlicher Treuhand

Láithreán picnící
Picnic site
Éres de Pique-nique
Picknickplatz

National Trust
ar oscailtar feadh na bliana
National Trust always open
Propriété du National Trust
ouverte toute l'année
National Trust immer geöffnet

Teilefón Poiblí
Public Telephone
Cabine Téléphonique
Telefonzelle

N T
Northern Ireland
National Trust
ar oscailt le linn an tséasúir
National Trust opening restricted
Propriété du National Trust
ouverte en saison
National Trust nur während
der saison geöffnet

Ionad dearctha
Viewpoint
Point de vue
Aussichtspunkt

N T
Northern Ireland

Relíf Relief
Relief Relief

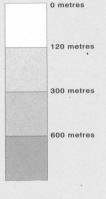
Altitudes in metres above Mean Sea Level
at Malin Head Co. Donegal

0 metres
120 metres
300 metres
600 metres

△ 647
Cuaille triantánachta
Triangulation Pillar
Pilier de Triangulation
Trigometrische Säule

123 •
Spota airde
Spot Height
Point Cuminant
Höhenpunkt

Bóithre Roads
Routes Straßen

M 1   1
Mótarbhealach
Motorway (Junction number)
Autoroute (Numero de l'échangeur)
Schnellstraße (Nummer der
Anschlussstelle)

N 11
A 2
Northern Ireland
Bóthar príoma náisiúnta
National Primary Road
Route nationale principale
Nationalstraße erster Ordnung

N 71
A 37
Northern Ireland
Bóthar tánaisteach náisiúnta
National Secondary Road
Route nationale secondaire
Nationalstraße zweiter Ordnung

Northern Ireland
Bóthar príoma / tánaisteach náisiúnta
beartaithe
Proposed Nat. Primary / Secondary Road
Route nationale principale / secondaire
projetée
Geplante Nationalstraße erster /
zweiter Ordnung

R 574
B 202
Northern Ireland
Bóthar Réigiúnach
Regional Road
Route Régionale
Landstraße

Bóthar den tríú grád
Third Class Road
Route de troisieme classe
Straße dritter Ordnung

In Northern Ireland roads are designated by the letter
A, B or M.
In the Republic of Ireland roads are designated by the
letter N, R or M.
The representation on these maps of a Road, Track or Path is
no evidence of a right of way.

Gnéithe ginearálta General features Traits généreaux Signaturen

Cathair / Baile mór
City / large town
Grande ville / ville
Großstadt / Stadt

Baile eile
Other towns
Autres villes
Andere Städte

✈ Aerfort
Airport
Aéroport
Flughafen

✈ Aerpháirc
Airfield
Champ d'aviation
Flugzeuglandeplatz

9   18
Galfchúrsa, machaire gailf
Golf Course or Links
Terrain de Golf
Golfplatz oder Golfbahnen

★ Garda Síochána
Police
Gendarmerie
Polizei

PO Oifig phoist
Post office
Bureau de Poste
Post

Crann teilifíse
T.V. Mast
Pylône de télévision
Fernsehmast

† Ardeaglais
Cathedral
Cathédrale
Kathedrale

○ Stáisiún cumhachta (uisce)
Power Station (Hydro)
Centrale électrique (hydraulique)
Kraftwerk (Wasser)

◉ Stáisiún cumhachta (breosla iontaiseach)
Power Station (Fossil)
Centrale électrique (fossile)
Kraftwerk (fossile Brennstoffe)

—+— Ferry V —+—
Bád fartha (feithiclí)
Ferry (Vehicle)
Ferry (véhicules)
Fähre (Fahrzeuge)

—+— Ferry P —+—
Bád fartha (paisinéirí)
Ferry (Passenger)
Ferry (Passager)
Fähre (Passagiere)

CH
Séadchomhartha Ainmnithe
Named Antiquities
Monuments mentionnes
Namentlich aufgeführte
Altetümer

✕
Láthair Chatha (le dáta)
Battlefield (with date) Champ
de bataille
(avec date)
Schlachtfeld (datiert)

Iarnróid Railways
Chemins de fer Bahnen

Iarnróid
Railways
Chemins de fer
Bahnlinie
Disused Railway

Stáisiún traenach
Station
Gare
Bahnhof

Tollán
Tunnel
Tunnel
Tunnel

LC
Crosaire comhréidh Level
Crossing
Passage á niveau
Bahnübergang

Teorainneacha Boundaries Frontières Grenzen

Teorainn idirnáisiúnta
International Boundary
Frontières internationales
Landesgrenze

Teorainn chontae
CountyBoundary
La Limite du Comté
Grafschaftsgrenze

Páirc Náisiúnta
National Park
Parc National
Nationaler Park

Páirc Foraoise
Forest Park
Parc Forestier
Waldpark

Gnéithe uiscí Water features
Traits aquatiques Gewasserzeichen

Loch
Lake
Lac
See

Canáil, canáil (thirim)
Canal, Canal (dry)
Canal, Canal à sec
Kanal, Kanalbecken (trocken)

Abhainn nó sruthán
River or Stream
Rivière ou Ruisseau
Fluß oder Bach

shingle,mud sand
or loose rock

Teach Solais in úsáid / as úsáid
Lighthouse in use / disuse
Phare que fonctionne / désaffecté
Leuchtturm benutzt / unbenutzt

Líne bharr láin
High Water Mark
Marque des hautes eaux
Hochwasserstand

Line lag trá
Low Water Mark
Marque des eaux basses
Niedrigwasserstand

Bádóireacht
Boating activities
Activités Nautiques
Bootssport

Trá
Beach
Plage
Strand

TORY ISLAND
TORAIGH

West Town
Baile Thiar

East Town
Baile Thoir

TORY SOUND

Ferry (P)

Inishbeg

Inishdooey

Inishbofin
Inis Bó Finne

BLOODY FORELAND
CNOC FOLA

R257

Meenlaragh
Mín Laragh

Meenaclady
Mín an Chladaigh

Brinlack
Bun na Leaca

GWEEDORE
Gaoth Dobhair

CL
Cloic

L Lagha

Inishsirrer

Inishmeane

Gola Island
Gabla

Gweedore
Bay

Derrybeg
Doirí Beaga

Tievealehid

Taobh an Leithid

431

The Stag Rocks

Inishinny

Inishfree
Lower

9

Bunbeg
An Bun Beag

R258

Owey Island

Uaigh

Inishfree
Bay

R257

N56

Cruit
Island

An Chruit

R266

Power Station Hydro

Gweedore
Gaoth Dobhair

Loch na C

Torneady Point

9

Kincaslough
Cionn Caslach

Annagary
Anagaire

Grogan More

Rosses Bay

ARAN
ISLAND

ARAINN MHÓR

Ferry

Crocknafarragh

Leabgarrow
An Leadhb Gharbh

BURTONPORT
Ailt an Chórráin

THE ROSSES
Na Rosa

Lough
Anure

A T

R260

L Meela

Rutland
Island

N56

Inishkeeragh

L Craghy

Lough
Croangar

Crocknahallin

Crockr

Inishfree Upper

R259

DUNGLOW
An Clochán Liath

Termon

Maghery
An Machaire

Crohy Head

L
Aleck
More

R252

OCEAN

ATLANTIC

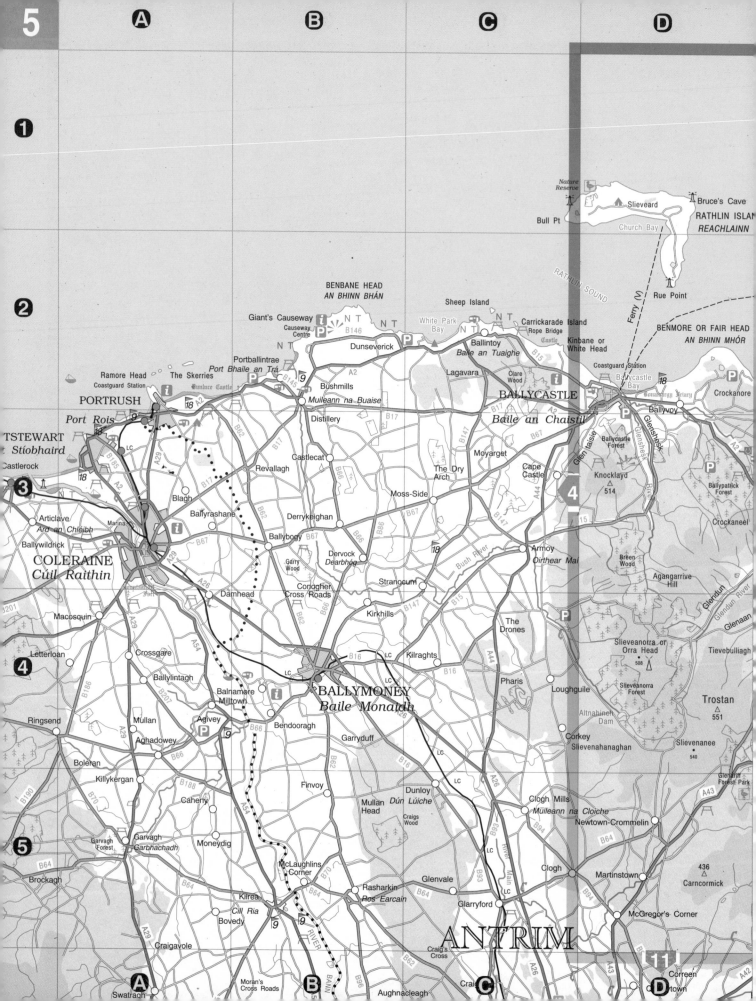

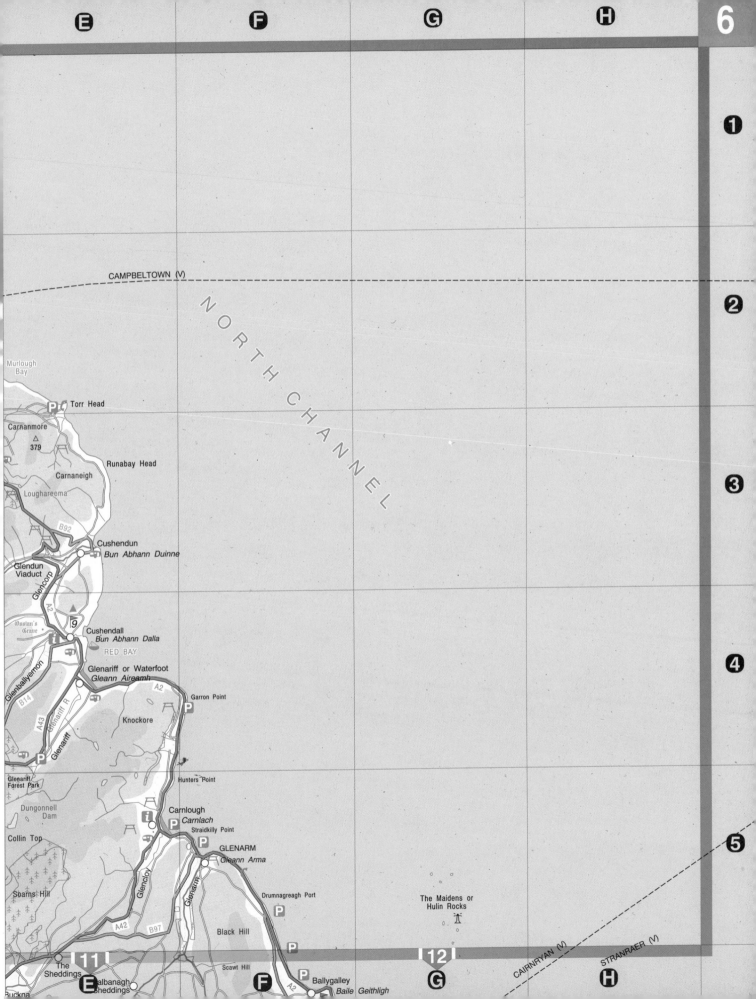

1

CAMPBELTOWN (V)

2

NORTH CHANNEL

Murlough Bay

Torr Head

Carnanmore

△ 379

Runabay Head

Carnaneigh

Loughareema

3

B92

Cushendun
Bun Abhann Duinne

Glendun Viaduct

Glencorp

A2

Ossian's Grave

9

Cushendall
Bun Abhann Dalla

RED BAY

Glenballyemon

Glenariff or Waterfoot
Gleann Aireamh

4

A2

B14

Garron Point

A43

Glenariff R

Knockore

Glenariff

Hunters Point

Glenariff Forest Park

Dungonnell Dam

Carnlough
Carnlach

Collin Top

Straidkilly Point

GLENARM
Gleann Arma

5

Glencloy

Glenarm

Soarns Hill

Drumnagreagh Port

The Maidens or
Hulin Rocks

A42

B97

Black Hill

CAIRNRYAN (V)

STRANRAER (V)

The Sheddings

Scawt Hill

Ballygalley
Baile Geithligh

Buckna

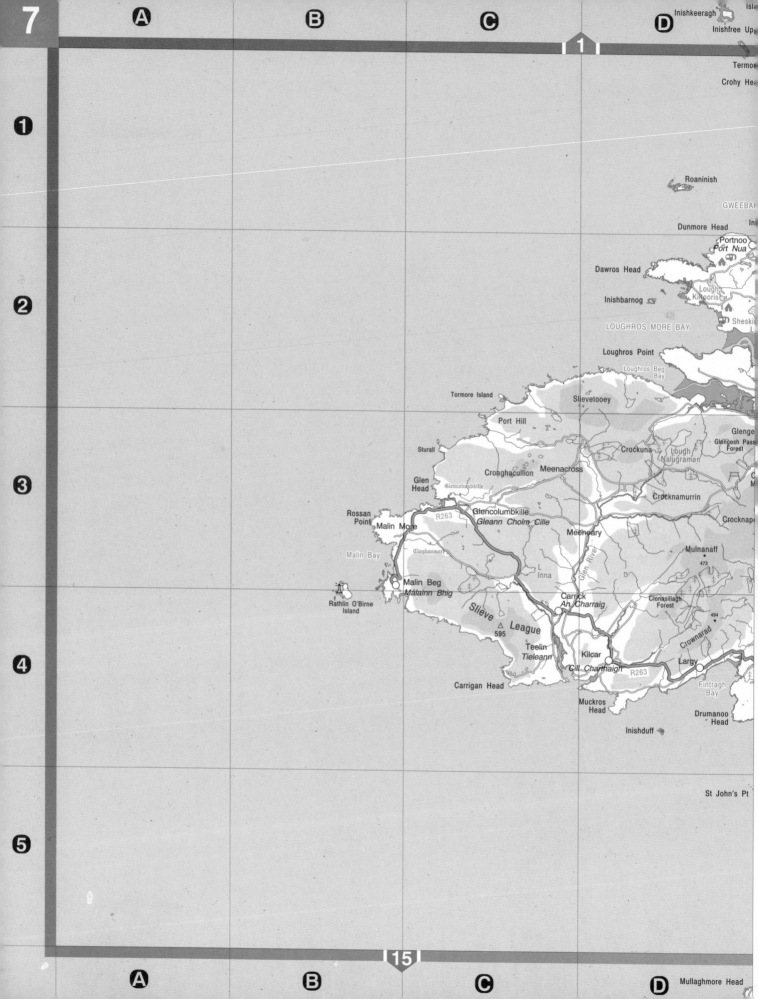

Ⓐ   Ⓑ   Ⓒ   Ⓓ Inishkeeragh

Isla

Inishfree Up

1

Termo

Crohy Hea

1

Roaninish

GWEEBAR

Dunmore Head   In

Portnoo
Port Nua

Dawros Head

Lough
Ki toori

2

Inishbarnog

Sheski

LOUGHROS MORE BAY

Loughros Point

Loughros Beg
Bay

Tormore Island

Slievetooey

Port Hill

Glenge

Glengesh Pass
Forest

Sturall

Crockuna

Lough
Nalugraman

Croaghacullion   Meenacross

Glen
Head   Glencolumbkille

Crocknamurrin

3

Rossan
Point   Glencolumbkille   Crocknap

Malin More   Gleann Cholm Cille

Meeneary

Malin Bay   Claghanmore

Mulnanaff

473

Malin Beg
Málainn Bhig

L
Inna

Glen River

Clonasillagh
Forest

Carrick
Ah Charraig

Rathlin O'Birne
Island   Slieve

League

595   494

Crownarad

Teelin
Tieleann

Kilcar
Cill Charthaigh

Largy

4

R263   Fintragh
Bay

Carrigan Head

Muckros
Head

Drumanoo
Head

Inishduff

St John's Pt

5

15

Ⓐ   Ⓑ   Ⓒ   Ⓓ Mullaghmore Head

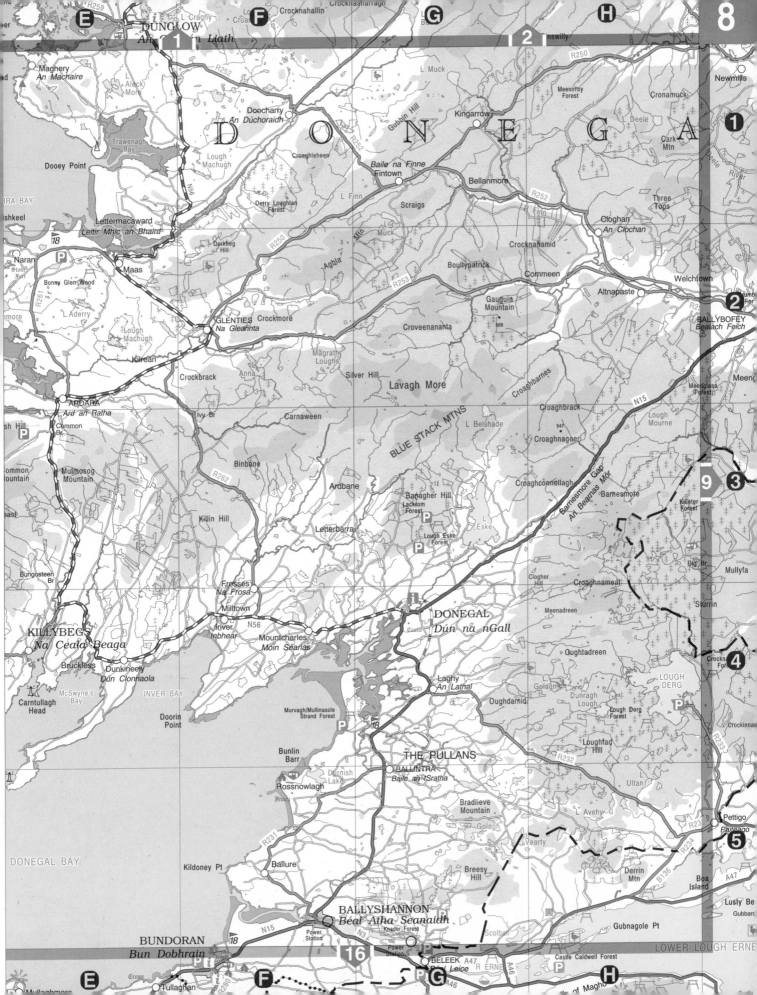

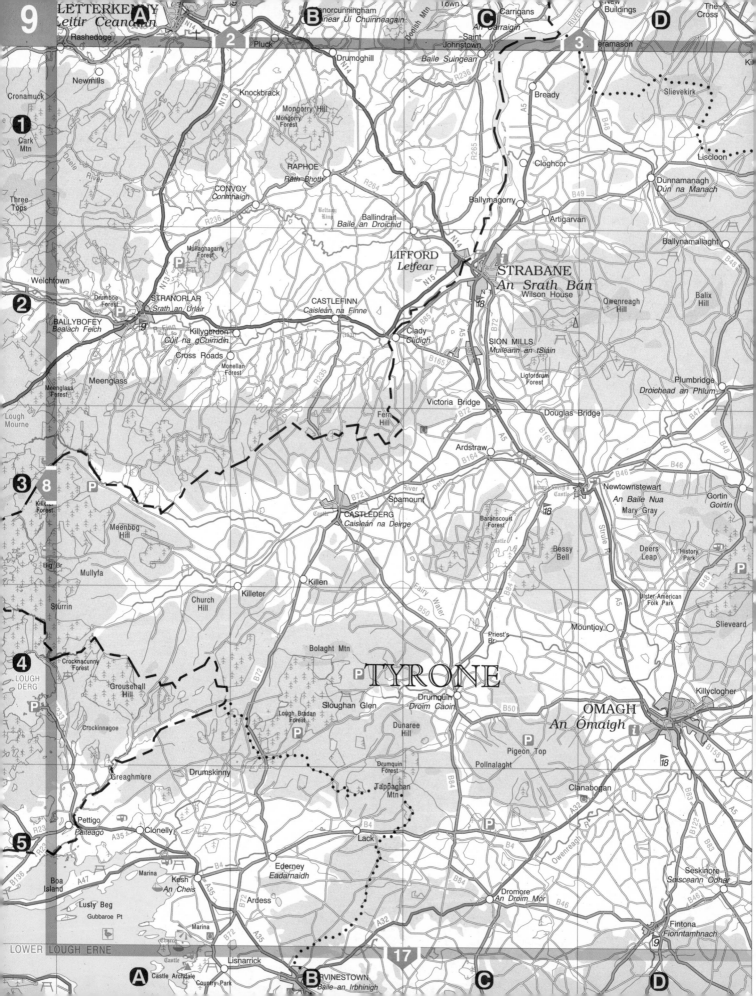

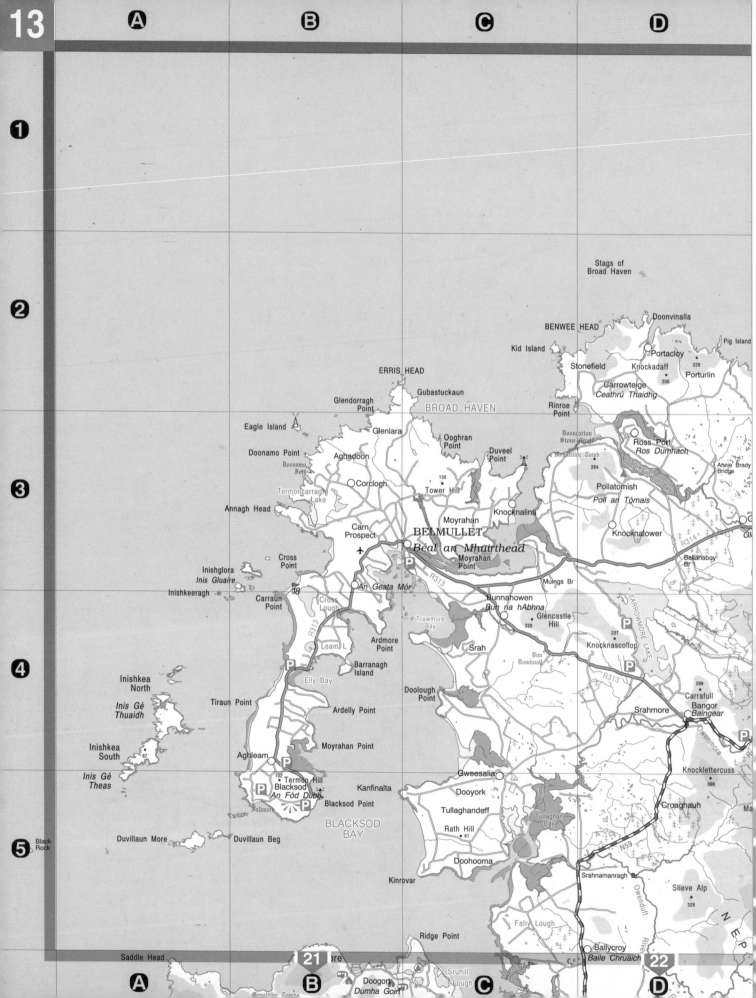

A   **B**   **C**   **D**

➊

➋

➌

➍

➎

Stags of
Broad Haven

BENWEE HEAD   Doonvinalla

Kid Island   Portacloy   Pig Island

Stonefield   Knockadaff   Porturlin
  229
  208

ERRIS HEAD   Carrowteige
   Ceathrú Thaidhg

Gubastuckaun   Rinroe
Point

Glendorragh   BROAD HAVEN   Dooncarton
Point   Stone Circle

Glenlara   Ross Port
     Ros Dumhach

Eagle Island   Ooghran
     Point   Meelthir Tomb   Annie Brady
     Duveel   Bridge

Doonamo Point   Aghadoon   Point   264
    Doonamo
    Fort   Pollatomish
     Poll an Tómais

130

Termoncarragh   Corclogh   Tower Hill
Lake   Knocknalina   Knocknalower

Annagh Head   Moyrahan   R314

Carn   BELMULLET
Prospect   Béal an Mhuirthead   Bellanaboy
     Moyrahan   Br
Cross   Point   **P**

Point   R313   Muings Br

Inishglora   An Geata Mór   CARROWMORE LAKE
Inis Gluaire   18   Bunnahowen
Inishkeeragh   Carraun   Cross   Bun na hAbhna
    Point   Lough   Glencastle   237
     Trawmore   Hill   Knocknascollop
     Bay   229   R313
   R313   Ardmore   Srah   **P**
   Leam L   Point   Dun
     Barranagh   Domhnall   269
P   Island   Carrafull
   Elly Bay   Doolough   Srahmore   Bangor
Inishkea   Point   Baingear
North   Tiraun Point   Ardelly Point   **P**
Inis Gé   Owenmore
Thuaidh   Moyrahan Point   Knocklettercuss
    Aghleam   Gweesalia   366
Inishkea   **P**   Dooyork   Croaghaun
South   102   Termon Hill
   67   Blacksod   Tullaghanduff
Inis Gé   **P**   An Fód Dubh   Kanfinalta
Theas   **P**   Blacksod Point   Rath Hill   Tullaghan
     Fallmore   61   Bay
Duvillaun More   BLACKSOD   Doohooma
   Duvillaun Beg   BAY   N59

Black   Kinrovar   Srahnamanragh Br
Rock   Slieve Alp
     328
     Owenduff
     River

Fahy Lough   Ridge Point   Ballycroy
     Baile Chruaich

Doogort
Dumha Goirt   Sruhill
Lough

A   **B**   **C**   **D**

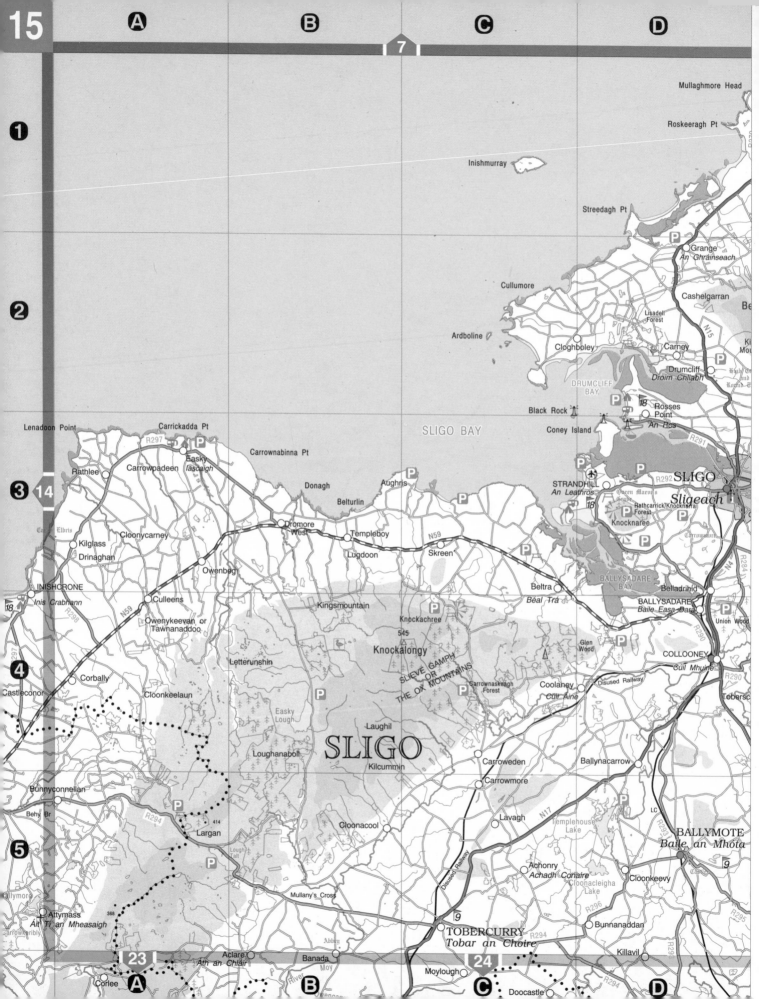

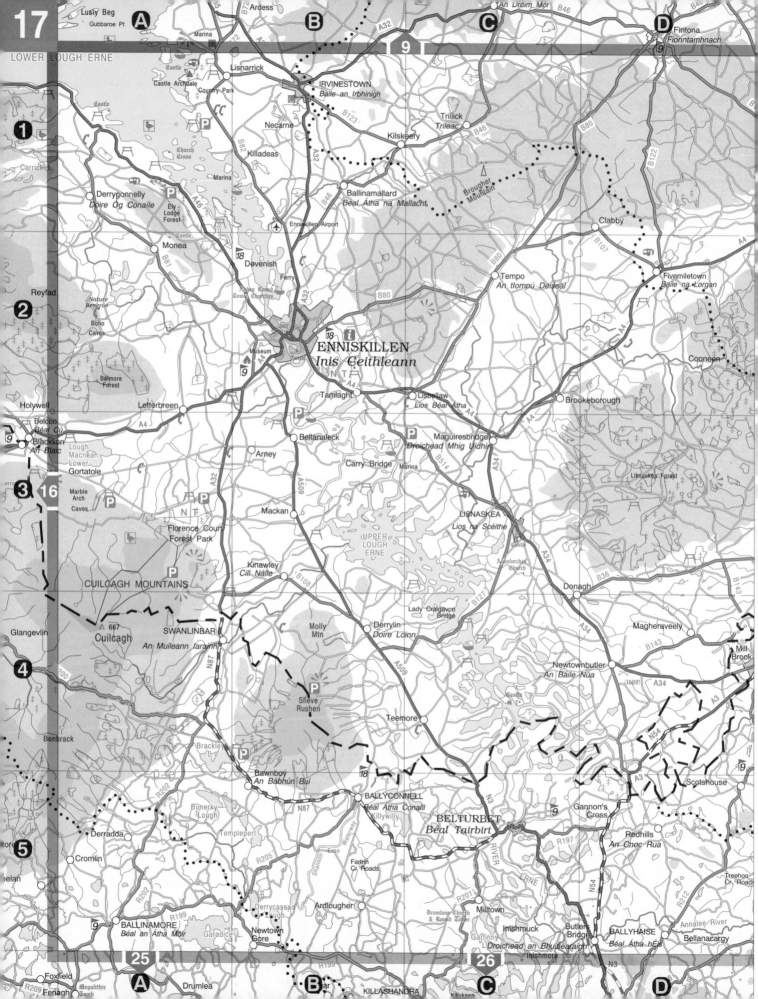

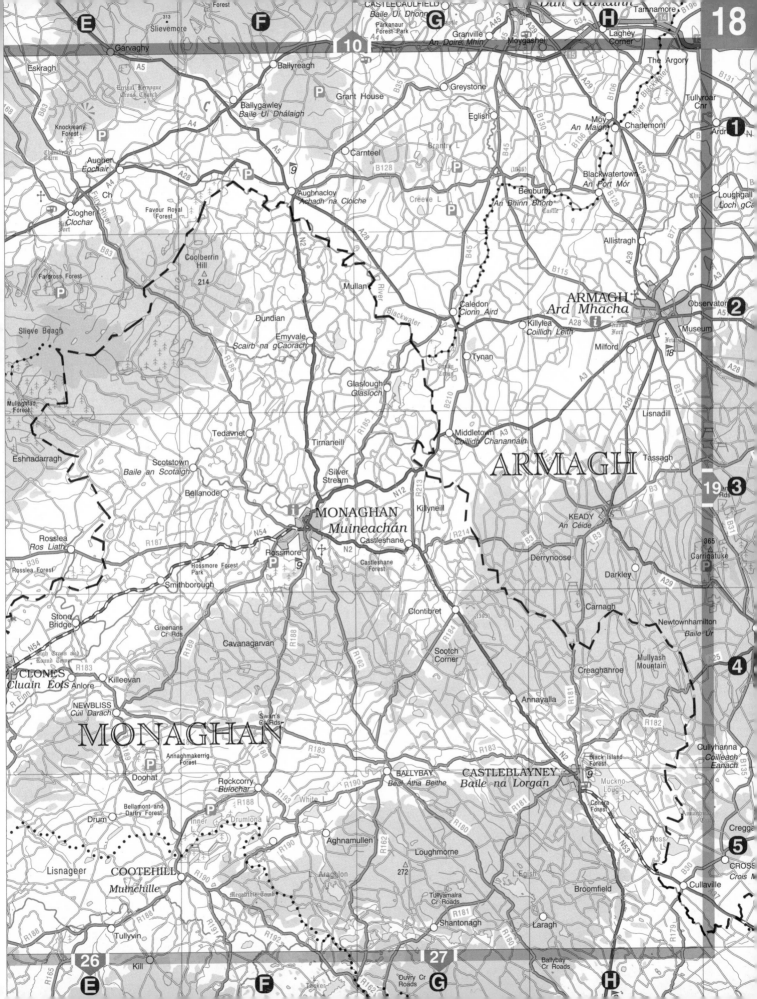

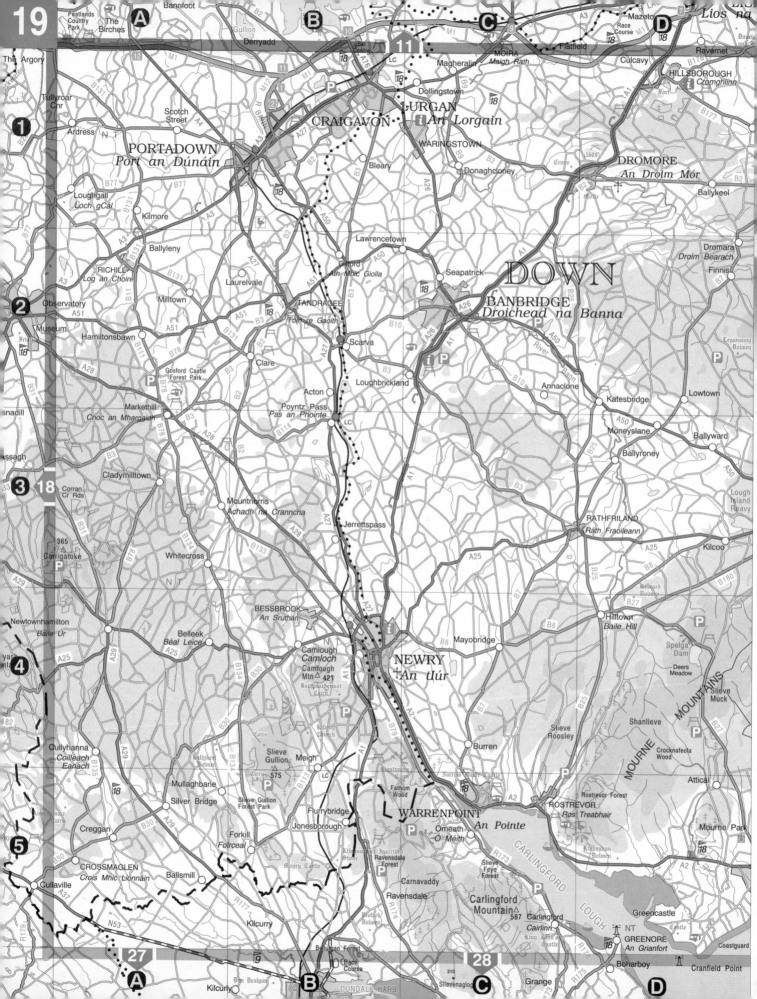

Sketrick Is
Killinchy
Cill Dhuinsí
Gransha Pt
Islandmore
Pawle Island
Ringburr Point
Island Taggart

E
The Temple
B6
Boardmills
Baileysmill
9
A49
Annahilt
A24
A21

F
SAINTFIELD
Tamhnaigh Naomh
Raffrey
Derryboy
B6

G
Cúastry
Rubane
Portavogie
Port an Bhogaigh
Kirkistown
Ardkeen
18
Cloghy
9

H
Motor Racing Circuit

1

BALLYNAHINCH
Baile na hInse
18
The Spa

Listooder
9
B7
Shrigley
KILLYLEAGH
Cill Ó Laoch
CROSSGAR
An Chrois Ghearr
Kilmore
A22
A7

Audley's Castle
Audleystown Cairn
Castleward Wood

PORTAFERRY
Port an Phéire
Kearney Point
Strangford
Baile Loch Cuan
Aquarium
Ferry (V)&(P)

532
Slieve Croob
Drumkeeragh Forest
Drumaness
Dróim an Easa
Annacloy
Loughinisland

Raholp
Balltculter
Museum
18
DOWNPATRICK
Dún Pádraig
Inch Abbey
Struell Wells

Nature Reserve
Kilclief
Ballyquintin Point
Bishops Court
Ballyhornan
Killard Point
Guns Island

2

Drumaroad
Slievegarran
A24
Seaforde
B175

Race Course
Ballynoe Stone Circle
A25

Chapeltown
Church

Leitrim
Castlewellan Forest Park
Annsborough
Baile Anna
CASTLEWELLAN
Caisleán Uidhilín
A50
A25

Clough
An Cloch
18
Ballykinler
Dundrum
Dún Droma
Baile Coinnleora
Tyrella
Minerstown
St John's Point
Church

Killough
Cill Locha
Ardglass
Ard Ghlais
18
Ringfad Point
Coastguard Station

3

Bryansford
Drumena Cashel
Tollymore Forest Park
B180
Maghera
Church Round Tower
18

NEWCASTLE
An Caisleán Nua

DUNDRUM BAY

4

Slieve Bearnagh
Slieve Commedagh
The Mourne Wall
850
Slieve Donard
Maggy's Leap
Slievelamagan
Reservoir
Bloody Bridge

Slieve Binnian
Annalong Wood
744
Reservoir

IRISH SEA

Marine Park
ANNALONG
Áth na Long
Ballinran
Ballymartin

5

Lee Stone Pt
Coastguard Station
KILKEEL
Cill Chaoil

E   F   G   H

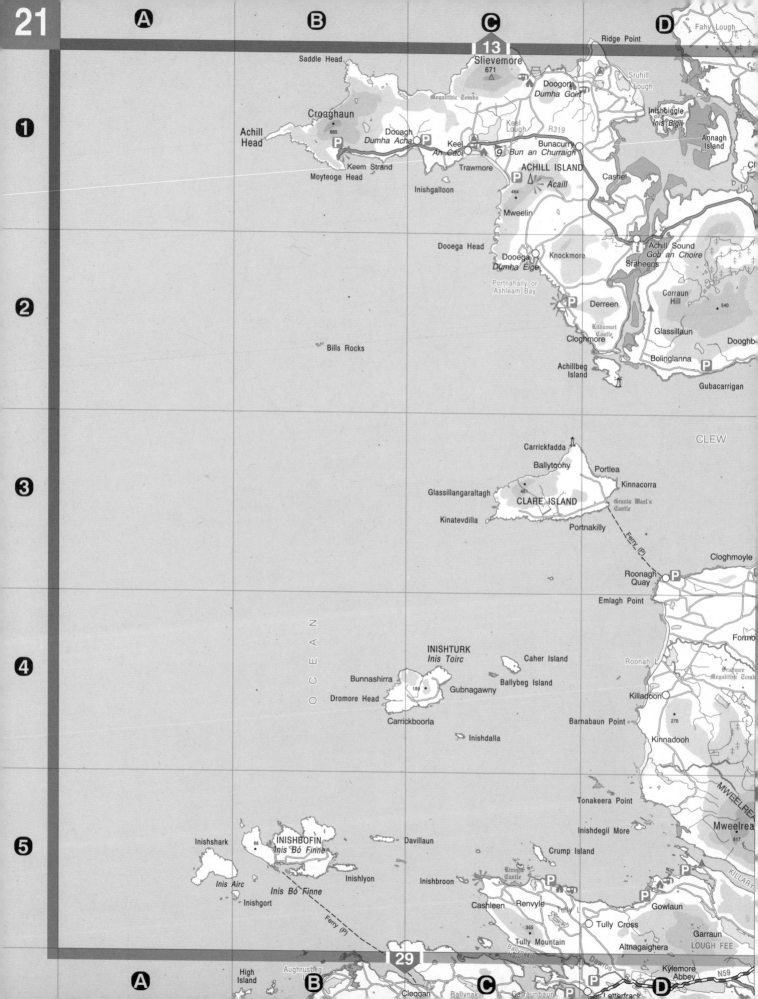

A   **B**   **C**   **D**

1

2

3

4

5

Ridge Point
Fahy Lough

Saddle Head

13
Slievemore
671

Doogort
Dumha Goirt

Sruhill
Lough

Inishbiggle
Inis Bigil

Megalithic Tombs

Croaghaun

665
Achill
Head

Dooagh
Dumha Acha

Keel
An Caol

Keem Strand
Moyteoge Head

Trawmore

Inishgalloon

Keel
Lough

R319

9 Bun an Churraigh
Bunacurry

ACHILL ISLAND

464

Acaill

Mweelin

Cashel

Annagh
Island

Dooega Head

Dooega
Dumha Éige

Knockmore

Achill Sound
Gob an Choire

Sraheens

Portnahally or
Ashleam Bay

Derreen

Corraun
Hill

540

Bills Rocks

Killdavnet
Castle

Cloghmore

Achillbeg
Island

Glassillaun

Bolinglanna

Dooghb

Gubacarrigan

Carrickfadda

Ballytoohy

Portlea

CLEW

Glassillangaraltagh

481

CLARE ISLAND

Kinnacorra

Grania Wael's
Castle

Kinatevdilla

Portnakilly

Cloghmoyle

Ferry (P)

Roonagh
Quay

Emlagh Point

Formo

Roonah L

O
C
E
A
N

INISHTURK
Inis Toirc

Caher Island

Bunnashirra

189

Ballybeg Island

Gubnagawny

Dromore Head

Killadoon

270

Barnabaun Point

Carrickboorla

Inishdalla

Kinnadooh

Tonakeera Point

Inishdegil More

Mweelrea

817

Inishshark

86

INISHBOFIN
Inis Bó Finne

Davillaun

Crump Island

KILLARY

Inis Airc

Inis Bó Finne

Inishlyon

Inishbroon

Rinvyle
Castle

Cashleen

Renvyle

Gowlaun

Inishgort

Ferry (P)

Tully Cross

Garraun

355

Tully Mountain

LOUGH FEE

Altnagaighera

High
Island

Aughrusbeg

29

Ballynakill
Harbour

Dawros

Kylemore
Abbey

N59

Cleggan

Ballynakill

Gerraunbaun

Letterfrack

A   **B**   **C**   **D**

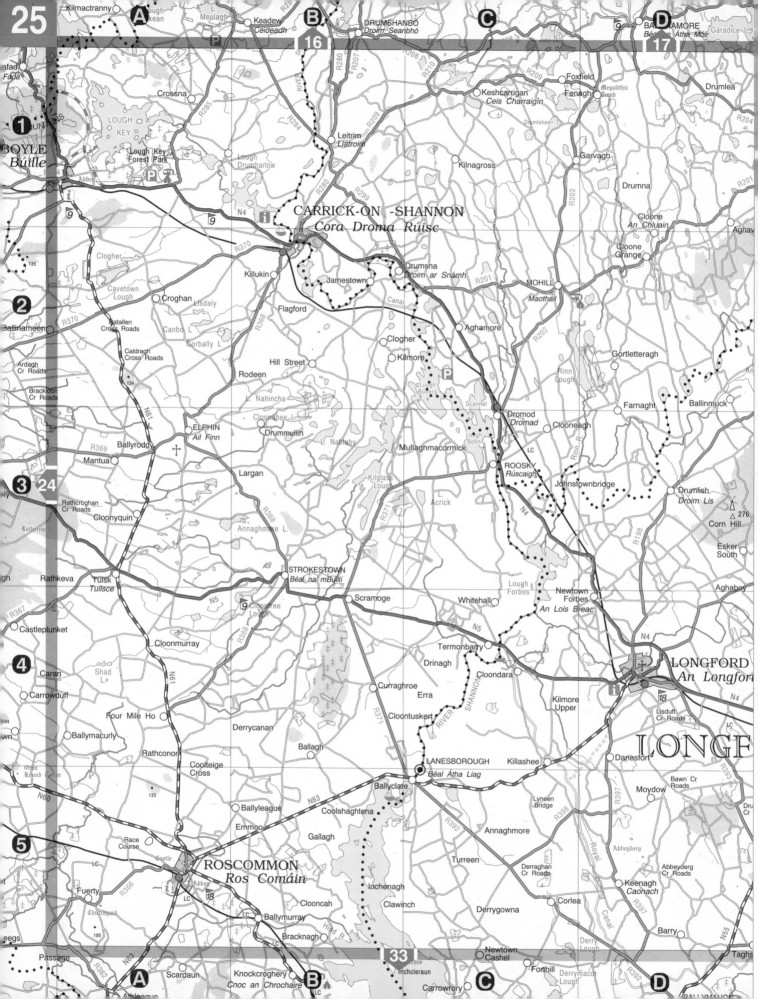

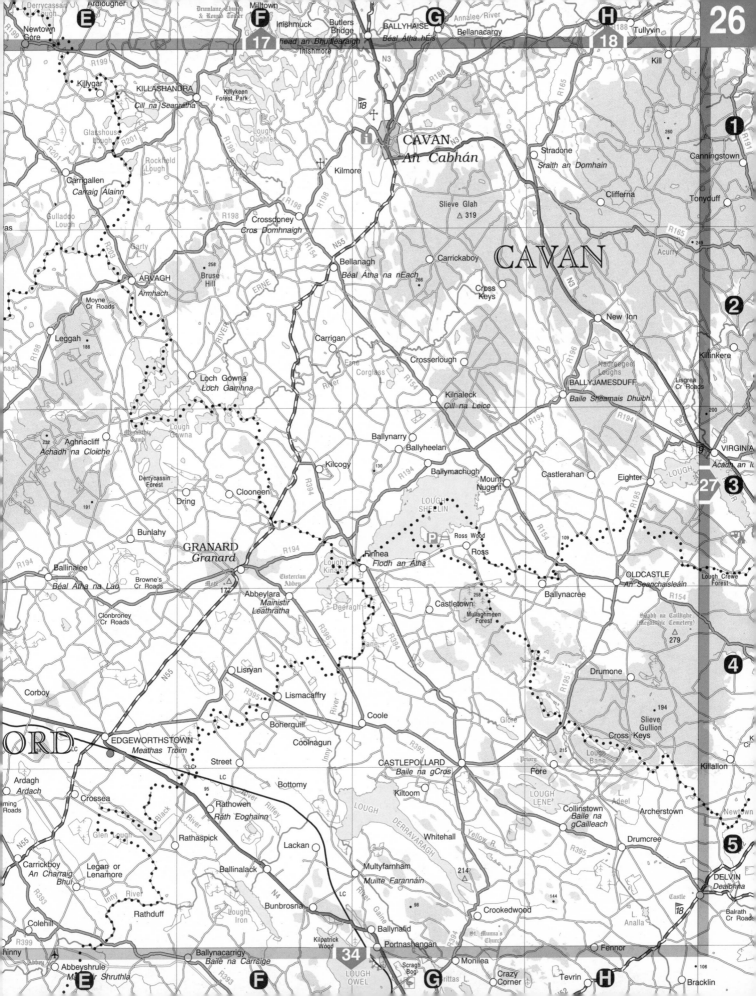

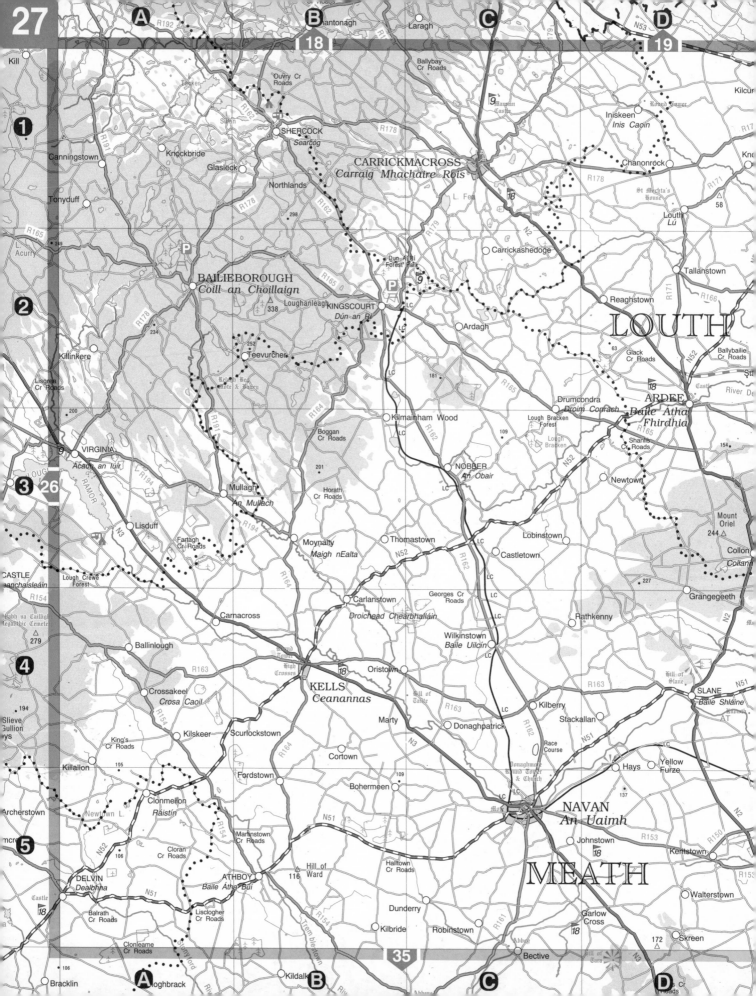

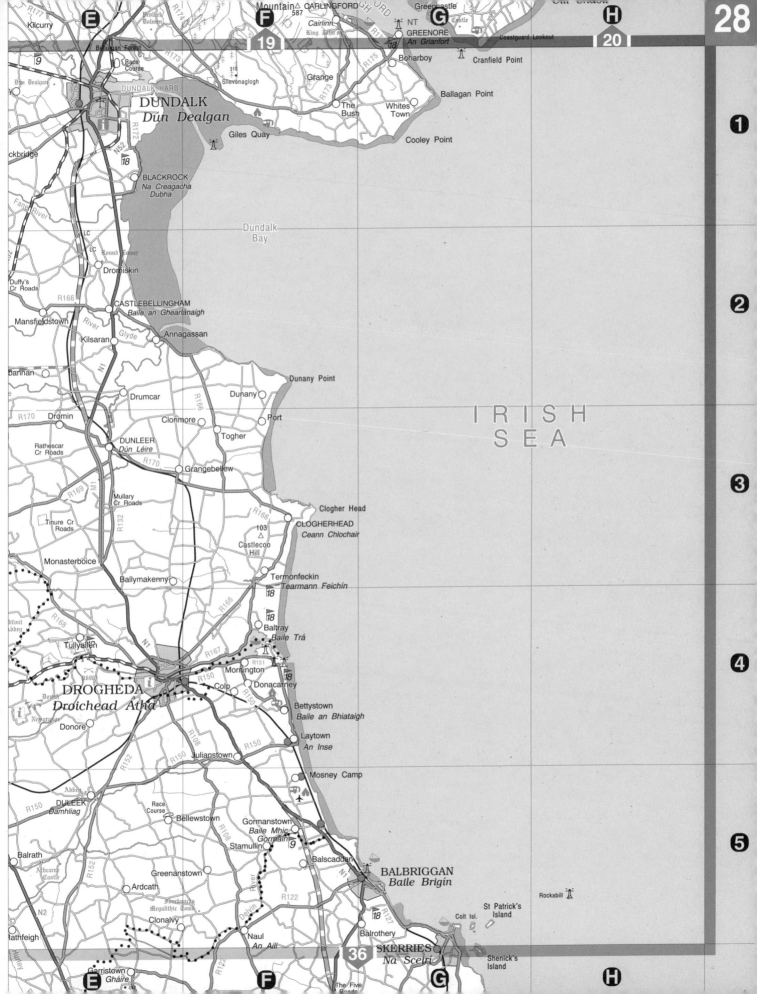

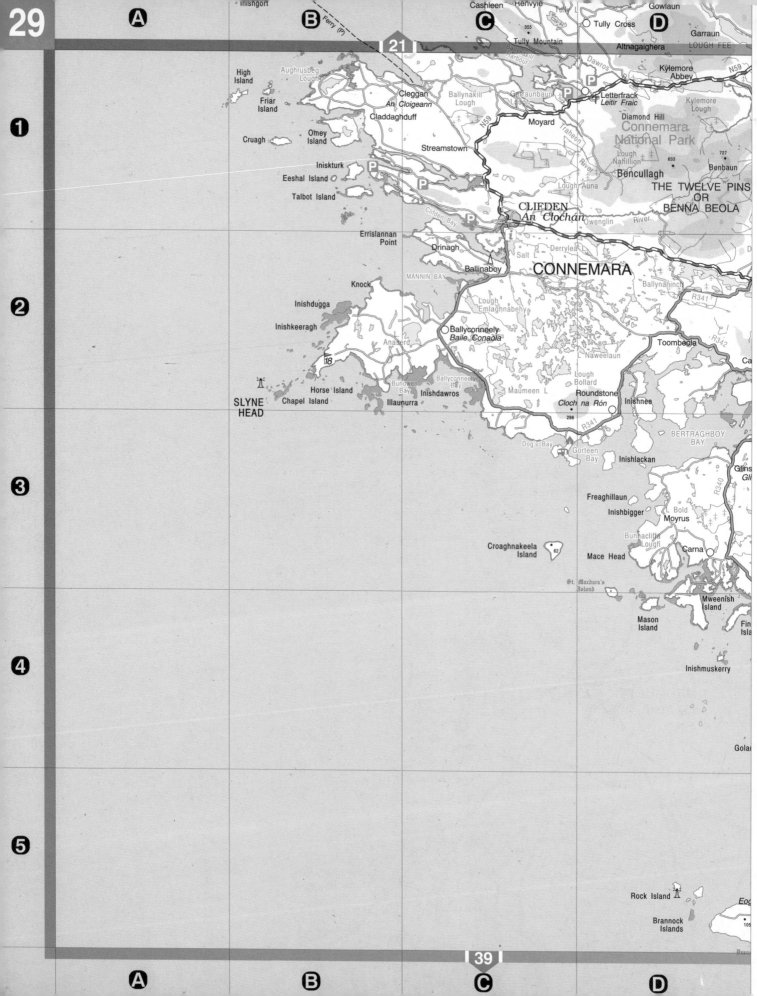

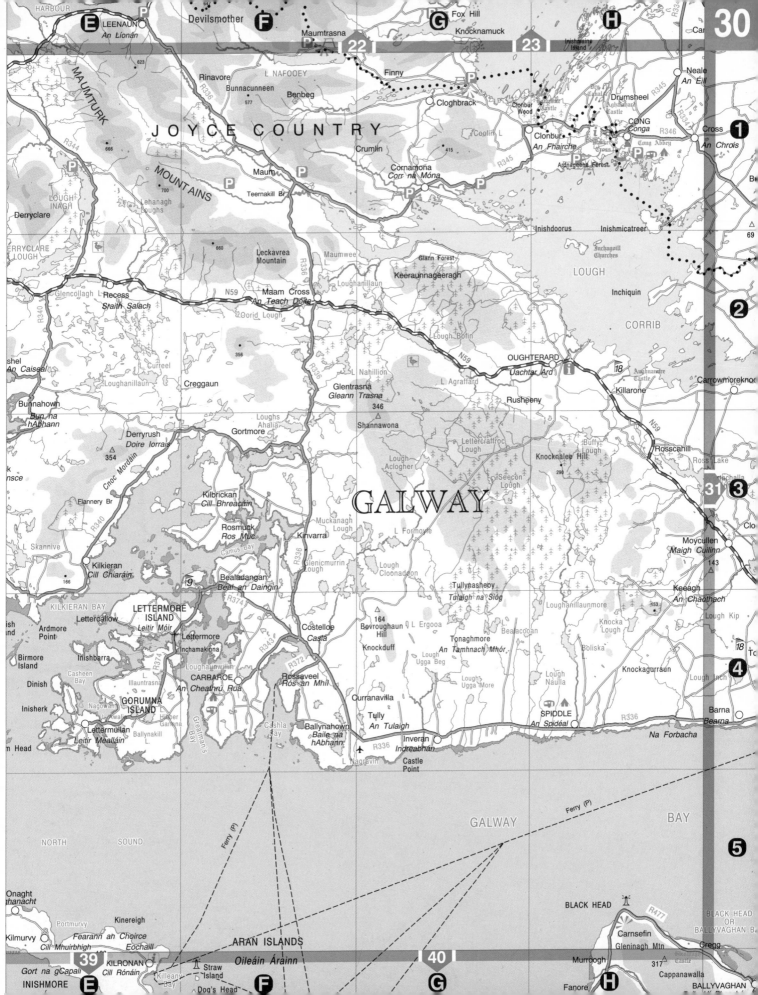

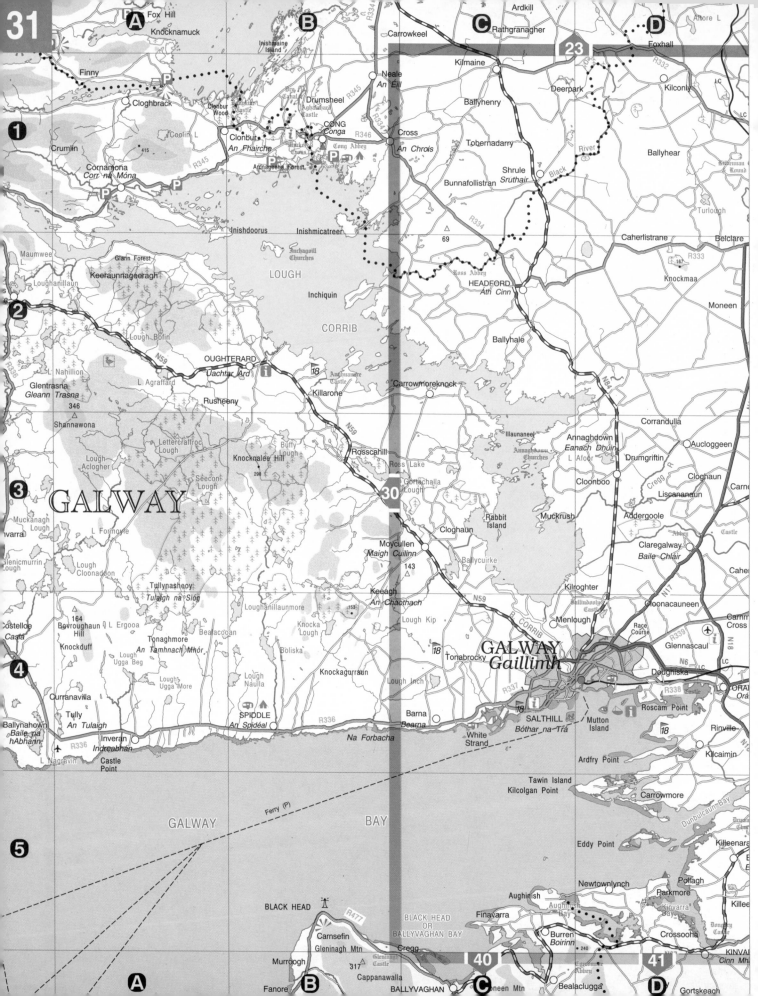

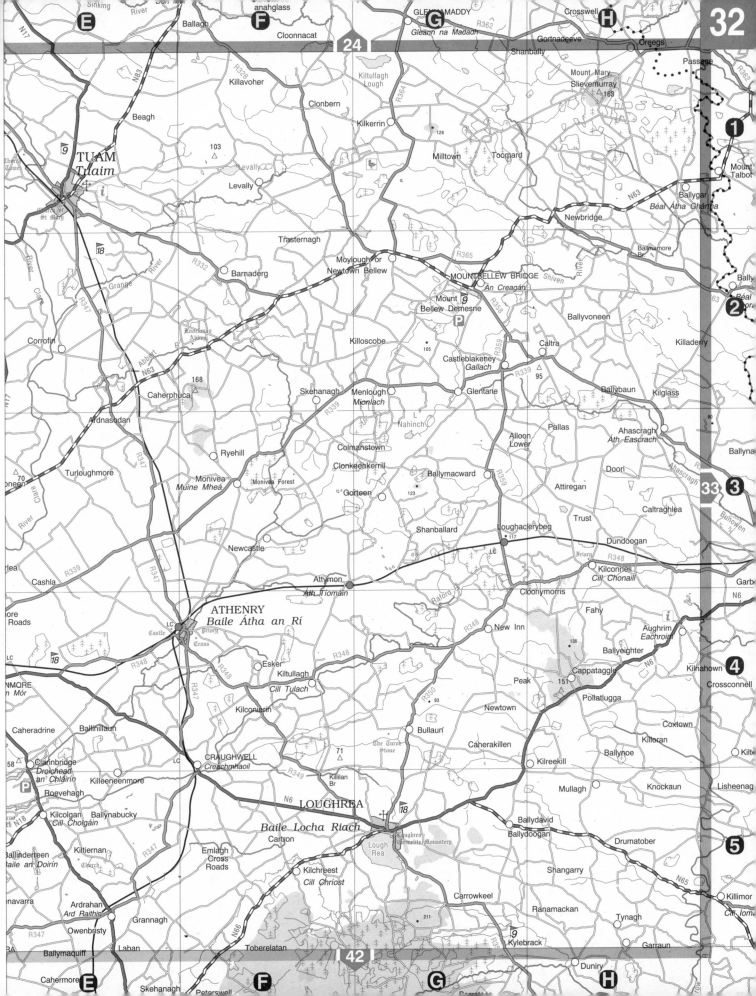

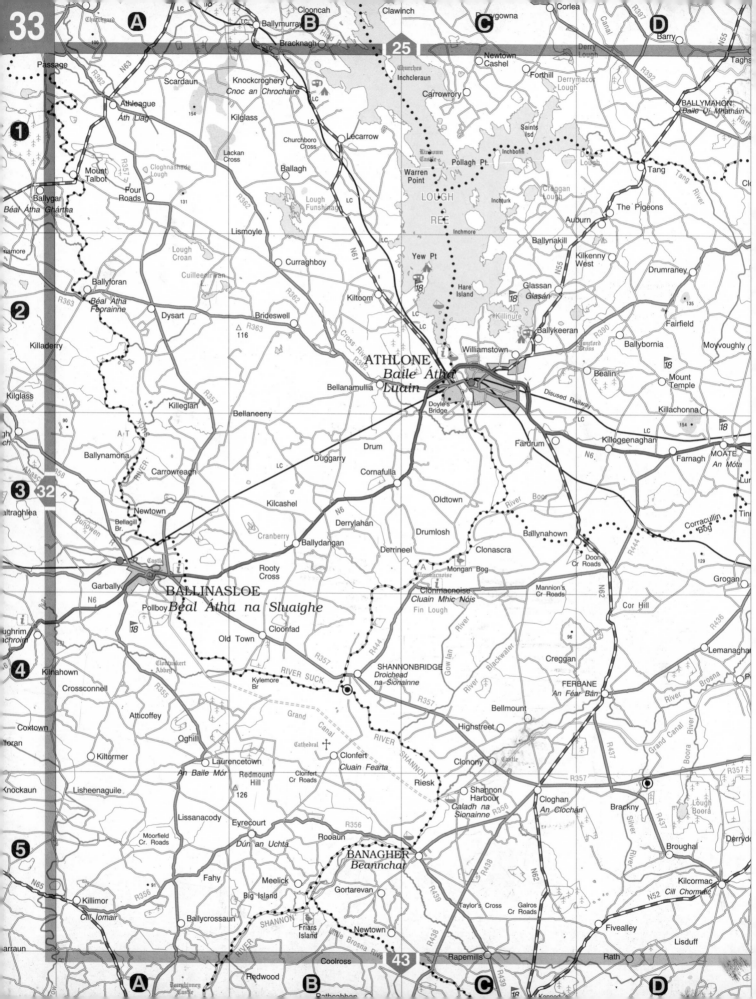

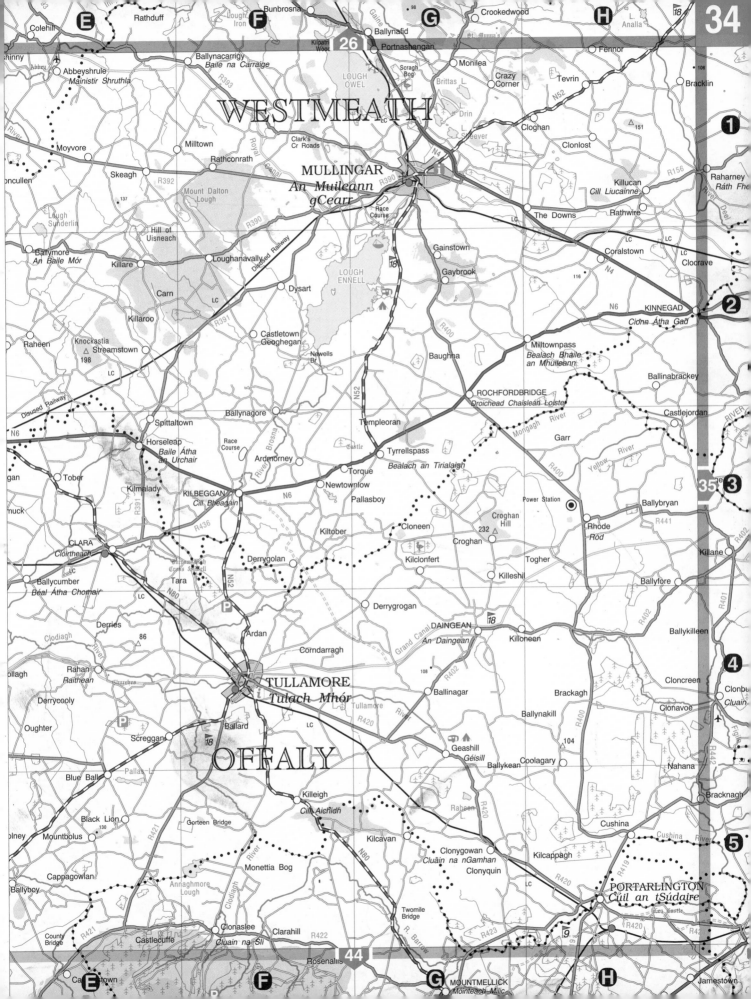

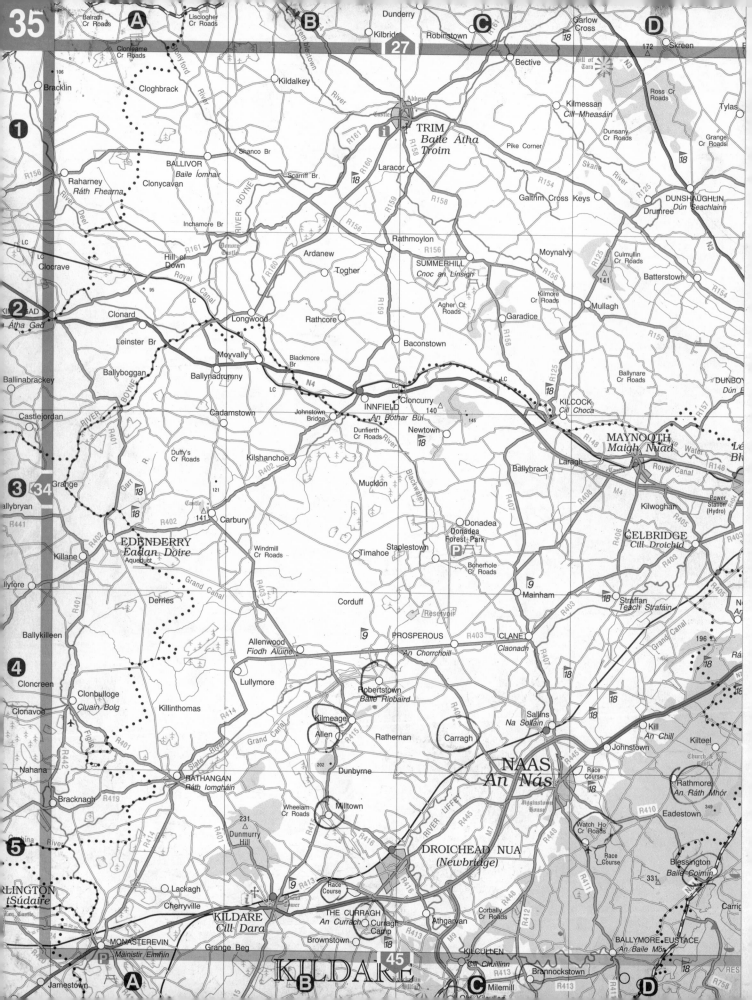

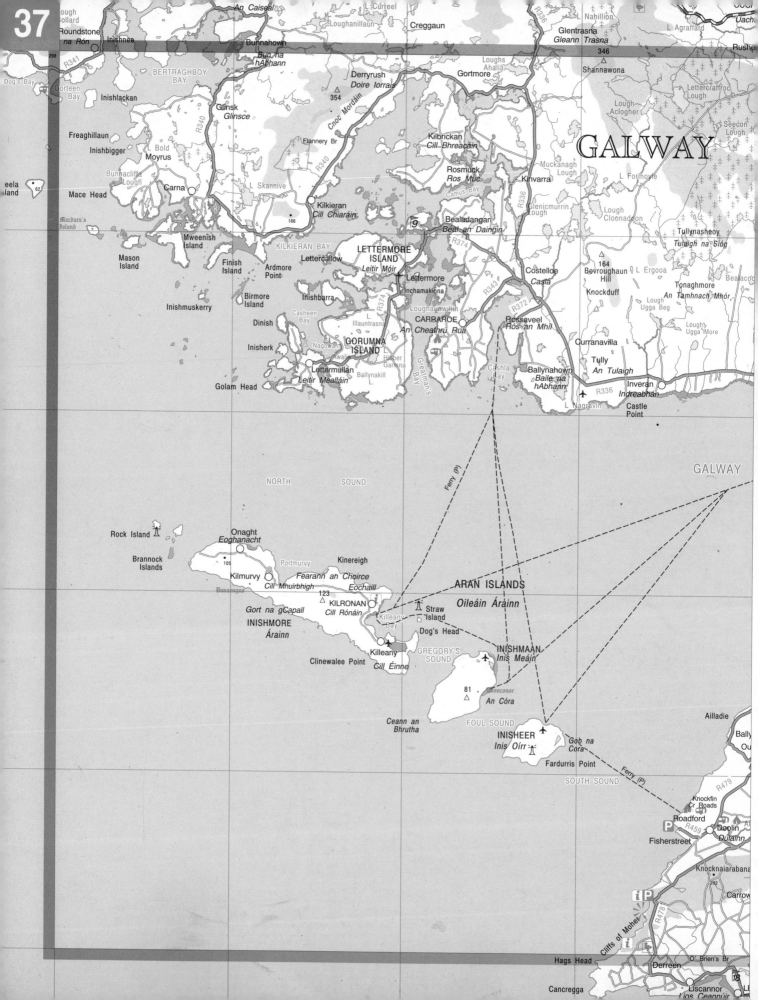

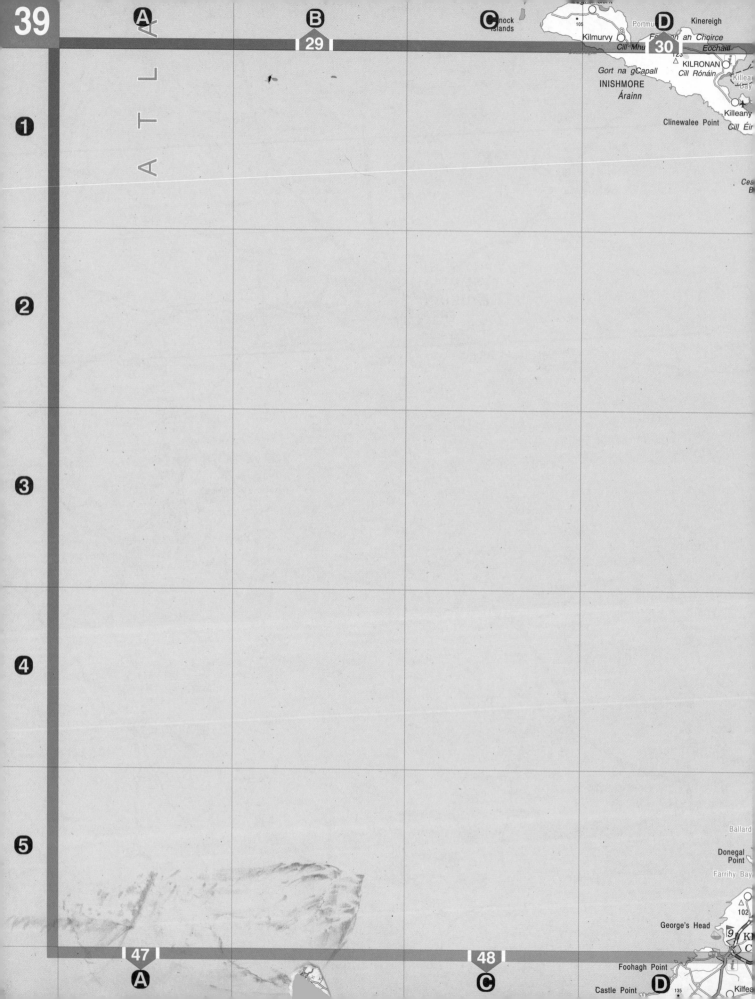

Knock
Islands

Portmu
Kilmurvy
Cill Mhu
Kinereigh
Fe on an Choirce
Cill
Eochaill
KILRONAN
Cill Rónáin
Killea
Bay

Gort na gCapall
INISHMORE
Árainn

Killeany
Cill Éir

Clinewalee Point

1

Cea
B

2

3

4

5

Ballard

Donegal
Point

Farrihy Bay

102

George's Head

9
KI
C

Foohagh Point

Castle Point

Kilfe

135

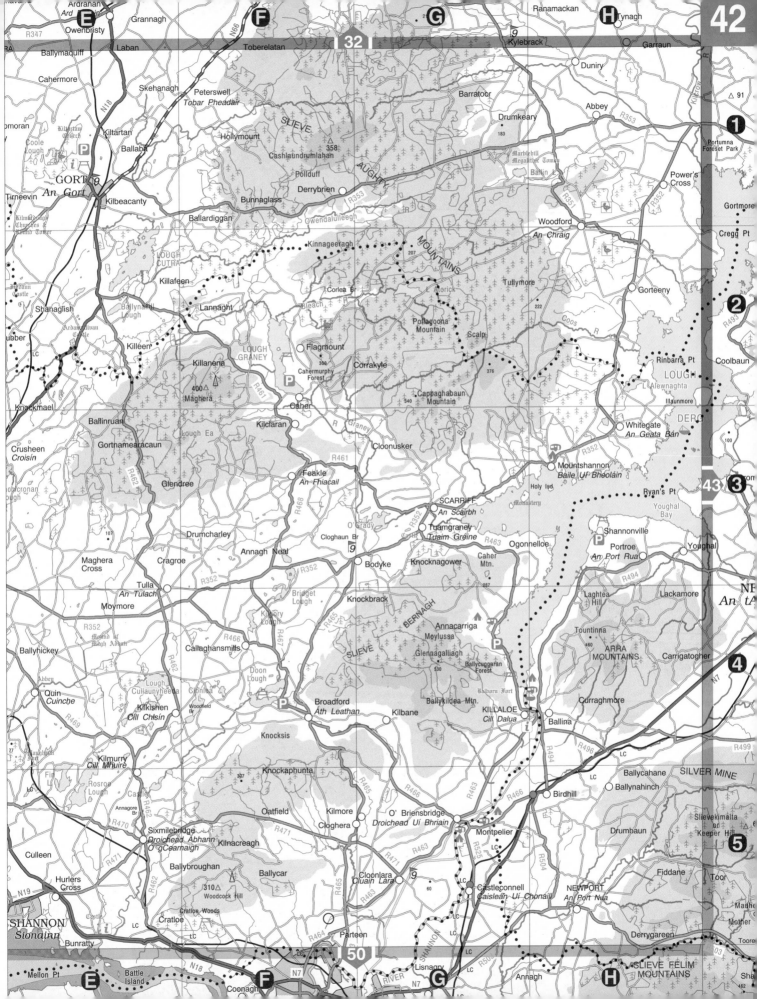

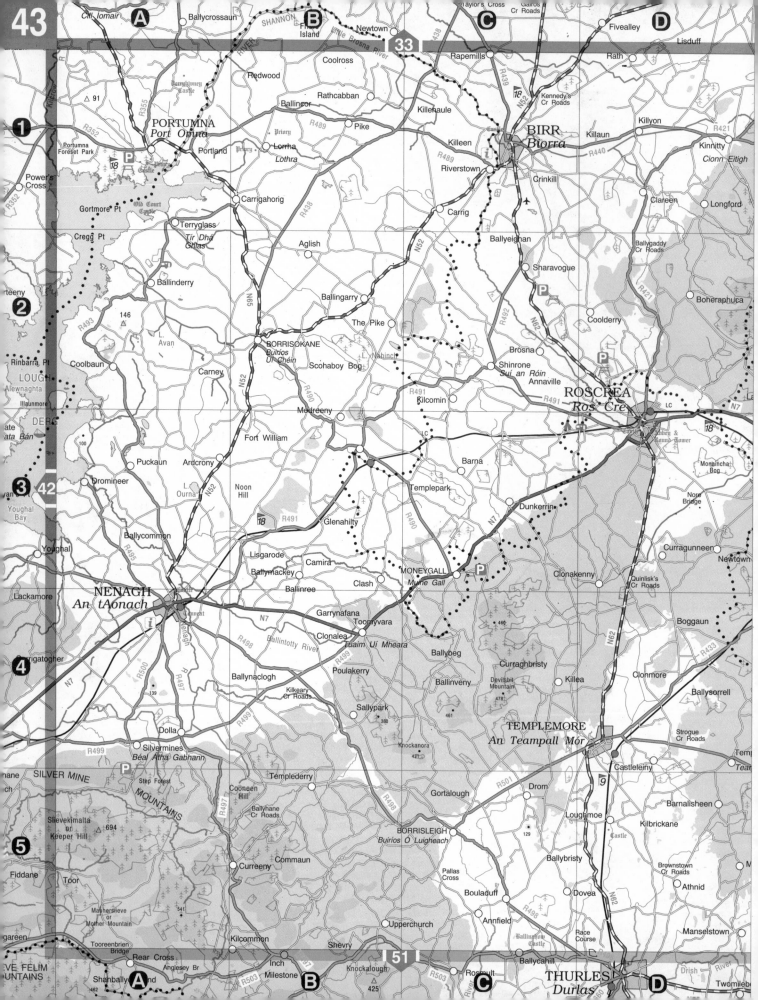

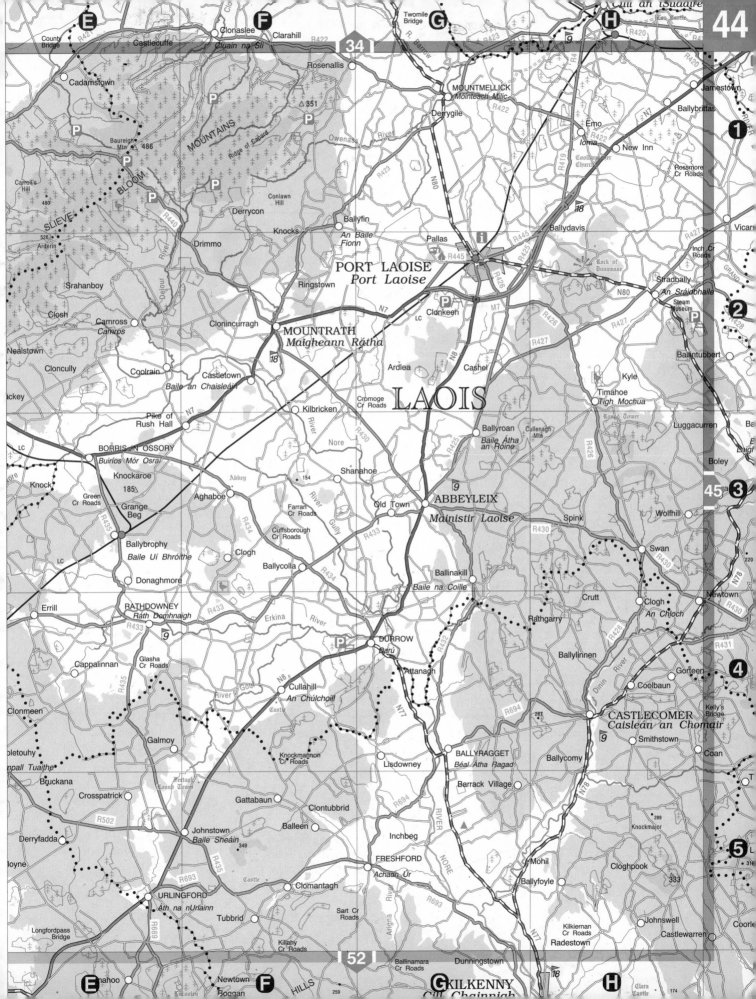

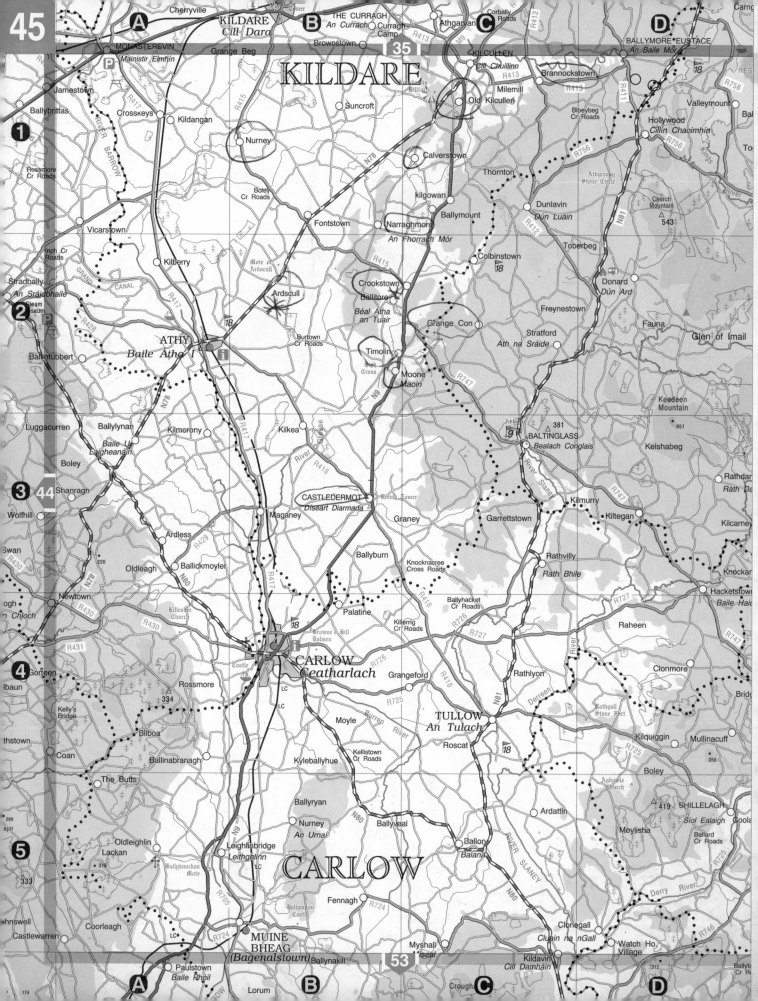

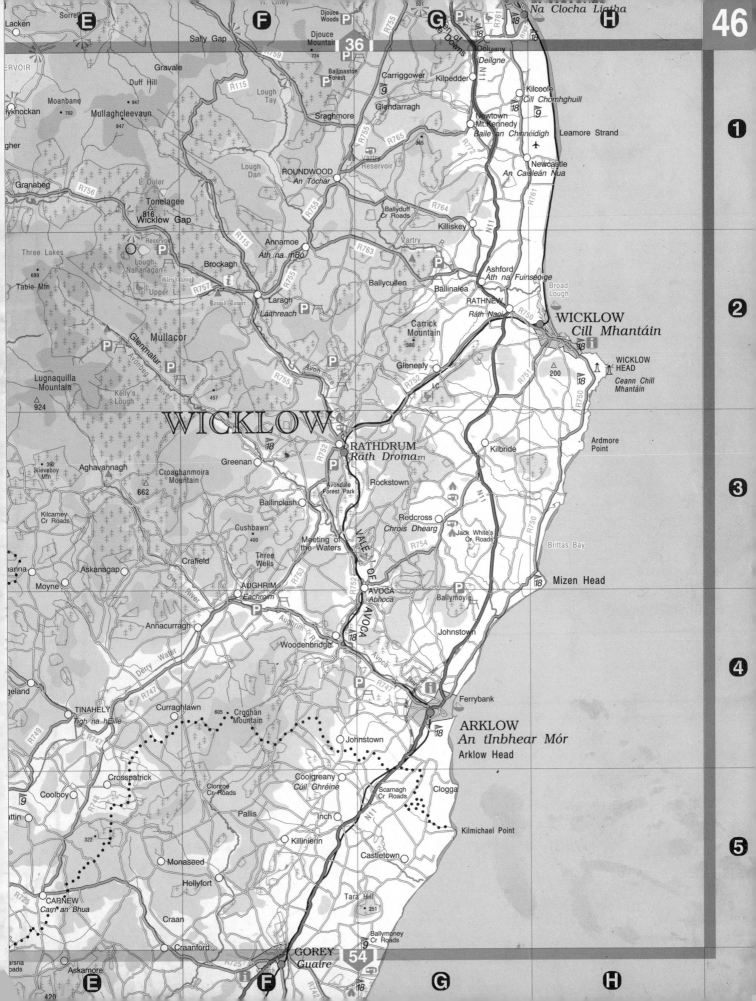

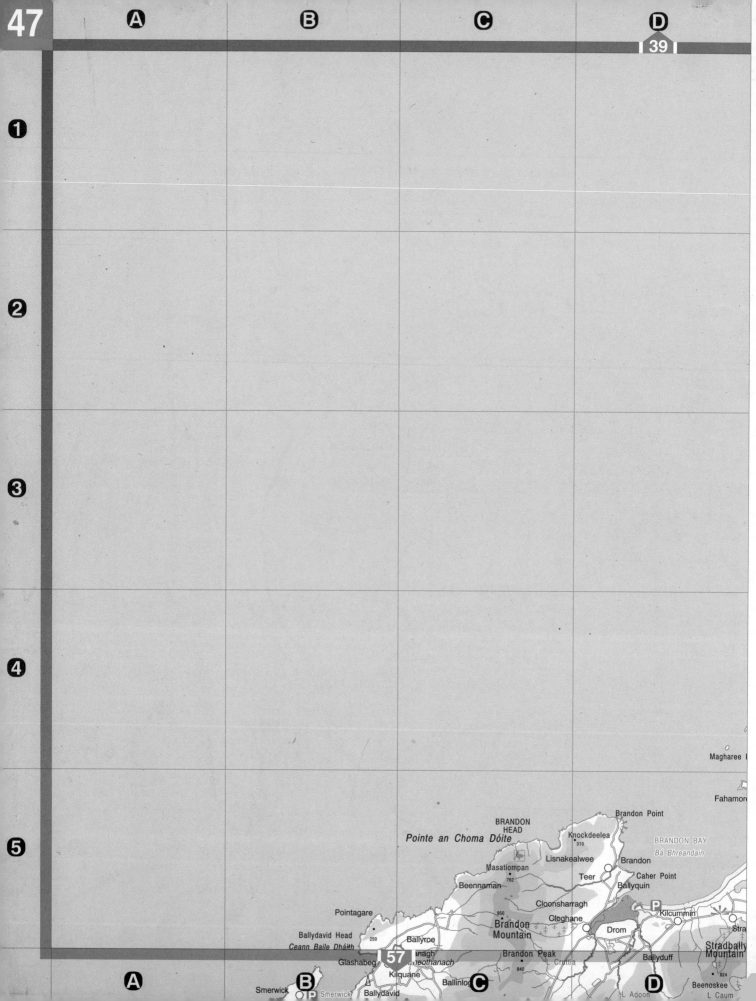

A B C D 39

1

2

3

4

Magharee

Fahamore

5

BRANDON HEAD
Pointe an Choma Dóite
Knockdeelea 310
BRANDON BAY
Bá Bhreandain
Lisnakealwee
Masatiompan
Brandon
Beennaman 762
Teer
Caher Point
Ballyquin
Pointagare
Cloonsharragh
P Kilcummin
Cloghane
Brandon 950
Mountain
Drom
Ballydavid Head
Ceann Baile Dháith 250
Ballyroe
Stradbally
Mountain
824
Glashabeg 57 anagh neothanach
Brandon Peak
L Cruttia 840
Ballyduff
Smerwick P Smerwick Ballydavid
Kilquane
Ballinloo
Beenoskee
L Adoon L Caum
Stra

A B C D

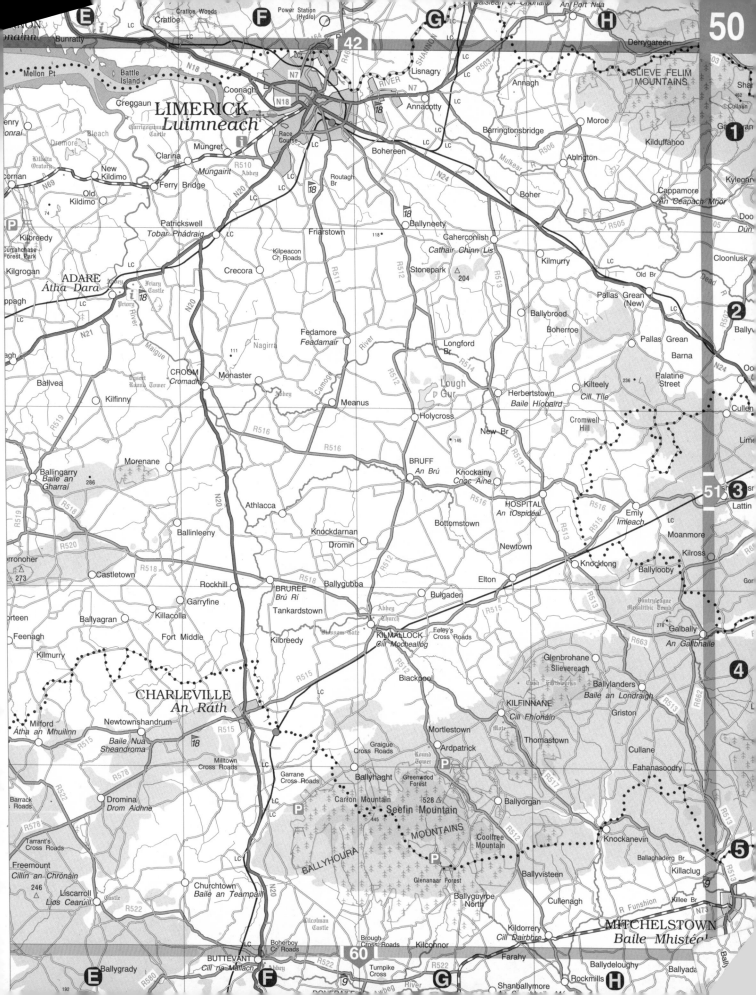

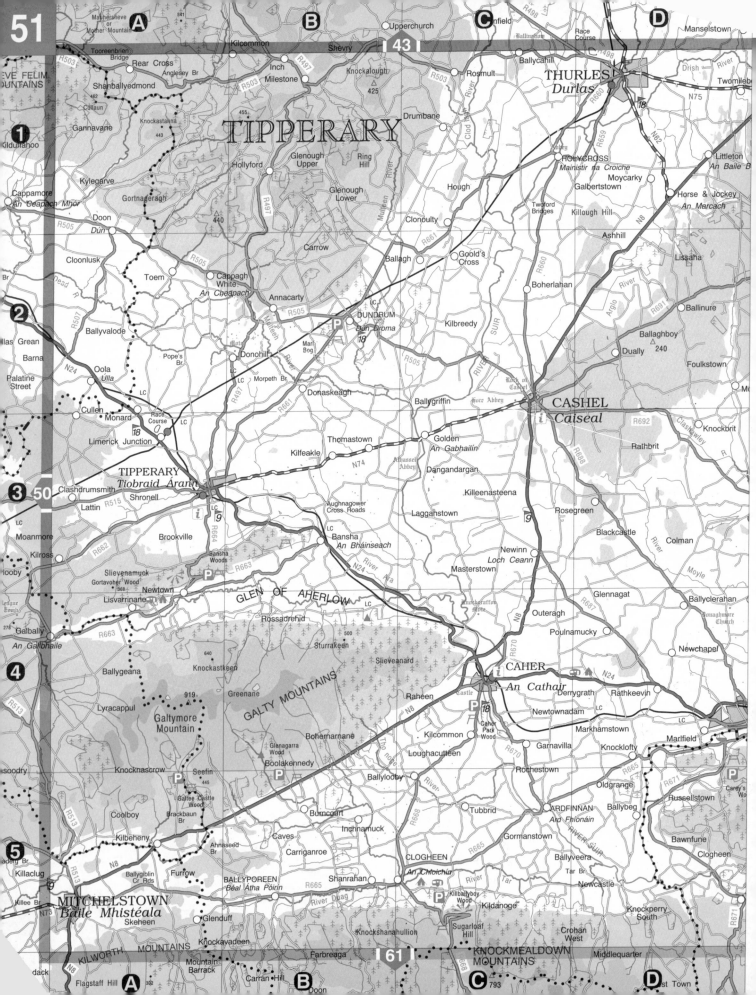

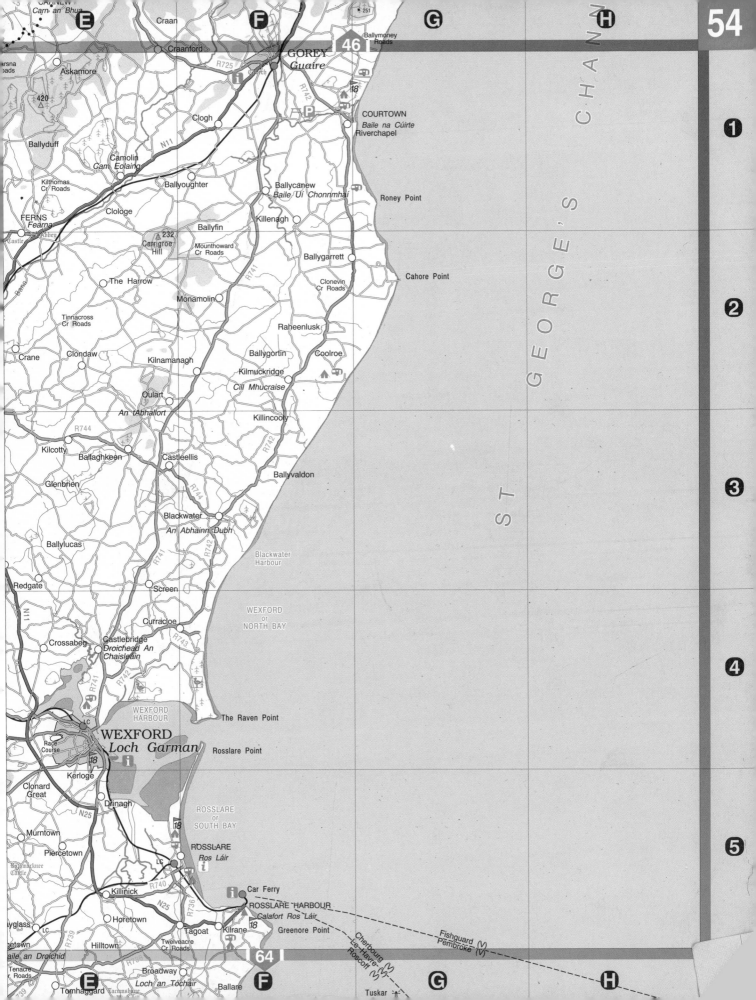

Magharee

Fahamor

BRANDON HEAD
Pointe an Choma Dóite

Brandon Point

Knockdeelea
310

BRANDON BAY
Bá Bhreandáin

Lisnakealwee

Brandon

Masatiompan
762

Teer

Caher Point

Ballyquin

Beennaman

Cloonsharragh

Cloghane

Drom

Kilcummin

Pointagare

Brandon
Mountain
950

Stradbally
Mountain

Ballydavid Head
Ceann Baile Dháith
250

Ballyroe

Brandon Peak
840

Ballyduff

Feohanagh
An Fheothanach

L Cruttia

Smerwick

Glashabeg

Kilquane

Ballinloghig

Beenoskee

Sybil Head

Smerwick
Harbour

Ballydavid
Baile na nGall

L Gal

L Adoon

L Caum

Araglen
Forest

Slievenagower
486

Murreagh
An Mhúlríoch

Kilmalkedar

Ballysitteragh

L Camclaun

Lough
Anscaul

Sybil Point

Ballinrannig

622

Conair
615

Slievanea

Coumanare
Lakes

BALLYFERRITER
Baile an Fheirtéaraigh

Gallarus
(Oratory)

Ballynana

Knockavrogeen

Knockmoylemore

Coumduff

Clogher
Head

Teeravane

Ballineanig

Ballyeightragh

Ballybowler

Lisdargan

Annagap

ANASCAUL
Abhainn an Scáil

18

R559
403

Milltown
Baile an Mhuilinn

Lispole
Lios Póil

DINGLE
An Daingean

N86

Croaghmarhin

Ventry

R559

Dunquin
Dún Chaoin

Kildurrihy

Dingle
Harbour

Aglish

Acres Point
284

Inishtooskert
172

Mount Eagle
514

Ventry
Harbour

Ballymacadoyle
Hill

Doonmanagh

Minard
Head

Gubranna

GREAT BLASKET
ISLAND

BLASKET
SOUND

Beginish

Beenacouma

Cloghaus

Fahan

Parkmore Pt

Reenbeg
Point

Bull's
Head

Garraun Pt

SLEA HEAD
Ceann Sléibhe

An Blascaod
Mór
290

Caher
(Promontory Fort)

Tearaght
Island

Canduff

DINGLE BAY
Bá an Daingin

Inishnabro
175

Inishvickillane
135

Feak

King's Head

Gleensk
Wood

Beenn

Darby's
Br

Mount Foley
668

Canglass Point

Killurly
Commons
686

Been Hill
662

Mullaghnarakill

Coosfadda

Slievagh

Knocknadobar

N70

Castlequin

Power Station
(Steam)

Foilmore Br

Teeromoyle

DOULUS HEAD

Killelan
Mountain

Leacanabuaile
Stone Fort

Coomduff

Caunoge
495

Beginish
Island

CAHERSIVEEN
Cathair Saidhbhín

Knockaneden
Cross

Reenadrolaun Pt

VALENCIA
HARBOUR

Reenard
Cross

Keelnagore

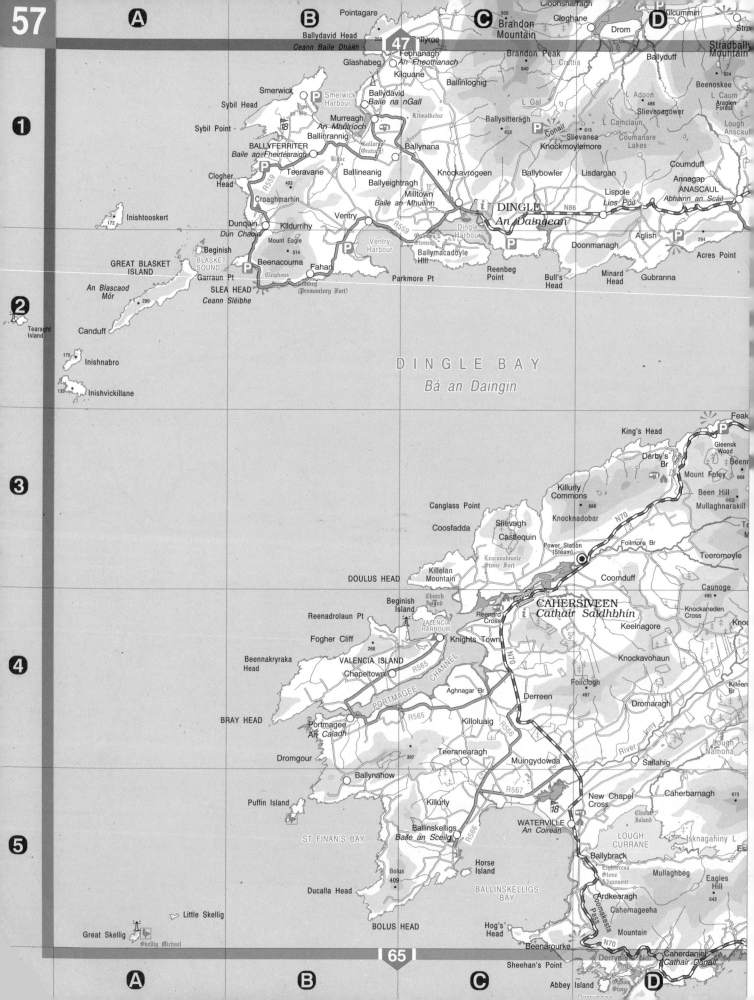

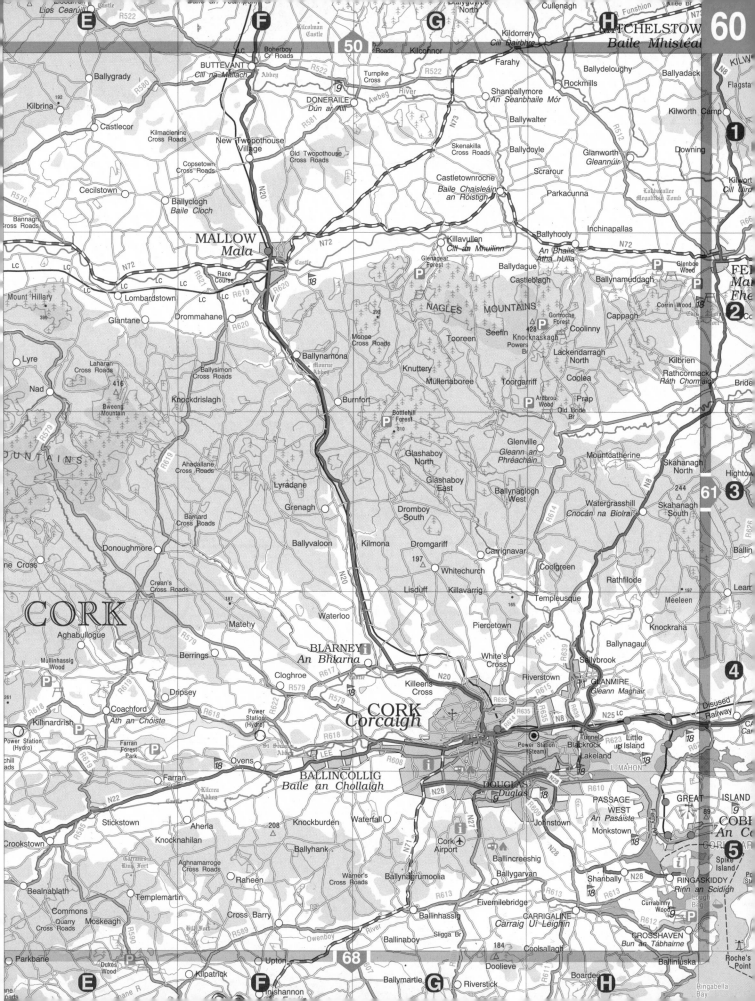

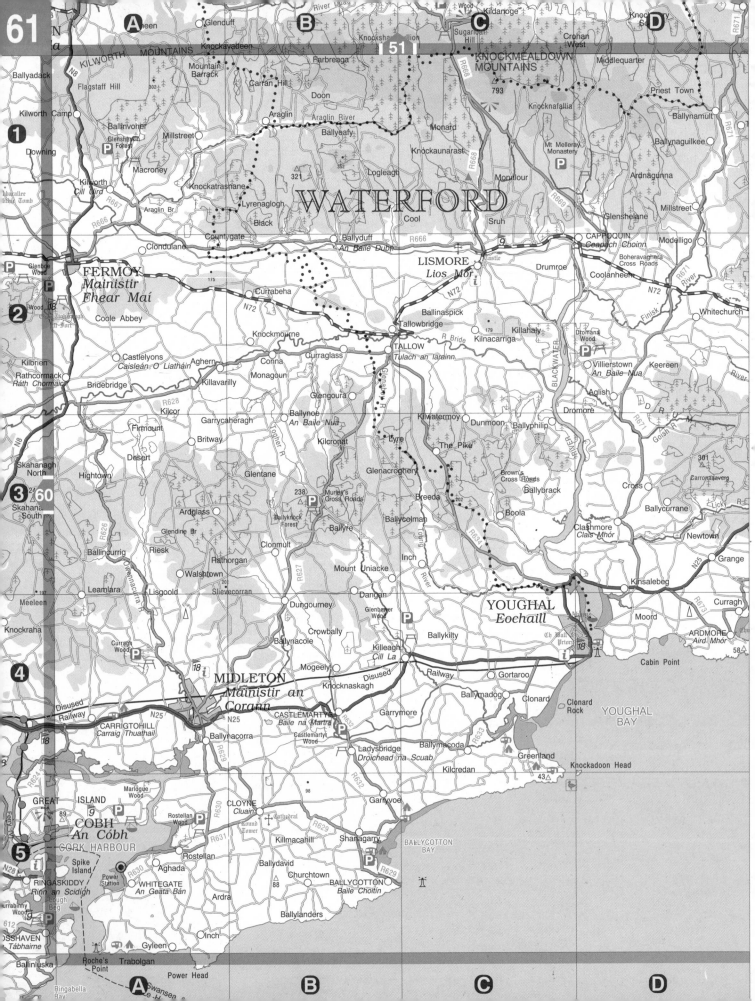

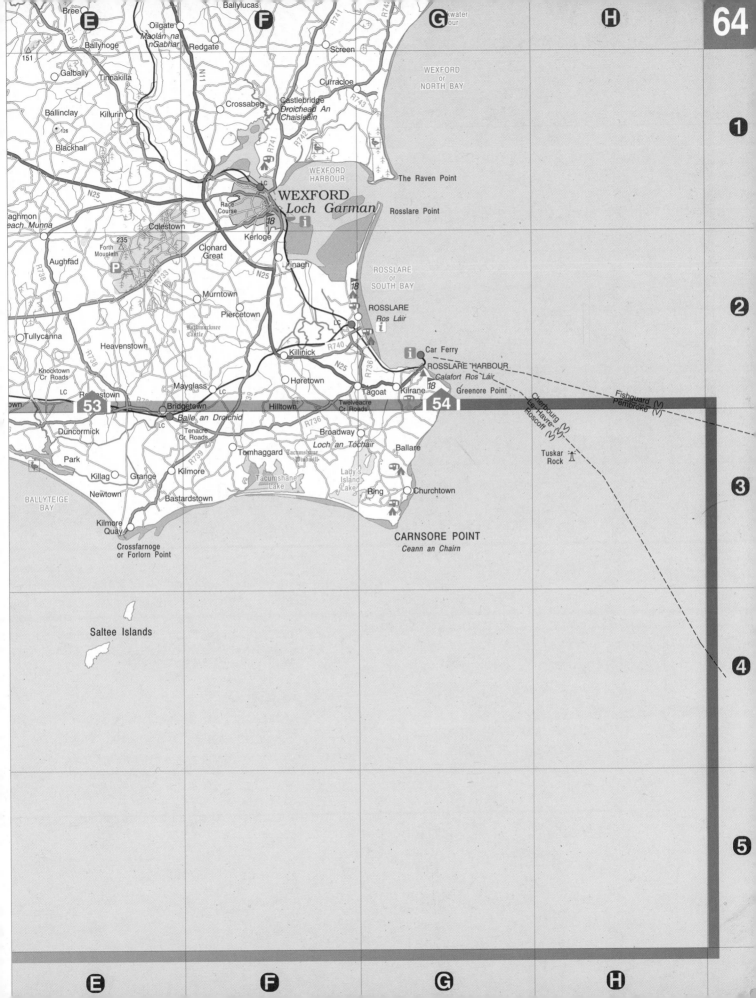

Bree
Ballylucas
E
F
Gwater
our
G
H
Oilgate
Maolán na nGabhar
Redgate
Screen
R741
R741
R741

Ballyhoge
151

Galbally
Tinnakilla
Crossabeg
Curracloe
R743

WEXFORD
or
NORTH BAY

Ballinclay
Kilurin
Castlebridge
Droichead An Chaisleáin
R742

126
Blackhall
R741

The Raven Point

WEXFORD
HARBOUR

aghmon
each Munna
Colestown
Race
Course
WEXFORD
Loch Garman
Rosslare Point

Aughfad
Forth
Mountain
235
P
Clonard
Great
Kerloge
18
i

R738
R733

Murntown
Finagh
ROSSLARE
or
SOUTH BAY

R738
N25

Piercetown
18

Tullycanna
Heavenstown
Ballymacnee
Castle
Killinick
ROSSLARE
Ros Láir
i

Knocktown
Cr Roads
LC
R740
LC
i
Car Ferry

LC
Høretown
N25
R736
ROSSLARE HARBOUR
Calafort Ros Láir

Mayglass
LC
Tagoat
Kilrane
18
Greenore Point

53
Bridgetown
Hilltown
Twelveacre
Cr Roads
54
Fishguard
Pembroke (V)

Duncormick
Baile an Droichid
LC
R736
Broadway
Cherbourg
Le Havre
Roscoff

Tenacre
Cr Roads
Loch an Tóchair
Ballare

Park
Tomhaggard
Tacumshane
Windmill
Tuskar
Rock

Killag
Grange
Kilmore
Tacumshane
Lake
Lady's
Island
Lake
Ring
Churchtown

BALLYTEIGE
BAY
Newtown
Bastardstown

Kilmore
Quay
CARNSORE POINT
Ceann an Chairn

Crossfarnoge
or Forlorn Point

Saltee Islands

E
F
G
H

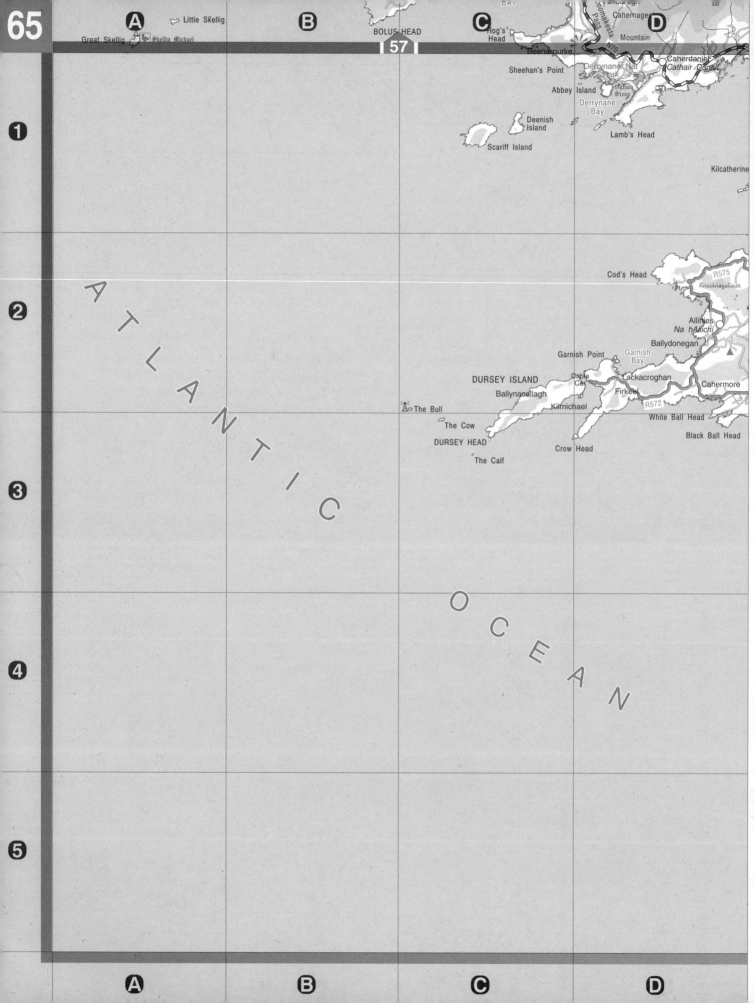

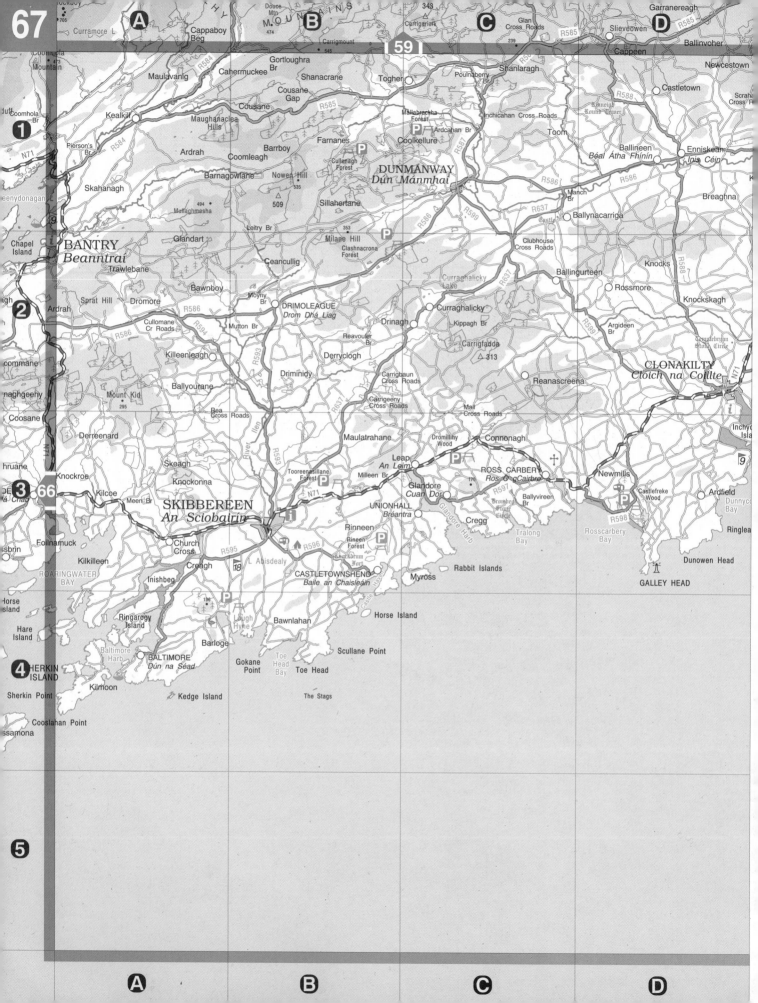

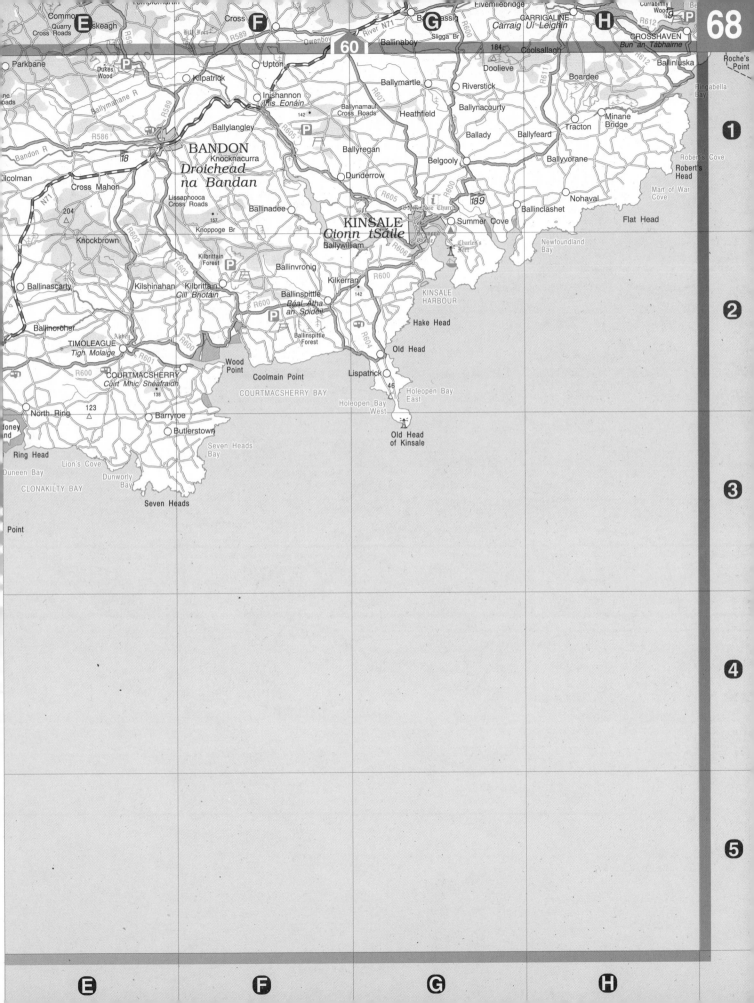

E   skeagh   Common   Cross   F   Ballynassig   G   Carraig Uí Leighin   H   Currabinny Wood   P   Fivemilebridge

CARRIGALINE

CROSSHAVEN
Bun an Tábhairne

Roche's Point

Quarry
Cross Roads

Hill Fort   R589

River N71   Owenboy

60   Ballinaboy   Sligga Br   R600   184   Coolsallagh   R612   Ballinluska

Parkbane   Dukes Wood   P   Kilpatrick   Upton   Doolieve   R611   Boardee   Ringabella Bay

oads   R559   Inishannon
Inis Eonáin   Ballymartle   Riverstick   Ballynacourty   Minane Bridge   Tracton

142   Ballynamaul
Cross Roads   Heathfield   Ballady   Ballyfeard   ❶

Ballylangley   R607   R605   P   Belgooly   Ballyvorane   Robert's Cove

BANDON   Ballyregan   Robert's Head

R586   18   Knocknacurra   R605   189   Nohaval   Mart of War Cove

Droichead
na Bandan   Dunderrow   R600   Ballinclashet

Bandon R   204   Lissaphooca
Cross Roads   157   St Multose Church   i   Flat Head

ilcolman   N71   Ballinadee   KINSALE   Summer Cove

Cross Mahon   Knoppoge Br   Cionn tSáile   Desmond Castle   ▲ Charles' Fort

Knockbrown   Kilbrittain
Forest   P   Ballywilliam   Newfoundland Bay

Ballinvronig

Ballinascarty   R602   Kilbrittain
Cill Briotáin   Ballinspittle
Béal Átha
an Spidéil   142   Kilkerran   KINSALE HARBOUR   ❷

Ballinoroher   R603   R600   P   Hake Head

Aiherl   Ballinspittle
Forest   R604   Old Head

TIMOLEAGUE
Tigh Molaige   R601   Wood
Point   Lispatrick

COURTMACSHERRY
Cúirt Mhic Shéafraidh   Coolmain Point   46   Holeopen Bay
East

R600   138   123   COURTMACSHERRY BAY   Holeopen Bay
West   ❸

North Ring   Barryroe   Old Head
of Kinsale

Butlerstown   Seven Heads
Bay

Ring Head   Lion's Cove   Dunworly
Bay

oney
nd   Duneen Bay   Seven Heads

CLONAKILTY BAY

Point

❹

❺

E   F   G   H

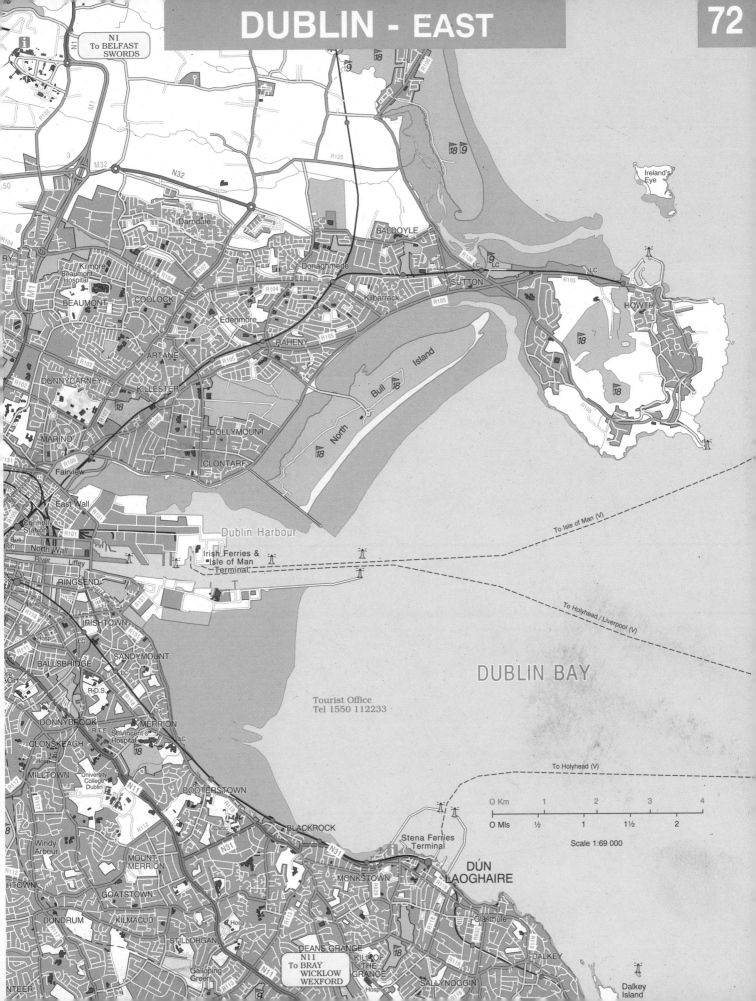

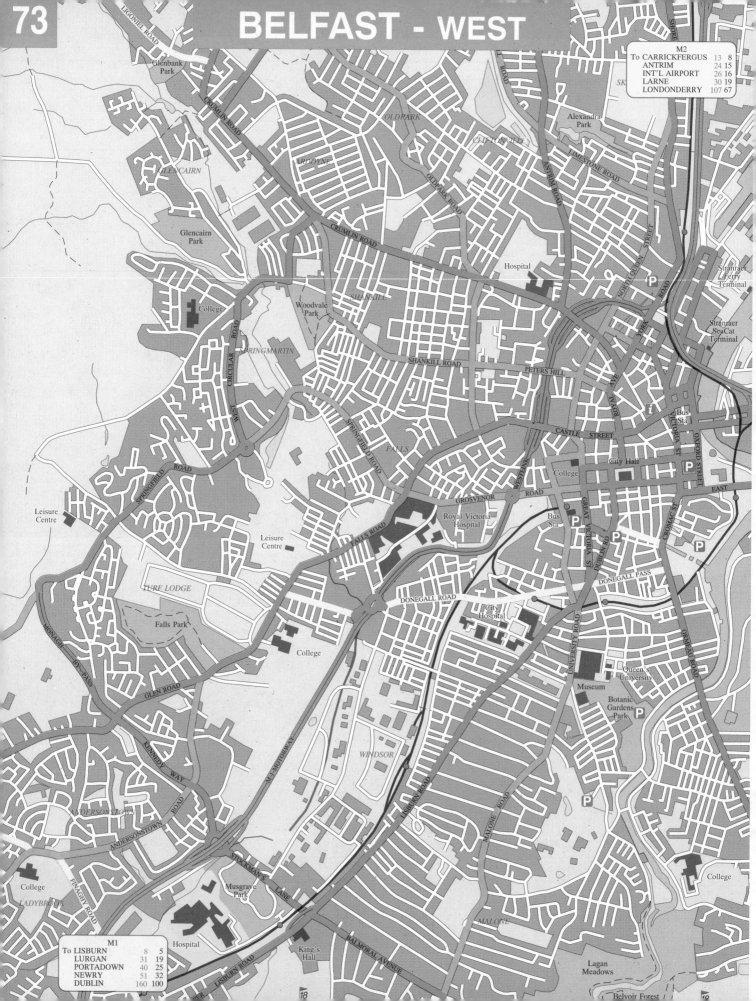

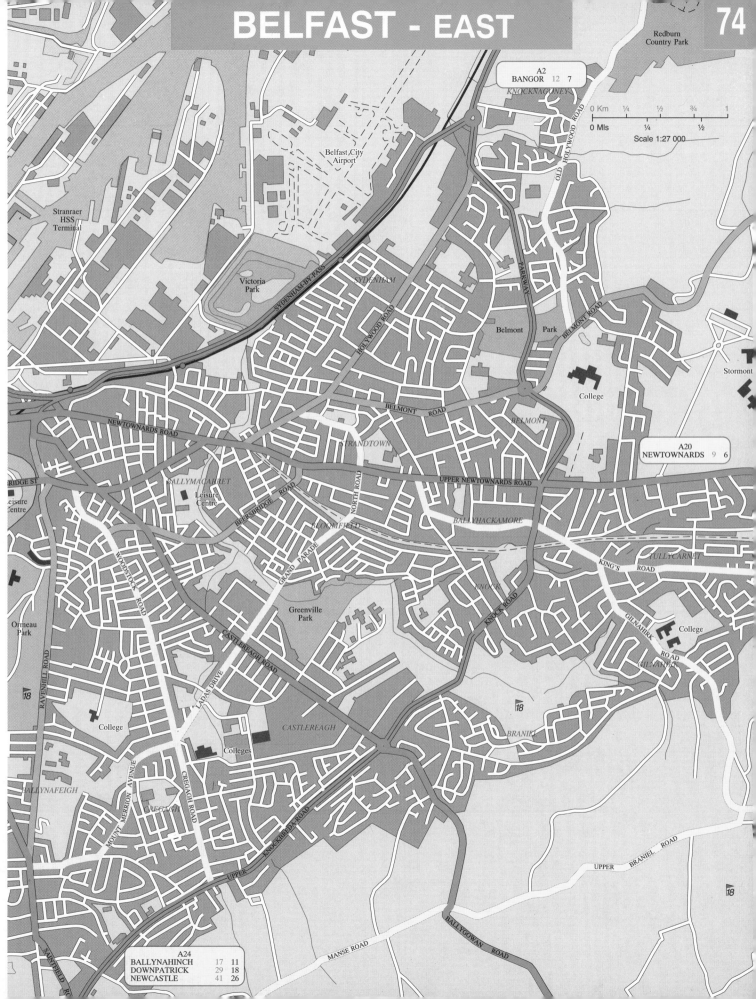

Redburn
Country Park

A2
BANGOR 12 7
KNOCKNAGONEY

0 Km ¼ ½ ¾ 1
0 Mls ¼ ½
Scale 1:27 000

OLD HOLYWOOD ROAD

Belfast City
Airport

Stranraer
HSS
Terminal

PARKWAY

Victoria
Park

SYDENHAM

Belmont Park

BELMONT ROAD

SYDENHAM-BY-PASS

HOLYWOOD ROAD

College

Stormont

BELMONT ROAD

NEWTOWNARDS ROAD

BELMONT

STRANDTOWN

A20
NEWTOWNARDS 9 6

BRIDGE ST

BALLYMACARRET

Leisure
Centre

BEERSBRIDGE ROAD

NORTH ROAD

UPPER NEWTOWNARDS ROAD

Leisure
Centre

BLOOMFIELD

BALLYHACKAMORE

TULLYCARNET

WOODSTOCK ROAD

GRAND PARADE

KNOCK

KING'S ROAD

Ormeau
Park

Greenville
Park

KNOCK ROAD

GILNAHIRK ROAD

College

RAVENHILL ROAD

18

CASTLEREAGH ROAD

18

GILNAHIRK

College

LADAS DRIVE

CASTLEREAGH

Colleges

BRANIEL

BALLYNAFEIGH

MOUNT MERRION AVENUE

CREGAGH ROAD

CREGAGH

KNOCKBREDA ROAD

UPPER

UPPER BRANIEL ROAD

18

SAINTFIELD R

MANSE ROAD

BALLYGOWAN ROAD

BALLYVOLANE

BALLYVOLANE ROAD

NEW ROAD

R614

MAYFIELD

Mayfield Cross

R615

Indust Estate

MONTENOTTE

TIVOLI

R635

Hosps

N8

LOWER GLANMIRE ROAD

Industrial Estate

RIVER LEE

Glashaboy River

BARNAVARA

R639

N8 TO DUBLIN

GLANMIRE

Lota

Hosps

Dunkettle

N25 TO WATERFORD

R623

Páirc Uí Chaoimh

Hosp

Hosp

BOREENMANAGH ROAD

BALLINLOUGH

BALLINTEMPLE

BLACKROCK

MAHON

Coll

BALLINURE

Hosp

DOUGLAS ROAD

R610

SOUTH DOUGLAS ROAD

Indust Estate

Hospital

BALLYPHEHANE

Goat Isd

Douglas

River

R610 TO PASSAGE WEST

ROCHESTOWN ROAD

R610

R610

N28

DOUGLAS

ROCHESTOWN

N28

GRANGE

CARRIG HILL

DONNYBROOK

Sch

N28 TO RINGASKIDDY AND FERRY

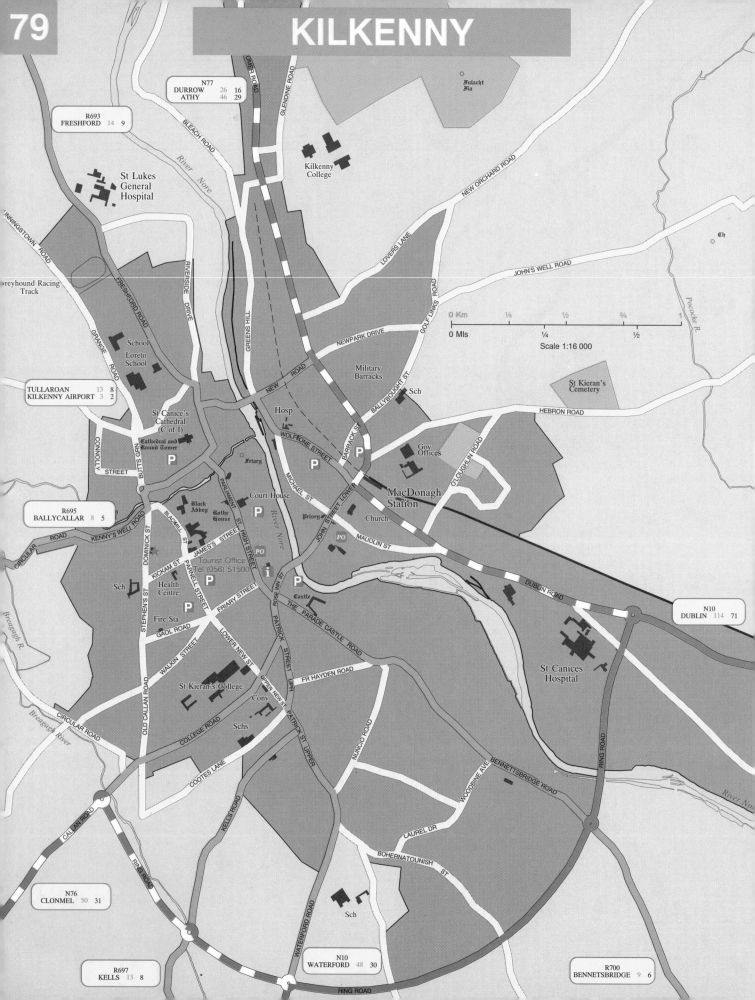

KILKENNY

Fulacht
Fia

N77
DURROW   26   16
ATHY   46   29

R693
FRESHFORD   14   9

Kilkenny
College

River Nore

St Lukes
General
Hospital

NEW ORCHARD ROAD

Ch

LOVERS LANE

JOHN'S WELL ROAD

Pococke R.

INNINGSTOWN ROAD

BLEACH ROAD

RIVERSIDE DRIVE

OMER ROAD

GLENDINE ROAD

GREENS HILL

NEW ROAD

greyhound Racing
Track

FRESHFORD ROAD

GRANGE ROAD

School
Loreto School

NEWPARK DRIVE

GOLF LINKS ROAD

Military
Barracks

BALLYBOUGHT ST

Sch

St Kieran's
Cemetery

HEBRON ROAD

TULLAROAN   13   8
KILKENNY AIRPORT   3   2

Hosp

WOLFEONE STREET

BARRACK ST

O'LOUGHLIN ROAD

St Canice's
Cathedral
(C of I)

Cathedral and
Round Tower

CONNOLLY STREET

BUTTS GRN

P

Friary

P

P

Gov
Offices

MacDonagh
Station

MICHAEL ST

PARLIAMENT

Court House

R695
BALLYCALLAR   8   5

KENNY'S WELL ROAD

DOMINICK ST

BLACKMILL ST

Black
Abbey

Rothe
House

P

River Nore

Priory

JOHN STREET LOWER

PO

MAUDLIN ST

Church

DUBLIN ROAD

N10
DUBLIN   114   71

CIRCULAR ROAD

Breagagh R.

ST HIGH STREET

JAMES'S STREET

KICKAM ST

PARNELL STREET

PO

i

Tourist Office
Tel (056) 51500

ROSE INN ST

P

Sch

Health
Centre

P

Fire Sta

Castle

St Canices
Hospital

STEPHEN'S ST

GAOL ROAD

WALKIN STREET

LOWER NEW ST

FRIARY STREET

PATRICK STREET

THE PARADE   CASTLE ROAD

FR HAYDEN ROAD

UPPER NEW ST

OLD CALLAN ROAD

St Kieran's College

Conv

Schs

COLLEGE ROAD

PATRICK ST UPPER

NUNCIO ROAD

WOODBINE AVE

BENNETTSBRIDGE ROAD

RING ROAD

River Nore

Breagagh River

CIRCULAR ROAD

COOTES LANE

KELLS ROAD

WATERFORD ROAD

LAUREL DR

BOHERNATOUNISH ST

CALLAN ROAD

RING ROAD

N76
CLONMEL   50   31

Sch

R697
KELLS   13   8

N10
WATERFORD   48   30

RING ROAD

R700
BENNETTSBRIDGE   9   6

0 Km   ¼   ½   ¾   1

0 Mls   ¼   ½

Scale 1:16 000

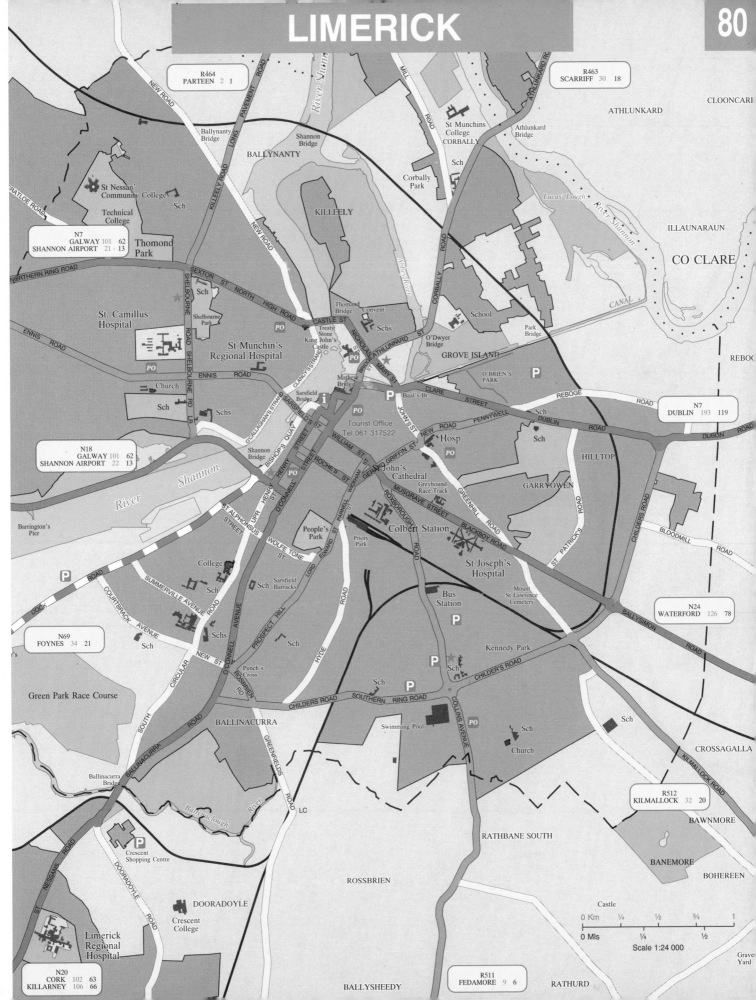

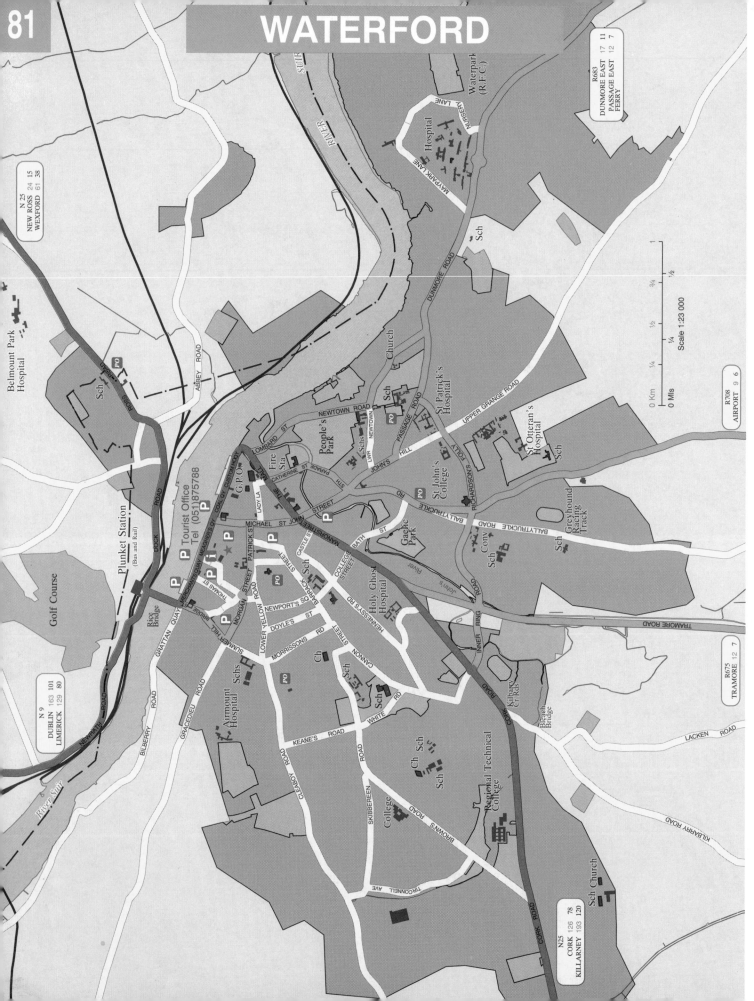

Scale 1:23 000

R683
DUNMORE EAST 17 11
PASSAGE EAST 12 7
FERRY

N 25
NEW ROSS 24 15
WEXFORD 61 38

Belmount Park Hospital

Golf Course

Plunket Station
(Bus and Rail)

P Tourist Office
Tel (051)875788

G.P.O.

Fire Sta

People's Park

Church

St Patrick's Hospital

UPPER GRANGE ROAD

St Otteran's Hospital

St John's College

Greyhound Racing Track

Gaelic Park

Holy Ghost Hospital

Airmount Hospital

R708
AIRPORT 9 6

TRAMORE ROAD

Rice Bridge

N 9
DUBLIN 163 101
LIMERICK 129 80

R675
TRAMORE 12 7

Regional Technical College

Kilbarry Cr Rds

N25
CORK 126 78
KILLARNEY 193 120

River Suir

Sch Church

LACKEN ROAD

KILBARRY ROAD

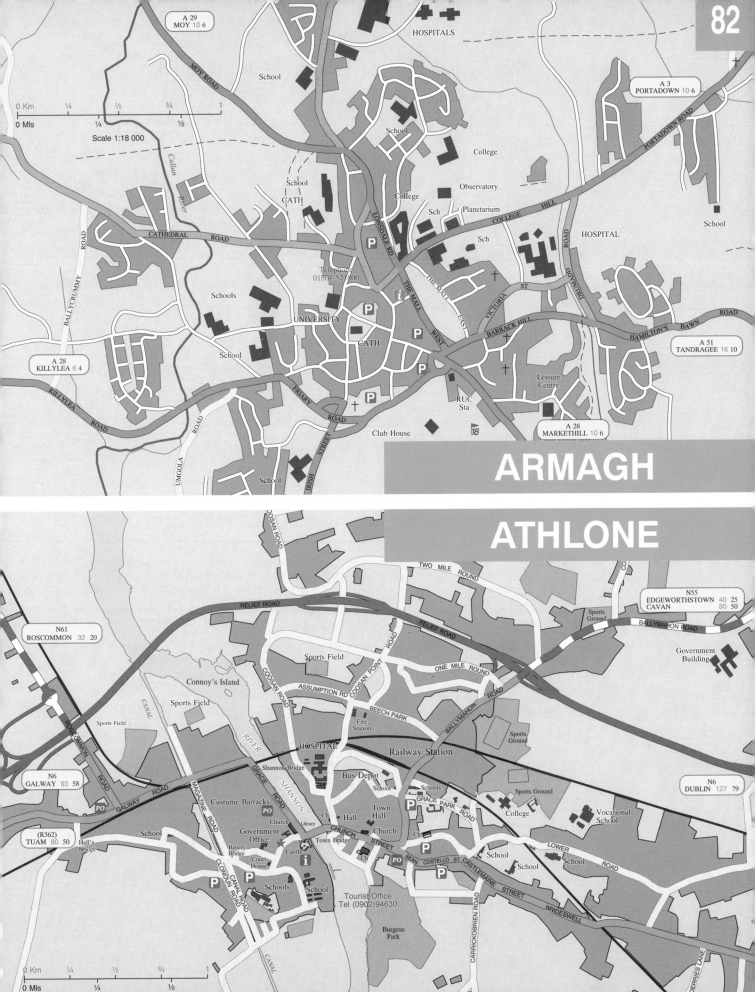

ARMAGH

ATHLONE

A 29
MOY 10 6

A 3
PORTADOWN 10 6

0 Km ¼ ½ ¾ 1
0 Mls ¼ ½
Scale 1:18 000

HOSPITALS

School

School

School

College

Observatory

Planetarium

Sch

Sch

College

College

CATH

MOY ROAD

Callan River

CATHEDRAL ROAD

BALLYCRUMMY ROAD

LONSDALE RD

COLLEGE HILL

COLLEGE ROAD

DRUMSILL

HOSPITAL

Telephone
01861-527800

P

P

Schools

P

UNIVERSITY

School

CATH

P

P

THE MALL EAST

THE MALL WEST

VICTORIA ST

BARRACK HILL

HAMILTON'S BAWN ROAD

A 51
TANDRAGEE 16 10

A 28
KILLYLEA 6 4

KILLYLEA ROAD

School

UMGOLA ROAD

FRIARY ROAD

IRISH STREET

P

Leisure
Centre

RUC
Sta

School

Club House

18

A 28
MARKETHILL 10 6

COOSAN ROAD

TWO MILE ROUND

N55
EDGEWORTHSTOWN 40 25
CAVAN 80 50

RELIEF ROAD

RELIEF ROAD

Sports
Ground

BALLYMAHON ROAD

N61
ROSCOMMON 32 20

CO

Government
Building

Sports Field

COOSAN ROAD

Connoy's Island

ASSUMPTION RD

COOSAN POINT ROAD

ONE MILE ROUND

Sports Field

Sports Field

CANAL

BEECH PARK

Fire
Station

BALLYMAHON ROAD

Sports
Ground

RIVER

HOSPITAL

Railway Station

ROSCOMMON ROAD

Shannon Bridge

Bus Depot

N6
GALWAY 93 58

SHANNON

GRACE ROAD

MAGAZINE ROAD

School

Schools

P

GRACE PARK ROAD

Sports Ground

College

PO

GALWAY ROAD

Custume Barracks

PO

Church

Library

Hall

Town
Hall

Church

School

Vocational
School

(R362)
TUAM 80 50

School

Government
Office

Battery
Bridge

Court
House

Castle

Town Bridge

CHURCH STREET

Church

Ch

PO

SEAN COSTELLO ST

CASTLEMAINE STREET

School

LOWER ROAD

School

N6
DUBLIN 127 79

Hall's
Bridge

CANAL ROAD

CLONOUN ROAD

P

P

Schools

School

i

Tourist Office
Tel (0902)94630

P

CARRICKOBRIEN ROAD

BRIDESWELL ROAD

DERRIES LANE

Burgess
Park

0 Km ¼ ½ ¾
0 Mls ¼ ½

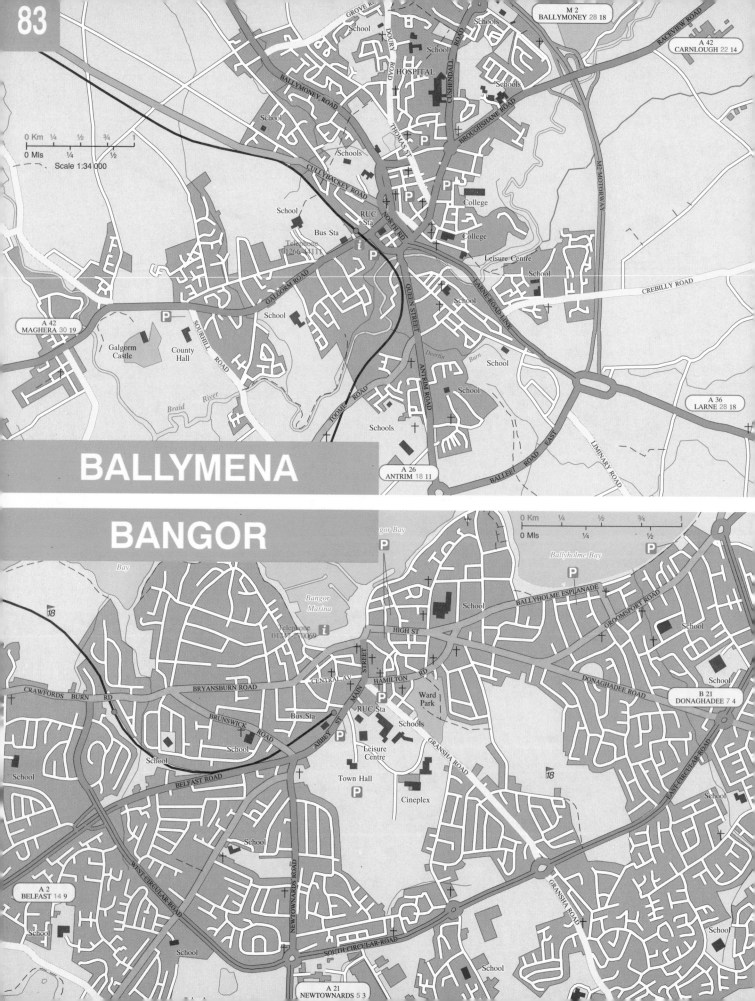

BALLYMENA

BANGOR

Ballymena map labels:

GROVE RD
School
DOURY ROAD
Schools
M 2
BALLYMONEY 28 18
RACEVIEW ROAD
A 42
CARNLOUGH 22 14
BALLYMONEY ROAD
School
HOSPITAL
CUSHENDALL ROAD
School
Schools
BROUGHSHANE ROAD
School
Schools
THOMAS ST
P
CULLYBACKEY ROAD
Schools
M2 MOTORWAY
College
School
RUC Sta
NORTH RD
P
College
Bus Sta
Leisure Centre
Telephone
01266 44111
i
P
School
CREBILLY ROAD
GALGORM ROAD
QUEEN STREET
LARNE ROAD LINK
School
A 42
MAGHERA 30 19
P
School
Deerfin
Burn
School
Galgorm
Castle
County
Hall
SOURHILL ROAD
Braid River
TOOME ROAD
ANTRIM ROAD
School
School
A 36
LARNE 28 18
Schools
BALLEE ROAD EAST
LIMINARY ROAD
A 26
ANTRIM 18 11

Bangor map labels:

Bangor Bay
P
Ballyholme Bay
P
0 Km ¼ ½ ¾ 1
0 Mls ¼ ½
Bay
P
School
BALLYHOLME ESPLANADE
School
Bangor Marina
Telephone
01247 270069
i
HIGH ST
GROOMSPORT ROAD
School
School
CENTRAL AV
MAIN STREET
HAMILTON RD
Ward Park
DONAGHADEE ROAD
B 21
DONAGHADEE 7 4
CRAWFORDS BURN RD
BRYANSBURN ROAD
P
RUC Sta
18
BRUNSWICK ROAD
Bus Sta
Schools
ABBEY ST
GRANSHA ROAD
School
School
Leisure Centre
18
School
BELFAST ROAD
Town Hall
P
EAST CIRCULAR ROAD
School
Cineplex
School
A 2
BELFAST 14 9
WEST CIRCULAR ROAD
NEWTOWNARDS ROAD
School
GRANSHA ROAD
School
SOUTH CIRCULAR ROAD
A 21
NEWTOWNARDS 5 3
School

Scale 1:34 000
0 Km ¼ ½ ¾ 1
0 Mls ¼ ½

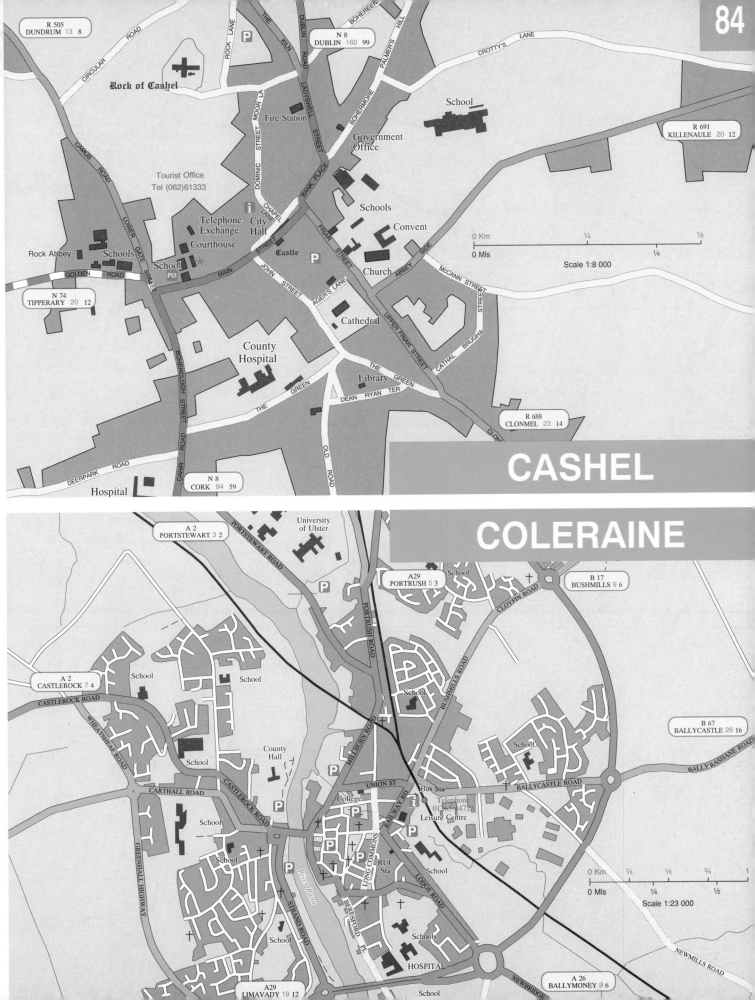

CASHEL

R 505
DUNDRUM 13 8

N 8
DUBLIN 160 99

R 691
KILLENAULE 20 12

Rock of Cashel

CIRCULAR ROAD

ROCK LANE

THE KILN

DUBLIN ROAD

PALMER'S HILL

BOHEREEN

CROTTY'S LANE

School

Fire Station

MOOR LA.

LADYSWELL STREET

BOHERMORE

Government
Office

DOMINIC STREET

BANK PLACE

Tourist Office
Tel (062)61333

Schools

Convent

Telephone
Exchange

CHAPEL
LANE

City
Hall

FRIAR STREET

ABBEY SIDE

Courthouse

Castle

Church

McCANN STREET

CAMUS ROAD

Rock Abbey

Schools

School

CHAPEL
STREET

JOHN STREET

AGER'S LANE

UPPER FRIAR STREET

CATHAL BRUGHA STREET

0 Km   ¼   ½

0 Mls   ¼

Scale 1:8 000

LOWER GATE STREET

PO

GOLDEN ROAD

MAIN

N 74
TIPPERARY 20 12

County
Hospital

Cathedral

THE GREEN

BOHERCLOUGH STREET

THE GREEN

Library

DEAN RYAN TER.

R 688
CLONMEL 23 14

CLON

DEERPARK ROAD

CAHIR ROAD

OLD ROAD

N 8
CORK 94 59

Hospital

COLERAINE

A 2
PORTSTEWART 3 2

PORTSTEWART ROAD

University
of Ulster

A29
PORTRUSH 5 3

School

B 17
BUSHMILLS 9 6

CLOYFIN ROAD

P

PORTRUSH ROAD

School

BUSHMILLS ROAD

A 2
CASTLEROCK 7 4

School

School

School

B 67
BALLYCASTLE 26 16

CASTLEROCK ROAD

WHEATSHEAF ROAD

County
Hall

School

MILBURN ROAD

School

BALLY RASHANE ROAD

CARTHALL ROAD

School

P

CASTLEROCK ROAD

P

UNION ST

Bus Sta

BALLYCASTLE ROAD

GREENHALL HIGHWAY

P

College

P

RAILWAY RD

Telephone
01265 44723
Leisure Centre

School

School

P

LONG COMMONS

P

RUC
Sta

LODGE ROAD

0 Km   ¼   ½   ¾   1

STRAND ROAD

River Bann

BERESFORD

0 Mls   ¼   ½

Scale 1:23 000

School

Schools

NEWMILLS ROAD

A29
LIMAVADY 19 12

HOSPITAL

A 26
BALLYMONEY 9 6

NEWBRIDGE

School

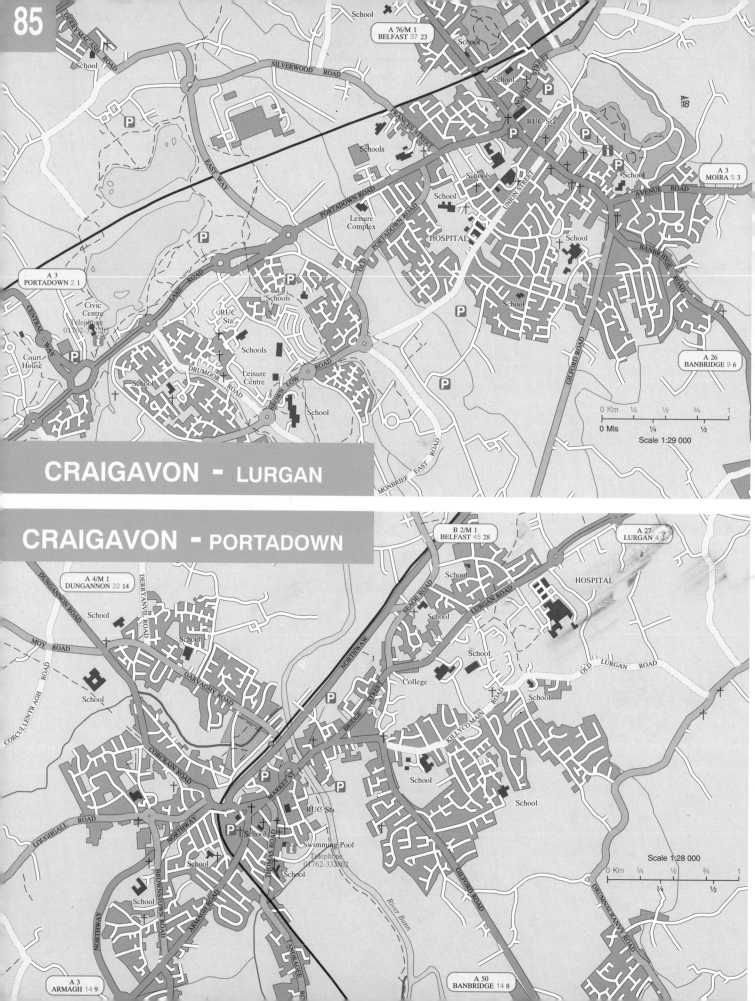

CRAIGAVON - LURGAN

CRAIGAVON - PORTADOWN

Map labels (Lurgan, top map):

A 76/M 1
BELFAST 37 23

A 3
MOIRA 5 3

A 3
PORTADOWN 2 1

A 26
BANBRIDGE 9 6

SILVERWOOD ROAD
DERRY MACASH ROAD
EAST WAY
FRANCES STREET
NORTH STREET
RUC Sta
UNION STREET
AVENUE ROAD
BANBRIDGE ROAD
PORTADOWN ROAD
OLD PORTADOWN ROAD
LAKE ROAD
CENTRAL WAY
BROWN LOW ROAD
GILFORD ROAD
MONBRIEF EAST ROAD

Leisure Complex
HOSPITAL
Civic Centre
Telephone 01762-341200
Court House
RUC Sta
DRUMGOR ROAD
Leisure Centre
Schools
School

Scale 1:29 000
0 Km ¼ ½ ¾ 1
0 Mls ¼ ½

Map labels (Portadown, bottom map):

B 2/M 1
BELFAST 45 28

A 27
LURGAN 4 2

A 4/M 1
DUNGANNON 22 14

HOSPITAL

DUNGANNON ROAD
DERRYANVIL ROAD
MOY ROAD
CORCULLENTRAGH ROAD
GARVAGHY ROAD
CORCRAIN ROAD
LOUGHGALL ROAD
NORTHWAY
BROWNSTOWN ROAD
ARMAGH ROAD
THOMAS ROAD
MARKET ST
BRIDGE STREET
NORTHWAY
SEAGOE ROAD
LURGAN ROAD
OLD LURGAN ROAD
KILLYCOMAIN ROAD
GILFORD ROAD
DRUMNACANVY ROAD
TANDRAGEE ROAD

College
RUC Sta
Swimming Pool
Telephone 01762-332802
River Bann

A 3
ARMAGH 14 9

A 50
BANBRIDGE 14 8

Scale 1:28 000
0 Km ¼ ½ ¾ 1
¼ ½

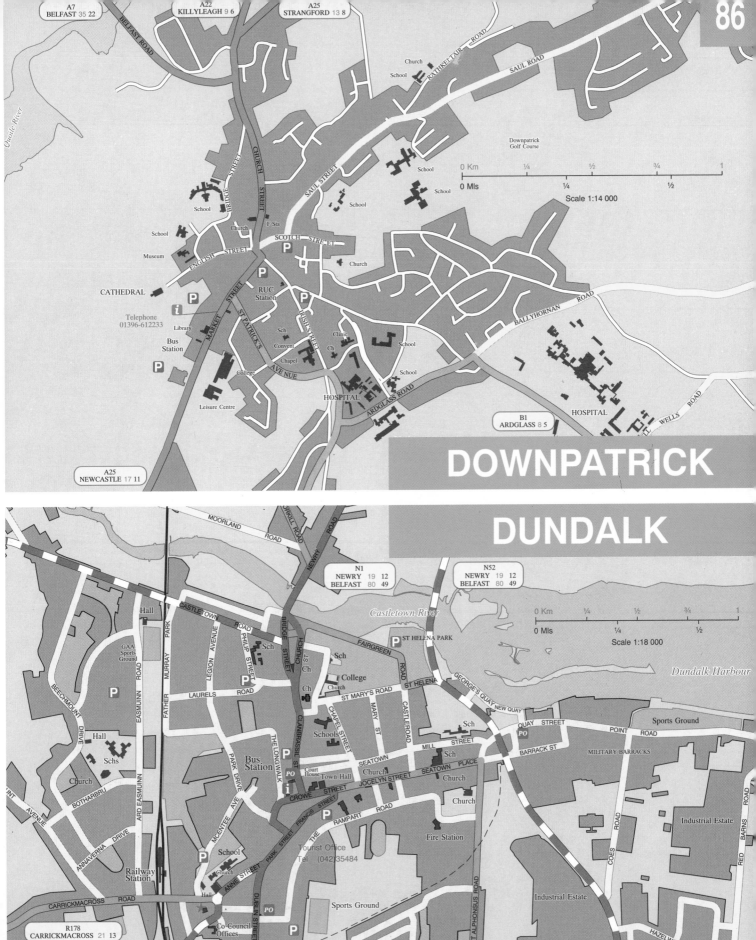

DOWNPATRICK

DUNDALK

A7
BELFAST 35 22

A22
KILLYLEAGH 9 6

A25
STRANGFORD 13 8

Church
School

SAUL ROAD

RATHKELTAIR ROAD

Quoile River

Downpatrick
Golf Course

0 Km   ¼   ½   ¾   1
0 Mls   ¼   ½
Scale 1:14 000

School
School

School

School

BRIDGE STREET

CHURCH STREET

SAUL STREET

F Sta

Church

SCOTCH STREET

School

English Street

Church

Museum

CATHEDRAL

P

RUC Station

Telephone
01396-612233

i

P

BALLYHORNAN ROAD

Library

MARKET STREET

ST PATRICK'S

Bus Station

Sch

IRISH STREET

Convent

Clinic

Ch

School

P

Chapel

AVENUE

School

College

HOSPITAL

ARDGLASS ROAD

School

HOSPITAL

WELLS ROAD

Leisure Centre

B1
ARDGLASS 8 5

A25
NEWCASTLE 17 11

MOORLAND ROAD

ORKILL ROAD

NEWRY ROAD

N1
NEWRY 19 12
BELFAST 80 49

N52
NEWRY 19 12
BELFAST 80 49

Castletown River

Dundalk Harbour

0 Km   ¼   ½   ¾   1
0 Mls   ¼   ½
Scale 1:18 000

Hall

CASTLETOWN ROAD

LEGION AVENUE

PHILIP STREET

BRIDGE STREET

CHURCH STREET

Sch

FAIRGREEN

P St Helena Park

GAA Sports Ground

MURRAY PARK

Sch

Ch

College

ST HELENA

GEORGE'S QUAY NEW QUAY

BEECHMOUNT DRIVE

EASMUINN ROAD

FATHER

LAURELS ROAD

P

Ch

Church

ST MARY'S ROAD

MARY ST

CASTLEROAD

QUAY STREET

POINT ROAD

Sports Ground

Hall

Schs

Church

Bus Station

P

THE LONGWALK

CLANBRASSIL ST

Chapel Street

Schools

SEATOWN

Sch

MILL STREET

Sch

PO

Church

BARRACK ST

MILITARY BARRACKS

BOTHARBRU

ARD EASMUINN

PARK DRIVE

PO

Court House

Town Hall

JOCELYN STREET

SEATOWN PLACE

Church

AVENUE

ANNAVERNA DRIVE

i

CROWE STREET

FRANCIS STREET

RAMPART ROAD

Church

Industrial Estate

P

School

Tourist Office
Tel (042)35484

Fire Station

ST ALPHONSUS ROAD

COES ROAD

RED BARNS ROAD

MCENTEE AVE

ANNE STREET

PARK STREET

Ch

Hall

Church

Sports Ground

Industrial Estate

Railway Station

DUBLIN STREET

HILL STREET

PO

HAZELWOOD AVE

R178
CARRICKMACROSS 21 13

CARRICKMACROSS ROAD

Co Council Offices

P

CHERRYVALE

N52
ARDEE 18 11

ARDEE ROAD

School
Bus Depot

N1
DUBLIN 81 50

P

N52
DUBLIN 81 50

Sch

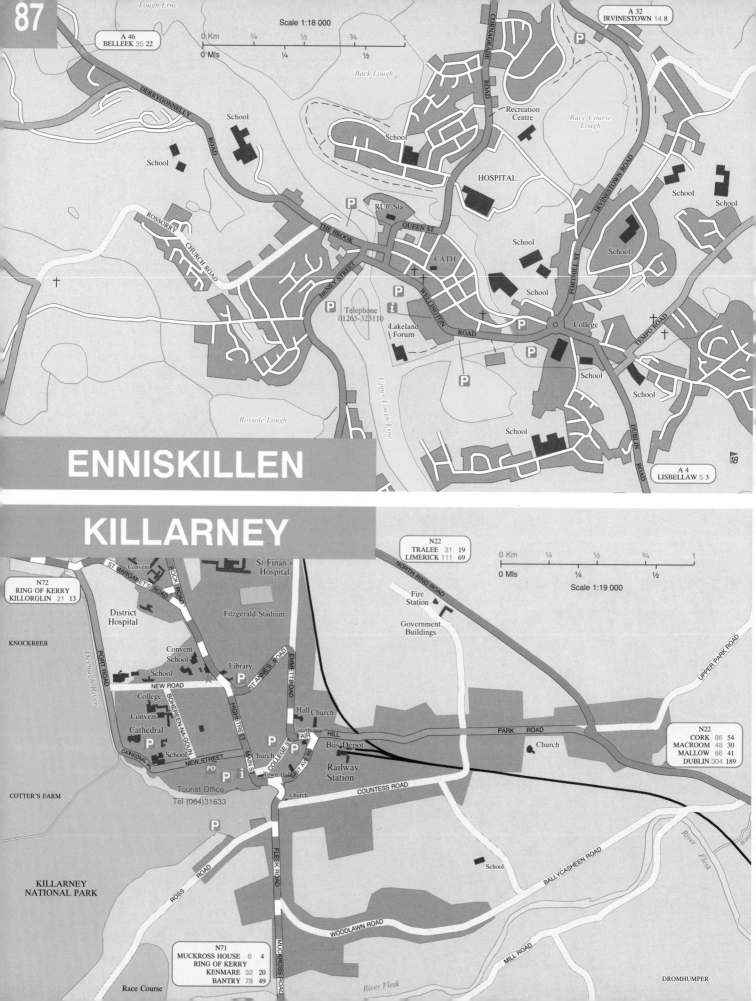

ENNISKILLEN

KILLARNEY

Scale 1:18 000

0 Km ¼ ½ ¾ 1

0 Mls ¼ ½

A 46
BELLEEK 35 22

A 32
IRVINESTOWN 14 8

DERRYGONNELLY ROAD

Lough Erne

Back Lough

CORNAGRADE ROAD

Recreation Centre

Race Course Lough

IRVINESTOWN ROAD

School

School

School

School

School

School

HOSPITAL

ROSSORRY

CHURCH ROAD

RUC Sta

THE BROOK

QUEEN ST

CATH

School

FORTHILL ST

School

HENRY STREET

WELLINGTON

School

College

TEMPO ROAD

P

Telephone
01265-323110

i

Lakeland
Forum

ROAD

P

P

P

School

School

Upper Lough Erne

Rossole Lough

P

School

DUBLIN ROAD

18

A 4
LISBELLAW 5 3

N22
TRALEE 31 19
LIMERICK 111 69

0 Km ¼ ½ ¾ 1

0 Mls ¼ ½

Scale 1:19 000

N72
RING OF KERRY
KILLORGLIN 21 13

St Finan's Hospital

ROCK ROAD

NORTH RING ROAD

Fire Station

Convent

ST MARGARET'S ROAD

Fitzgerald Stadium

Government Buildings

KNOCKREER

District Hospital

PORT ROAD

Deenagh River

Convent School

School

Library

ST ANNE'S ROAD

EMMETT ROAD

UPPER PARK ROAD

NEW ROAD

HIGH STREET

College

BOHEREEN-NA-GOUN

Convent

Cathedral

Hall
Church

PARK ROAD

Church

N22
CORK 86 54
MACROOM 48 30
MALLOW 66 41
DUBLIN 304 189

P

Courthouse

School

NEW STREET

FAIR

HILL

Bus Depot

MAIN ST

P

P

CATHEDRAL PL

PO

i

Church

COLLEGE ST

ST AVE RD

Railway Station

COTTER'S FARM

Town Hall

Tourist Office
Tel (064)31633

Church

COUNTESS ROAD

BALLYCASHEEN ROAD

P

FLESK ROAD

School

River Flesk

KILLARNEY
NATIONAL PARK

ROSS ROAD

MUCKROSS ROAD

WOODLAWN ROAD

MILL ROAD

River Flesk

DROMHUMPER

N71
MUCKROSS HOUSE 6 4
RING OF KERRY
KENMARE 32 20
BANTRY 78 49

Race Course

River Flesk

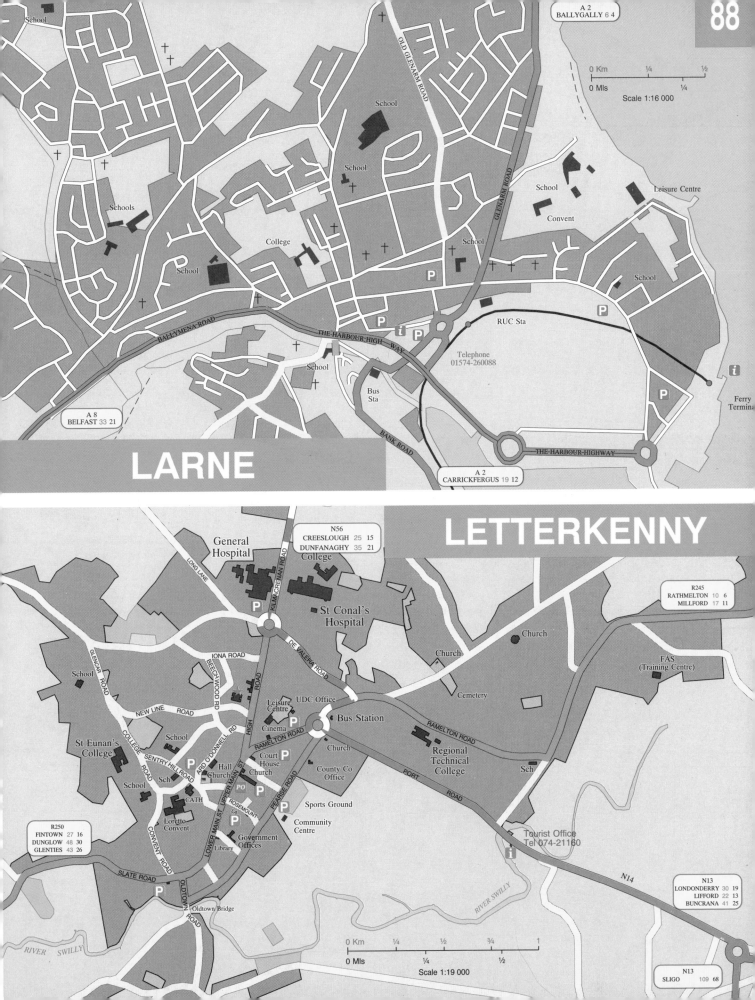

LARNE

LETTERKENNY

Larne map labels:

A 2
BALLYGALLY 6 4

School
School
School
School
School
Leisure Centre
Convent
School
School
School
Schools
College
School
School
P
P
P
OLD GLENARM ROAD
GLENARM ROAD
BALLYMENA ROAD
THE-HARBOUR-HIGH-WAY
i P
RUC Sta
Telephone
01574-260088
School
Bus Sta
P
i
Ferry Termina
BANK ROAD
THE-HARBOUR-HIGHWAY
A 8
BELFAST 33 21
A 2
CARRICKFERGUS 19 12

0 Km   ¼   ½
0 Mls   ¼
Scale 1:16 000

Letterkenny map labels:

N56
CREESLOUGH 25 15
DUNFANAGHY 35 21

R245
RATHMELTON 10 6
MILLFORD 17 11

General Hospital
College
St Conal's Hospital
Church
Church
Church
Cemetery
FÁS (Training Centre)
School
LONG LANE
KILMACRENAN ROAD
DE VALERA ROAD
IONA ROAD
BEECHWOOD RD
GLENCAR ROAD
NEW LINE ROAD
HIGH ROAD
P
Leisure Centre
UDC Office
Bus Station
Cinema
RAMELTON ROAD
St Eunan's College
COLLEGE ROAD
SENTRY HILL ROAD
ARD O'DONNELL RD
School
School
Sch
Hall
Church
PO
Court House
Church
P
P
P
P
County Co Office
Church
Sch
Regional Technical College
RAMELTON ROAD
PORT ROAD
CATH
Loretto Convent
LOWER MAIN ST
UPPER MAIN ST
ROSEMOUNT LA
PEARSE ROAD
Sports Ground
Community Centre
Government Offices
Library
CONVENT ROAD
SLATE ROAD
OLDTOWN ROAD
P
Oldtown Bridge
Tourist Office
Tel 074-21160
i
N14
RIVER SWILLY

R250
FINTOWN 27 16
DUNGLOW 48 30
GLENTIES 43 26

N13
LONDONDERRY 30 19
LIFFORD 22 13
BUNCRANA 41 25

RIVER SWILLY

0 Km   ¼   ½   ¾   1
0 Mls   ¼   ½
Scale 1:19 000

N13
SLIGO   109 68

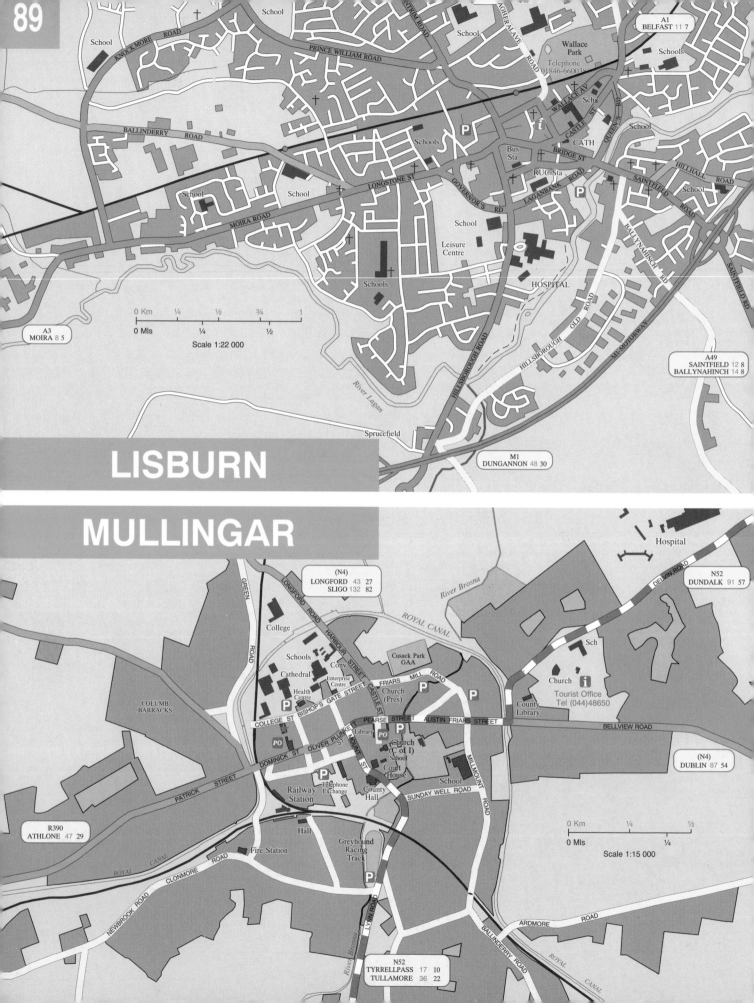

LISBURN

MULLINGAR

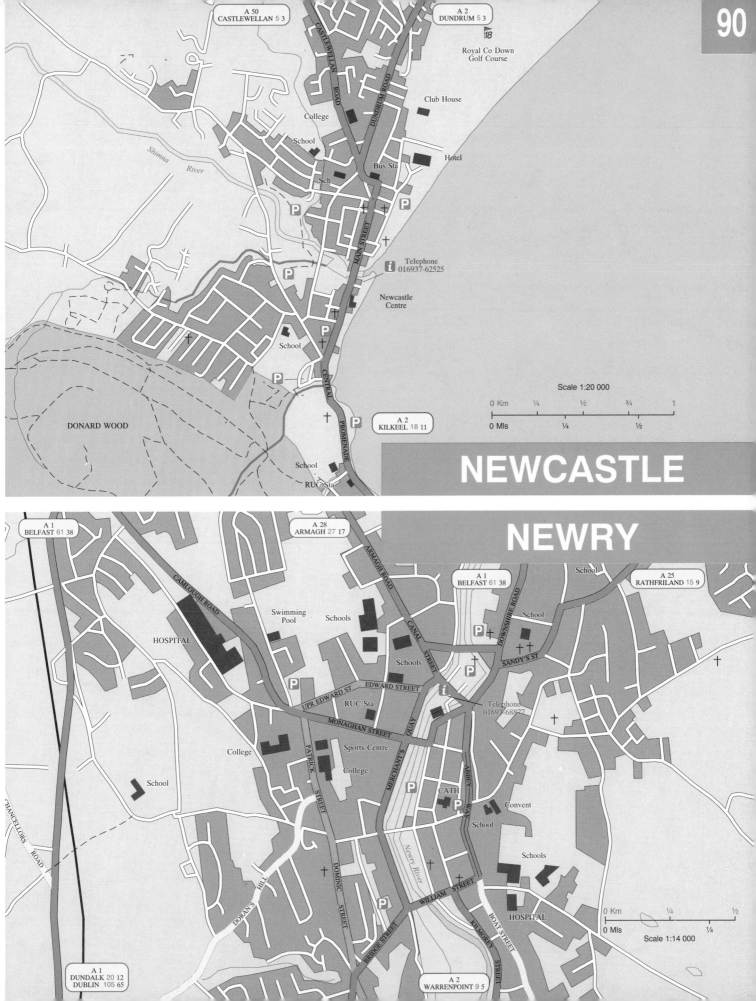

NEWCASTLE

NEWRY

A 50
CASTLEWELLAN 5 3

A 2
DUNDRUM 5 3

18

Royal Co Down
Golf Course

Club House

College

School

Hotel

Sch

Bus Sta

MAIN STREET

CASTLEWELLAN ROAD

DUNDRUM ROAD

P

P

P

i Telephone
016937-62525

Newcastle
Centre

P

School

P

CENTRAL

PROMENADE

P

A 2
KILKEEL 18 11

DONARD WOOD

School

RUC Sta

Shimna River

Scale 1:20 000

0 Km   ¼   ½   ¾   1

0 Mls   ¼   ½

A 1
BELFAST 61 38

A 28
ARMAGH 27 17

School

A 1
BELFAST 61 38

A 25
RATHFRILAND 15 9

CAMLOUGH ROAD

Swimming
Pool

Schools

ARMAGH ROAD

CANAL STREET

DOWNSHIRE ROAD

School

P

HOSPITAL

Schools

SANDY'S ST

P

EDWARD STREET

UPR EDWARD ST

i

P

RUC Sta

Telephone
01693-68877

MONAGHAN STREET

MERCHANT'S QUAY

College

Sports Centre

PATRICK STREET

College

P

CATH

P

Convent

School

DORAN'S HILL

DOMINIC STREET

BRIDGE STREET

School

Newry River

ABBEY WAY

Schools

CHANCELLORS ROAD

P

WILLIAM STREET

KILMOREY STREET

BOAT STREET

HOSPITAL

A 1
DUNDALK 20 12
DUBLIN 105 65

A 2
WARRENPOINT 9 5

0 Km   ¼   ½

0 Mls   ¼

Scale 1:14 000

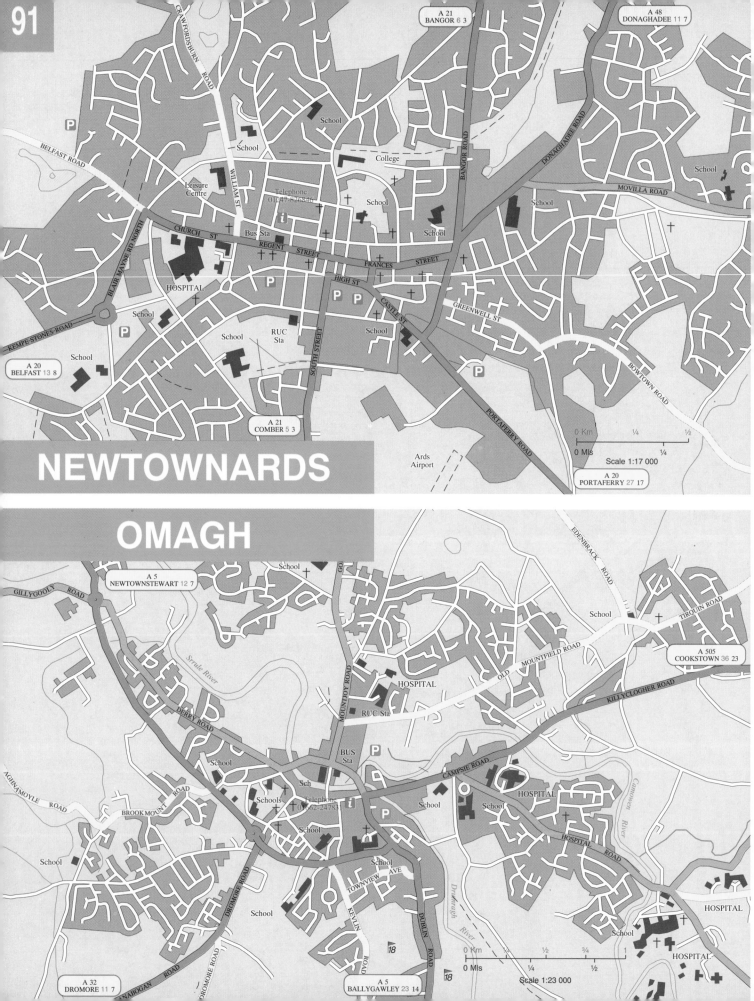

NEWTOWNARDS

OMAGH

NEWTOWNARDS

A 21
BANGOR 6 3

A 48
DONAGHADEE 11 7

CRAWFORDSBURN ROAD

BANGOR ROAD

DONAGHADEE ROAD

MOVILLA ROAD

School

School

College

School

BELFAST ROAD

WILLIAM ST

Leisure Centre

Telephone (01247-826830)

School

School

School

CHURCH ST

Bus Sta

BLAIR MAYNE RD NORTH

REGENT STREET

FRANCES STREET

HOSPITAL

High St

CASTLE ST

GREENWELL ST

School

School

RUC Sta

SOUTH STREET

School

KEMPE-STONES-ROAD

A 20
BELFAST 13 8

School

School

A 21
COMBER 5 3

Ards Airport

PORTAFERRY ROAD

BOWTOWN ROAD

0 Km   ¼   ½
0 Mls   ¼
Scale 1:17 000

A 20
PORTAFERRY 27 17

OMAGH

A 5
NEWTOWNSTEWART 12 7

GILLYGOOLY ROAD

School

EDENBRACK ROAD

School

TIRQUIN ROAD

A 505
COOKSTOWN 36 23

Strule River

OLD MOUNTFIELD ROAD

KILLYCLOGHER ROAD

DERRY ROAD

MOUNTJOY ROAD

HOSPITAL

RUC Sta

AGHNAMOYLE ROAD

BROOKMOUNT ROAD

School

Sch

Schools

Telephone (01662-24783)

BUS Sta

CAMPSIE ROAD

School

HOSPITAL

School

DROMORE ROAD

School

School

School

TOWNVIEW AVE

School

Camowen River

HOSPITAL HOSPITAL ROAD

School

A 32
DROMORE 11 7

NABOGAN ROAD

KEVLIN ROAD

DUBLIN ROAD

Drumragh River

HOSPITAL

18

A 5
BALLYGAWLEY 23 14

18

0 Km   ¼   ½   ¾   1
0 Mls   ¼   ½
Scale 1:23 000

School

HOSPITAL

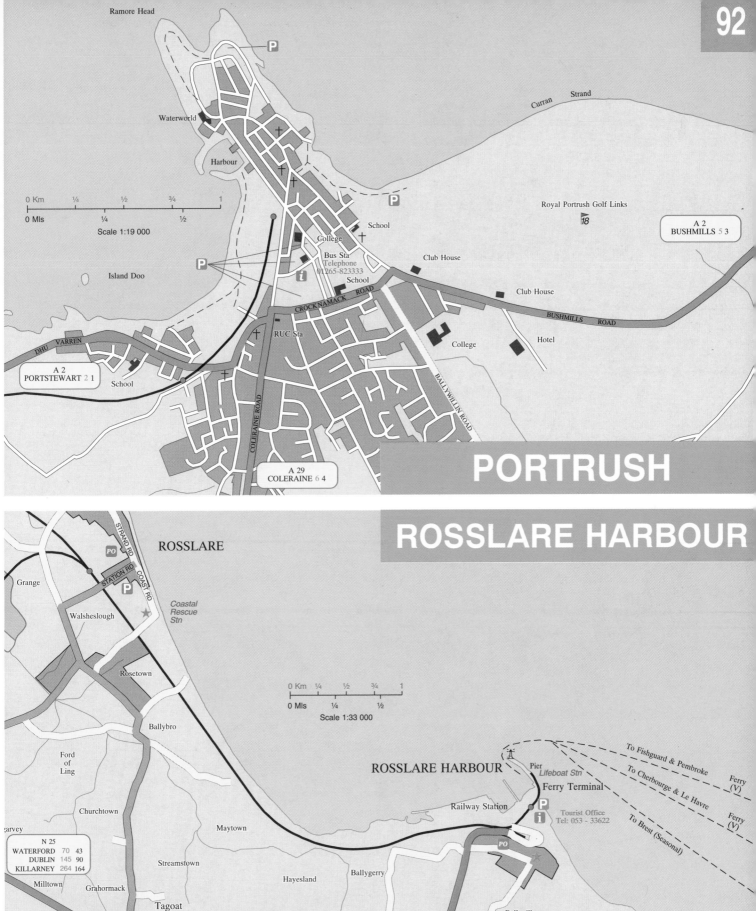

PORTRUSH

Ramore Head

P

Waterworld

Harbour

Curran   Strand

0 Km   ¼   ½   ¾   1
0 Mls   ¼   ½
Scale 1:19 000

Island Doo

P

P

Royal Portrush Golf Links
18

A 2
BUSHMILLS 5 3

School

College

School

Bus Sta
Telephone
91265-823333
i

School

Club House

Club House

BUSHMILLS   ROAD

DHU VARREN

A 2
PORTSTEWART 2 1

School

RUC Sta

CROCKNAMACK   ROAD

College

Hotel

COLERAINE ROAD

BALLYWILLIN ROAD

A 29
COLERAINE 6 4

ROSSLARE HARBOUR

ROSSLARE

STRAND RD
PO

STATION RD

COAST RD

P

Grange

Walsheslough

Coastal
Rescue
Stn

Rosetown

Ballybro

0 Km ¼   ½   ¾   1
0 Mls   ¼   ½
Scale 1:33 000

Ford
of
Ling

To Fishguard & Pembroke

Churchtown

Maytown

ROSSLARE HARBOUR

Pier

Lifeboat Stn
Ferry Terminal

To Cherbourge & Le Havre

Ferry
(V)

garvey

Railway Station

P
Tourist Office
Tel: 053 - 33622
i

Ferry
(V)

N 25
WATERFORD 70 43
DUBLIN 145 90
KILLARNEY 264 164

Streamstown

Hayesland

Ballygerry

PO

To Brest (Seasonal)

Milltown

Grahormack

Tagoat

Sch
PO

Church

P

Ballybing

Kilscoran

Slad

Ballycowan

Kilrane

Church
Sch

i
Tourist Office
Tel: 053 - 33232

Ballygillane

Ballyaddragh   Waddingsland

Churchtown

Bing

Greenore
Point

Car
Bea

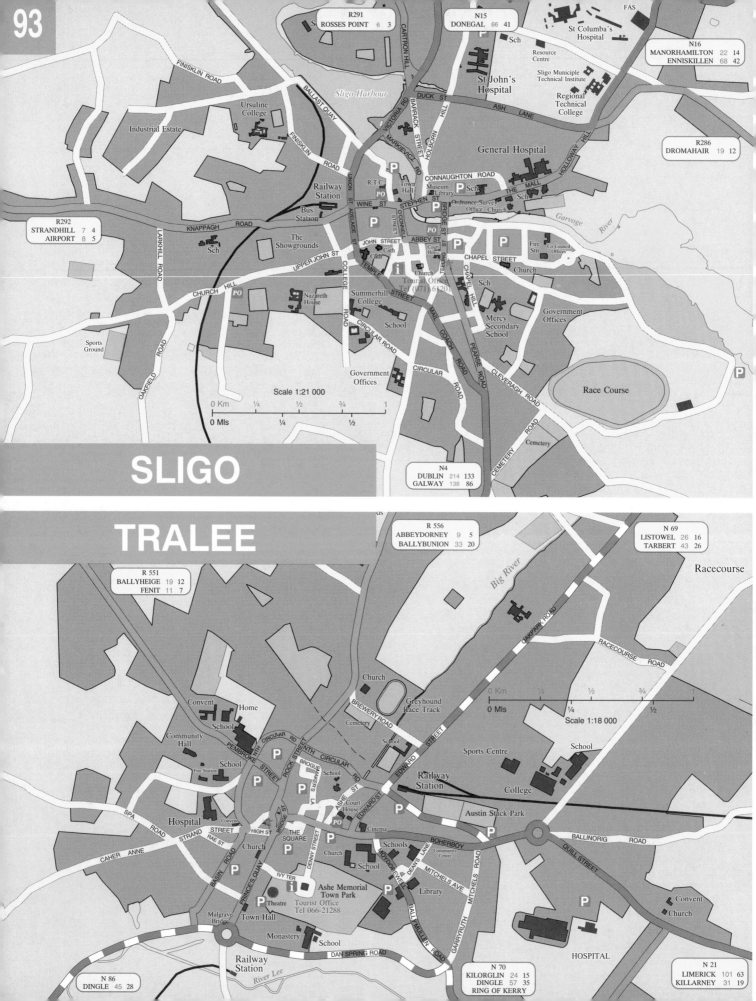

SLIGO

St Columba's Hospital
FÁS
Sch
Resource Centre
Sligo Municiple Technical Institute
Regional Technical College
St John's Hospital
General Hospital

FINISKLIN ROAD
BALLAST QUAY
CARTRON HILL
Sligo Harbour
VICTORIA RD
DUCK ST
BARRACK STREET
MARKIEVICZ RD
HOLBORN HILL
ASH LANE
HOLLOWAY HILL
THE MALL
CONNAUGHTON ROAD

Ursuline College
Industrial Estate
FINISKLIN ROAD
UNION ST
ADELAIDE ST
O'CONNELL ST
R.T.C.
PO
Town Hall
WINE ST
STEPHEN ST
BRIDGE ST
Museum Library
Sch
Sch
Ordnance Survey Office Church
Garvoge River

Railway Station
Bus Station
KNAPPAGH ROAD
LARKHILL ROAD
CHURCH HILL
The Showgrounds
Sch
UPPER JOHN ST
JOHN STREET
COLLEGE ROAD
TEMPLE STREET
Cath
Cath
Court House
Church
ABBEY ST
CASTLE ST
CHAPEL STREET
Fire Stn
Co Council Offices
Church

PO
Nazareth House
Summerhill College
School
CIRCULAR ROAD
SUMMERHILL STREET
MAIL COACH ROAD
PEARSE ROAD
Sch
CHAPEL HILL
Mercy Secondary School
Government Offices
Church

Sports Ground
OAKFIELD ROAD
Government Offices
CIRCULAR ROAD
CLEVERAGH ROAD
Race Course

Scale 1:21 000
0 Km ¼ ½ ¾ 1
0 Mls ¼ ½

CEMETERY ROAD
Cemetery

i
Tourist Office
Tel (071) 61201

TRALEE

Big River
Racecourse
OAKPARK ROAD
RACECOURSE ROAD

Convent
Home
School
Community Hall
School
Fire Station
PEMBROKE STREET
NTH CIRCULAR RD
ROCK STREET
BROGUE MAKERS LA
BREWERY ROAD
Church
Cemetery
Greyhound Race Track
School
EDWARD STREET

Sports Centre
School
College
Railway Station
Austin Stack Park

SPA ROAD
CAHER ANNE
Hospital
STRAND STREET
RAE ST
Convent
BASIN ROAD
PRINCES QUAY
HIGH ST
BRIDGE ST
DENNY STREET
THE SQUARE
Church
ASHE STREET
Court House
PO
EDWARD ST
Cinema
Schools
MOYDERWELL
DEANS LANE
BOHERBOY
MITCHELS ROAD
Community Centre
BALLINORIG ROAD
QUILL STREET

IVY TER
i
Tourist Office
Tel 066-21288
Ashe Memorial Town Park
Theatre
Town Hall
Mulgrave Bridge
Monastery
School
DAN SPRING ROAD
River Lee
Railway Station
Church
School
Library
GARRYRUTH
BALLYMULLEN ROAD
MITCHELS AVE
Convent
Church
HOSPITAL

0 Km ¼ ½ ¾
0 Mls ¼ ½
Scale 1:18 000

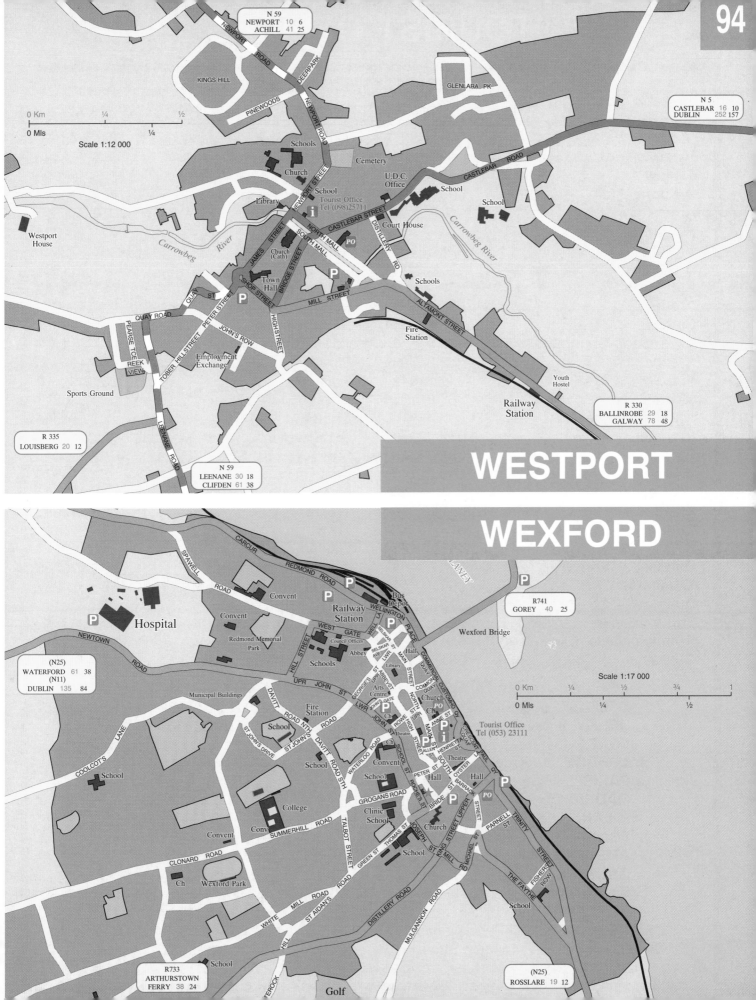

WESTPORT

WEXFORD

Scale 1:12 000

0 Km   ¼   ½
0 Mls   ¼

N 59		
NEWPORT	10	6
ACHILL	41	25

N 5		
CASTLEBAR	16	10
DUBLIN	252	157

R 330		
BALLINROBE	29	18
GALWAY	78	48

R 335		
LOUISBERG	20	12

N 59		
LEENANE	30	18
CLIFDEN	61	38

Tourist Office
Tel (098)25711

KINGS HILL
PINEWOODS
NEWPORT ROAD
DEERPARK
GLENLARA PK
Schools
Cemetery
Church
CASTLEBAR ROAD
U.D.C. Office
School
School
Carrowbeg River
Library
School
Castlebar Street
Court House
NORTH MALL
Westport House
Carrowbeg River
James Street
South Mall
PO
Distillery Rd
Schools
Church (Cath)
Town Hall
Shop Street
Bridge Street
Mill Street
Altamont Street
Quay Road
Quay St
Peter Street
John's Row
Highstreet
Fire Station
Pearse Tce
Reek View
Tober Hillstreet
Employment Exchange
Youth Hostel
Sports Ground
Railway Station
Leenane Road
Carrowbeg River

Scale 1:17 000

0 Km   ¼   ½   ¾   1
0 Mls   ¼   ½

R741		
GOREY	40	25

(N25)		
WATERFORD	61	38
(N11)		
DUBLIN	135	84

R733		
ARTHURSTOWN FERRY	38	24

(N25)		
ROSSLARE	19	12

Tourist Office
Tel (053) 23111

SPAWELL ROAD
CARCUR
REDMOND ROAD
Convent
Railway Station
Bus Depot
WELLINGTON PLACE
Hospital
NEWTOWN ROAD
Convent
Redmond Memorial Park
WEST GATE
Council Offices
Abbey
Main Street
Wexford Bridge
Wexford Bridge
HILL STREET
Schools
Library
SELSKAR AVE
Commercial Quay
Custom House Quay
Church
PO
Municipal Buildings
UPR JOHN ST
Arts Centre
Georges St
John's Gate
Rowe St
High St
North Main St
Church
Theatre
Anne St
Henrietta St
Theatre
COOLCOT'S LANE
DAVITT ROAD NTH
Fire Station
John St
St John's Drive
School
Waterloo Road
Convent
School
Allen St
Peter St
Oyster Lane
South Main St
Hall
Hall
School
DAVITT ROAD STH
School
Convent
School
Thomas St
Roches St
Bride St
King Street Upper
Parnell St
Trinity St
PO
Fishers Row
College
Grogans Road
Clinic
Joseph St
Green St
Church
School
SUMMERHILL ROAD
Talbot Street
Michael St
Barrack St
The Faythe
CLONARD ROAD
Convent
Ch
Wexford Park
ST AIDAN'S ROAD
WHITE MILL ROAD
DISTILLERY ROAD
MULGANNON ROAD
King Mill Rd
School
School
School
Golf

TOURIST OFFICES

REPUBLIC OF IRELAND

The Tourist Offices listed below operate throughout the year, except for those marked thus (*) which are open during the summer months. A full list is availabe from any Bord Fáilte - Irish Tourist Board Office.

*Adare	061 396255	*Glendalough	0404 45581
*Aran Islands (Kilronan)	099 61263	Gorey, Town Centre	055 21248
Arklow	0402 32484	*Kildare	045 522696
*Athlone	0902 94630	Kilkenny, Rose Inn Street	056 51500
Athy	0507 31859	Killarney, Town Hall	064 31633
Baggot St. Bridge (Head Office)	01 602 4000	*Kinsale	021 772234
Blarney	021 381624	*Knock Airport	094 67247
Brú na Bóinne Visitor Centre (Newgrange)	041 24274	Letterkenny, Derry Road	074 21160
Bundoran	072 41350	Limerick City, Arthur's Quay	061 317522
*Cahir	052 41453	Longford	043 46566
Carlow, College Street	0503 31554	*New Ross	051 21857
*Carrick-on-Shannon	078 20170	*Monaghan, Market House	047 81122
*Cashel (Town Hall)	062 61333	Mullingar, Dublin Road	044 48650
*Cavan, Farnham Street	049 31942	Portlaoise	0502 21178
*Cliffs of Moher, Liscannor	065 81171	*Rosslare Terminal	053 33622
*Clonmacnoise	0905 74134	Shannon Airport	061 471664
Clonmel	052 22960	Skibbereen, Town Hall	028 21766
Cork City, Tourist House, Grand Parade	021 273251	Sligo, Temple Street	071 61201
*Dingle	066 51188	Tipperary	062 51457
Donegal Town, The Quay	073 21148	*Tramore	051 381572
*Drogheda	041 37070	Tralee, Ashe Memorial Hall	066 21288
Dublin, Suffolk Street, Dublin 2.	01 605 7799	Trim	046 37111
	1550 112233	*Tullamore	0506 52617
Dundalk, Market Square	042 35484	Waterford, 41 The Quay	051 875788
*Dungarvan	058 41741	*Waterford Crystal Visitor Centre	051 358397
Dunglow	075 21297	Westport, The Mall	098 25711
Ennis, Clare Road	065 28366	Wexford, Crescent Quay	053 23111
*Enniscorthy (The Castle)	054 34699	Wicklow, Fitzwilliam Square	0404 69117
Galway, Victoria Place, Eyre Square	091 563081		

INTERNATIONAL OFFICES

BELFAST, 53 Castle Street	01232 327888
DERRY, 8 Bishop Street	01504 369501
LONDON, 150 New Bond Street	0171 493 3201
LONDON, 12 Regent Street	0171 839 8416
PARIS, 33 Rue de Miromesnil	0153 43 1212
MADRID, Claudio Coello 73	91 577 1787
MILAN, via S Maria Segreta 6	02 869 0541
FRANKFURT, Untermainanlage 7	069 236492
AMSTERDAM, Spuistraat 106-108	020 622 3101
BRUSSELS, Avenue de Beaulieu 25	02 673 9940
STOCKHOLM, Sipyllegatan 49	08 662 8510
COPENHAGAN, Klostergarden, Amagertory 293	33 15 8045
NEW YORK, 345 Park Avenue	212 418 0800
SYDNEY, 36 Carrington Street	02 9299 6177
TOKYO, 2-10-7 Kojimachi, Chiyoda-ku	03 5275 1611

NORTHERN IRELAND TOURIST BOARD

HEAD OFFICE			01 232 23 1221
59 North Street, Belfast. BT1 1NB	Fax		01 232 24 0960
DUBLIN			01 679 1977
16 Nassau Street, Dublin 2.	Fax		01 679 1863
LONDON			0171 355 5040
11 Berkley Street, London. W1X 5AD	Fax		0171 409 0487
GLASGOW			0141 204 4454
135 Buchanon Street, Glasgow. G1 2JA	Fax		0141 204 4033
U.S.A.			212 922 0101
551 Fifth Avenue, Suite 701, New York NY 10176	Fax		212 922 0099
CANADA			416 925 6368
111 Avenue Road, Suite 450, Toronto. M5R 3J8	Fax		416 961 2175
FRANCE			139 21 9380
3 Rue de Pontoise, 78100 St, Germain-en-Laye	Fax		139 21 9390
GERMANY			069 23 4504
Taunusstrasse 52-60, 60329 Frankfurt/Main.	Fax		069 23 3480

NETWORKED TOURIST INFORMATION CENTRES

The Tourist Information Centre Network provides a first-class information service for visitors to Northern Ireland and for local residents.Services available at these offices include : free information on the local area - tourist attractions, accommodations, where to eat, events; free information on holidays throughout Northern Ireland; accommodation booking for Ireland and the U.K.

Belfast, St. Anne's Court, 59 North Street - Head Office	01232-246609
Antrim, Pogues Entry, Church Street	01849-428331
Armagh. Old Bank Building, 40 English Street	01861-521800
Ballycastle, Sheskburn House, 7 Mary Street	012657-62024
Banbridge, Gateway Tourist Information Centre, 200 Newry Road	018206-23322
Bangor, 34 Quay Street	01247-270069
Belfast City Airport, Sydenham Bypass	01232-457745
Belfast International Airport	01849-422888
Carrickfergus, Heritage Plaza, Antrim Street	01960-366455
Coleraine, Railway Road	01265-44723
Cookstown, 48 Molesworth Street	016487-66727
Downpatrick, 74 Market Street	01396-612233
Enniskillen, Wellington Road	01365-323110
Giant's Causeway, 44 Causeway Road, Bushmills	012657-31855
Kilkeel, 6 Newcastle Street	016937-62525
Killymaddy, Ballygawley Road, Dungannon	01868-767259
Larne, Narrow Gauge Road	01574-260088
Limavady, Council Offices, 7 Connell Street	015047-22226
Lisburn, Irish Linen Centre & Lisburn Museum, Market Square	01846-660038
Londonderry, 8 Bishop Street	01504-267284
Newcastle, 10-14 Central Promenade	013967-22222
Newtownards, 31 Regent Street	01247-826846
Omagh, 1 Market Street	01662-247831
Portrush, Dunluce Centre, Sandhill Drive	01265-823333
Strabane, Abercorn Square	01504-883735

GOLFING INFORMATION

Affiliated to the Golf Union of Ireland
This listing is by Province and County
The name of the Golf Club is preceded by the number of holes and followed
by a page number and a reference for the grid square in which the golf location symbol appears.

CONNAUGHT

Co.GALWAY
9 Ardacong	32	E1
18 Athenry	32	E4
18 Ballinasloe	33	A4
18 Barna	31	C4
18 Connemara	29	B2
9 Connemara Isles	30	F3
9 Curra	32	G5
18 Galway	31	C4
18 Galway Bay	31	D4
9 Gort	42	E1
18 Loughrea	32	G5
9 Mountbellew	32	G2
18 Oughterard	30	H2
18 Portumna	43	A1
18 Tuam	32	E2

Co LEITRIM
9 Ballinamore	17	A5
9 Carrick-on-Shannon	25	A1

Co MAYO
9 Achill Island	21	C1
18 Ballina	14	H5
18 Ballinrobe	22	H5
9 Ballyhaunis	24	E3
18 Belmullet	13	B3
18 Castlebar	22	H3
9 Claremorris	23	D4
9 Mulranny	22	E2
9 Swinford	23	D2
18 Westport	22	F3

Co ROSCOMMON
18 Athlone	33	C2
9 Ballaghaderreen	24	G2
9 Boyle	25	A1
9 Castlerea	24	G3
18 Roscommon	25	A5
9 Strokestown	25	B4

Co SLIGO
9 Ballymote	15	D5
18 Co Sligo	15	D2
18 Enniscrone	14	H4
18 Strandhill	15	D3

LEINSTER

Co CARLOW
9 Borris	53	B2
18 Carlow	45	B4
18 Mount Wolseley	45	C4

Co DUBLIN
18 Balbriggan	28	G5
18 Balcarrick	36	G2
18 Ballinascorney	36	E4
18 Beaverstown	36	G1
18 Beech Park	35	D4
18 City West	36	E4
18 Coldwinters	36	F2
18 Corballis	36	G2
27 Corrstown	36	F2
18 Donabate	36	G2
18 Dublin Mountain	36	E4
18 Dun Laoire	36	G4
9 Finnstown	36	E3
18 Forrest Little	36	F2
18 Hermitage	36	F2
11 Hazel Grove	36	E4
18 Hollywood Lakes	36	F1
18 The Island	36	G2
9 Killiney	36	G4
18 Kilternan	36	G4
18 Lucan	36	E3
18 Luttrellstown	36	E3
27 Malahide	36	G2
18 Old Conna	36	G4
27 Portmarnock	36	G2
9 Rush	36	G1
18 St Margarets	36	F2
18 Skerries	36	G1
18 Slade Valley	36	E4
18 Swords	36	F2
9 Turvey	36	G1
18 Westmanstown	36	E3
18 Woodbrook	36	G4

DUBLIN CITY
9 Carrickmines	36	G4
18 Castle	36	F4
18 Clontarf	36	F3
34 Deer Park	36	G3
18 Edmondstown	36	F4
18 Elmgreen	36	E3
18 Elm Park	36	F4
9 Foxrock	36	G4
24 Grange	36	F4
18 Hollystown	36	E2
11 Hazel Grove	36	E4
18 Howth	36	G3
9 Kilmashogue	36	F4
18 Milltown	36	F4
18 Newlands	36	E4
9 Rathfarnham	36	F4
18 Royal Dublin	36	G3
18 St. Anne's	36	G3
18 Stackstown	36	F4
9 Sutton	36	G3

Co LAOIS
9 Abbeyleix	44	G3
18 The Heath	44	H1

18 Mountrath	44	F2
34 Portarlington	34	H5
9 Rathdowney	44	E4

Co KILDARE
18 Athy	45	B2
36 Bodenstown	35	C4
18 Castlewarden	35	D4
9 Cíll Dara	35	B5
9 Clongowes	35	C3
18 Craddockstown	35	D5
18 Curragh	35	B5
27 Highfield	35	A3
18 Killeen	35	D4
18 Knockanally	35	C3
18 K Club	35	D4
9 Leixlip	36	E3
18 Naas	35	D4
9 Woodlands	35	B4

Co KILKENNY
12 Callan	52	G2
9 Castlecomer	44	H4
18 Kilkenny	52	H1
18 Mount Juliet	52	H2
18 Waterford	53	A5

Co LONGFORD
18 Co Longford	25	D4

Co LOUTH
18 Ardee	27	D2
18 Co Louth	28	F4
18 Dundalk	28	E1
18 Greenore	19	D5
18 Killinbeg	28	E1
9 Townley Hall	28	E4
18 Seapoint	28	F3

Co MEATH
18 Ashbourne	36	E1
27 Black Bush	35	D1
9 Gormanstown	28	F5
18 Headfort	27	B4
18 Kilcock	35	C2
18 Laytown & Bettystown	28	F4
18 Moor Park	27	D5
27 Royal Tara	27	C5
18 Trim	35	B1

Co OFFALY
18 Birr	43	C1
18 Castle Barna	34	G4
18 Edenderry	35	A3
18 Tullamore	34	F4

Co WESTMEATH
18 Delvin Castle	26	H5
21 Glasson	33	C2

18 Moate	33	D3
18 Mount Temple	33	D2
18 Mullingar	34	G2

Co WEXFORD
18 Courtown	54	F1
18 Enniscorthy	53	D3
18 New Ross	53	A4
18 Rosslare	54	E5
18 St.Helen's Bay	54	F5
9 Tara Glen	46	G5
18 Wexford	54	E4

Co WICKLOW
18 Arklow	46	G4
9 Baltinglass	45	C3
18 Blainroe	46	H2
9 Bray	36	G5
18 Charlesland	36	H5
9 Coollattin	46	E5
18 Delgany	36	G5
9 Djouce Mountain	46	G1
18 Druid's Glen	46	G1
18 Glenmalure	46	F3
18 Greystones	36	G5
9 Kilcoole	46	H1
18 Powerscourt	36	G5
18 Rathsallagh	45	C2
18 Roundwood	46	G1
18 The European Club	46	H3
18 Tulfarris	45	D1
18 Wicklow	46	H2
18 Woodenbridge	46	F4

MUNSTER

Co CLARE
9 Clonlara	42	G5
18 Dromoland	41	D4
9 East Clare	42	F3
18 Ennis	41	D4
9 Kilkee	39	D5
18 Kilrush	49	A1
36 Lahinch	40	F3
18 Shannon	41	D5
9 Spanish Point	40	F4
18 Woodstock	41	D4

Co CORK
18 Bandon	68	E1
9 Bantry Park	66	H1
9 Berehaven	66	F2
18 Charleville	50	F4
9 Cobh	61	A5
9 Coosheen	66	H3
18 Cork	60	H4
9 Doneraile	60	F1

18 Douglas — 60 H5
9 Dunmore — 67 D3
18 East Cork — 61 A4
18 Fermoy — 60 H2
18 Fernhill — 60 H5
18 Fota Island — 60 H4
9 Frankfield — 60 G5
9 Glengarriff — 66 H1
18 Harbour Point — 60 H4
18 Kanturk — 59 D1
27 Kinsale — 68 G1
18 Lee Valley — 60 F4
9 Macroom — 59 D4
18 Mahon — 60 H4
18 Mallow — 60 F2
15 Mitchelstown — 50 H5
18 Monkstown — 60 H5
18 Muskerry — 60 F4
9 Raffeen Creek — 60 H5
18 Skibbereen — 67 B3
18 Youghal — 61 D4

Co KERRY
9 Ardfert — 48 G4
36 Ballybunion — 48 G2
9 Ballyheigue Castle — 48 F4
18 Beaufort — 58 G2
9 Castlegregory — 48 E5
18 Ceann Sibeal — 57 B1
18 Dooks — 58 E2
18 Kenmare — 58 H4
9 Kerries — 48 G5
36 Killarney — 58 H2
18 Killorglin — 58 G2
9 Parknasilla — 58 F5
9 Ross — 58 H3
18 Tralee — 48 F5
18 Waterville — 57 C5

Co LIMERICK
9 Abbeyfeale — 49 B4
18 Adare Manor — 50 E2
18 Castletroy — 50 G1
18 Killeline — 49 C3
18 Limerick — 50 F1
18 Limerick Co — 50 G1

Co TIPPERARY
18 Ballykisteen — 51 A3
18 Cahir Park — 51 C4
18 Clonmel — 52 E4
18 Co Tipperary — 51 B2
18 Nenagh — 43 B3
9 Rockwell — 51 C3
18 Roscrea — 43 D3
9 Templemore — 43 D4
18 Thurles — 51 D1
9 Tipperary — 51 A3

Co WATERFORD
18 Carrick-on-Suir — 52 G4
18 Dungarvan — 62 E2
18 Dunmore East — 63 B3
18 Faithlegg — 53 A5
9 Gold Coast — 62 F2
9 Lismore — 61 C2
18 Tramore — 62 H1
18 Waterford Castle — 53 A5

18 West Waterford — 62 E2

ULSTER

Co ANTRIM
18 Ballycastle — 5 D2
18 Ballyclare — 11 D2
18 Ballymena — 11 C1
18 Burnfield House — 12 E3
18 Bushfoot — 4 G2
18 Cairndhu — 12 E1
18 Carrickfergus — 11 D3
9 Cushendall — 6 E4
9 Gracehill — 5 B3
9 Greenisland — 12 E3
9 Lambeg — 11 D5
9 Larne — 12 F1
18 Lisburn — 11 D5
9 Mallusk — 11 D3
18 Massereene — 11 C3
45 Royal Portrush — 4 H3
18 Whitehead — 12 F2

Co ARMAGH
18 Ashfield — 19 A5
18 Co Armagh — 18 H2
18 Edenmore — 19 C1
18 Lurgan — 19 B1
18 Portadown — 19 B1
18 Silverwood — 19 B1
18 Tandragee — 19 B2

BELFAST
18 Balmoral — 12 E4
18 Belvoir Park — 12 E5
9 Cliftonville — 12 E4
18 Dunmurry — 12 E5
18 Fortwilliam — 12 E4
9 Gilnahirk — 12 F4
18 Knock — 12 F4
27 Malone — 12 E5
18 Mount Ober — 12 E5
9 Ormeau — 12 E4
18 Shandon Park — 12 E4

Co CAVAN
9 Belturbet — 17 C5
9 Blacklion — 16 H3
9 Cabra Castle — 27 B2
18 Co Cavan — 26 G1
18 Slieve Russell — 17 B4
9 Virginia — 27 A3

Co DONEGAL
18 Ballybofey & Stranorlar — 9 A2
18 Ballyliffin — 3 A2
9 Buncrana — 3 A3
18 Bundoran — 8 F5
9 Chloic Cheann Fhaola — 2 E3
9 Cruit Island — 1 C5
18 Donegal — 8 G4

18 Dunfanaghy — 2 F3
9 Gaoth Dobhair — 1 D4
18 Greencastle — 3 D2
18 Letterkenny — 2 H5
18 Naran & Portnoo — 8 E2
18 North West — 3 A4
9 Otway — 3 A3
18 Portsalon — 2 H2
9 Redcastle — 3 C3
18 Rosapenna — 2 G3

Co DOWN
18 Ardglass — 20 G3
18 Banbridge — 19 C2
18 Bangor — 12 G3
36 Blackwood — 12 F4
18 Bright Castle — 20 F3
18 Carnalea — 12 F3
36 Clandeboye — 12 F4
9 Crossgar — 20 F1
18 Donaghadee — 12 G3
18 Downpatrick — 20 G2
9 Helen's Bay — 12 F3
18 Holywood — 12 F4
18 Kilkeel — 19 D5
18 Kirkistown Castle — 20 H1
9 Mahee Island — 12 G5
18 Ringdufferin — 20 G1
18 Rockmount — 12 E5
18 Royal Belfast — 12 F4
36 Royal Co Down — 20 E3
18 Scrabo Newtownards — 12 F4
18 Spa Ballynahinch — 20 E1

9 Temple — 20 E1
18 Warrenpoint — 19 C5

Co FERMANAGH
18 Castle Hume — 17 B2
18 Enniskillen — 17 B2

Co LONDONDERRY
9 Brown Trout — 4 H4
27 Castlerock — 4 E3
27 City of Derry — 3 B5
27 Foyle — 3 B4
9 Kilrea — 4 G5
9 Manor — 5 A5
18 Moyola Park — 11 A2
45 Portstewart — 4 E3
18 Roe Park — 3 D4

Co MONAGHAN
9 Castleblaney — 18 H5
9 Clones — 17 D4
9 Mannan Castle — 27 C1
18 Nuremore — 27 C1
18 Rossmore — 18 F3

Co TYRONE
9 Aughnacloy — 18 F1
18 Dungannon — 10 G5
9 Fintona — 9 D5
18 Killymoon Cookstown — 10 H4
18 Newtownstewart — 9 C3
18 Omagh — 9 D4
18 Strabane — 9 C2

GAZETTEER

This Gazetteer lists place-names in alphabetical order. The figure in bold type immediately following the name is the number of the page on which the place appears and the alphanumeric reference indicates the appropriate grid square.

Example:- Allenwood / *Fiodh Alúine*   **35** B4

Allenwood will be found on page **35** square B4

A

Abbey / *An Mhainistir*	**42** H1
Abbeydorney / *Mainistir Ó dTorna*	**48** G4
Abbeyfeale / *Mainistir na Feile*	**49** B4
Abbeylara / *Mainistir Leathratha*	**26** F4
Abbeyleix / *Mainistir Laoise*	**44** G3
Abbeyshrule / *Mainistir Shruthla*	**34** E1
Abington	**50** H1
Achill Sound / *Gob an Choire*	**21** D2
Achonry / *Achadh Conaire*	**15** C5
Aclare / *Áth An Chláir*	**15** B5
Acton	**19** B2
Adamstown / *Maigh Arnai*	**53** C4
Adare / *Áth Dara*	**50** E2
Addergoole Co Mayo	**23** D3
Addergoole Co Galway	**31** D3
Adrigole	**66** G1
Aghaboe / *Achadh Bhó*	**44** F3
Aghaboy	**25** D3
Aghabullogue / *Achadh Bolg*	**60** E4
Aghada	**61** A5
Aghadifn	**24** F2
Aghadoon	**13** B3
Aghadowey / *Achadh Dubhtaigh*	**4** F4
Aghagallon / *Achadh Gallan*	**11** C5
Aghagower / *Achadh Ghobhair*	**22** G4
Aghalee / *Achadh Lí*	**11** C5
Aghamore / *Achadh Mór* Co Leitrim / *Liatroim*	**25** C2
Aghamore / *Achadh Mór* Co Mayo / *Maigh Eo*	**24** E3
Aghavas / *Achadh an Mheasa*	**25** D1
Aghern	**61** A2
Aghleam	**13** B4
Aghnacliff / *Achadh na Cloiche*	**26** E3
Aghnamullen / *Achadh na Muileann*	**18** F5
Agivey	**4** F4
Aglish / *An Eaglais* Co Kerry / *Ciarraí*	**57** D2
Aglish / *An Eaglais* Co Tipperary / *Tiobraid Árann*	**43** B2
Aglish / *An Eaglais* Co Waterford / *Port Láirge*	**61** D2
Ahafona	**48** G2
Ahakista	**66** G3
Ahascragh / *Ath Eascrach*	**32** H3
Aherla / *An Eatharla*	**60** F5
Ahoghill / *Achadh Eochaille*	**11** B1
Ailladie	**40** F1
Aldergrove / *An Garrán Fearnóigo*	**11** C4
Allen	**35** B4
Allenwood / *Fiodh Alúine*	**35** B4
Allihies / *Na hAitichi*	**65** D2
Allistragh / *An tAilastrach*	**18** H2
Alloon Lower	**32** G3
Altnapaste	**8** H2
An Greata Mór	**13** B3
Anascaul / *Abhainn an Scáil*	**57** D1

Anlore	**18** E4
Annacarriga	**42** G4
Annacarty / *Áth na Cairte*	**51** B2
Annaclone / *Eanach Cluana*	**19** C2
Annacloy / *Áth na Cloiche*	**20** F2
Annacotty	**50** G1
Annacurragh	**46** E4
Annacurragh	**46** E4
Annadorn	**20** F2
Annagap	**57** D1
Annagary / *Anagaire*	**1** C5
Annagassan / *Áth na gCasán*	**28** E2
Annagh Co Limerick	**50** G1
Annagh Co Roscommon	**24** G4
Annagh Neal	**42** F3
Annaghdown	**31** C3
Annaghmore / *Eanach Mór*	**25** C5
Annahilt / *Eanach Eilte*	**20** E1
Annalong / *Áth na Long*	**20** E5
Annamoe	**46** F2
Annascaul / *Abhainn an Scáil*	**57** D1
Annaville	**43** C2
Annayalla / *Eanaigh Gheala*	**18** G4
Annestown / *Bun Abha*	**62** G2
Annfield	**43** C5
Annsborough / *Baile Anna*	**20** E3
Antrim / *Aontroim*	**11** C3
Araglin / *Airglinn*	**61** B1
Archerstown / *Baile an Airsirigh*	**26** H5
Ardagh / *Ardach* Co Limerick / *Luimneach*	**49** C3
Ardagh / *Ardach* Co Longford / *An Longfort*	**26** E5
Ardagh / *Ardach* Co Meath / *An Mhí*	**27** C2
Ardagunna	**61** D1
Ardan	**34** F4
Ardanew	**35** B2
Ardara / *Ard an Rátha*	**8** E2
Ardattin / *Ard Aitinn*	**45** C5
Ardbane	**8** F3
Ardcath	**28** E5
Ardconnell	**48** F4
Ardcrony / *Ard Cróine*	**43** A3
Ardee / *Baile Átha Fhirdhia*	**27** D2
Ardfert / *Ard Fhearta*	**48** F4
Ardfeld / *Ard ó bhFicheallaigh*	**67** D3
Ardfinnan / *Ard Fhionáin*	**51** C5
Ardglass Co Cork	**61** A3
Ardglass / *Ard Ghlais* Co. Down / *An Dún*	**20** G3
Ardgroom / *Dhá Dhrom*	**66** E1
Ardkearagh	**57** D5
Ardkeen / *Ard Caoin*	**20** H1
Ardkill	**23** C5
Ardlea	**44** G2
Ardlougher / *Ard Luachra*	**17** B5
Ardmore / *Aird Mhór*	**61** D4
Ardmorney	**34** F3
Ardnasodan	**32** E3

Ardpatrick / *Ard Pádraig*	**50** G4
Ardra	**61** A5
Ardrah Co Cork	**67** A1
Ardrah Co Cork	**67** A2
Ardrahan / *Ard Raithin*	**32** E5
Ardress	**19** A1
Ardrigole	**66** G1
Ardscull	**45** B2
Ardstraw / *Ard Sratha*	**9** C3
Ardtrea / *Ard Tré*	**10** H4
Arigna / *An Airgnigh*	**16** G5
Arklow / *An tInbhear Mór*	**46** G4
Arless	**45** A3
Armagh / *Ard Mhacha*	**18** H2
Armoy / *Oirthear Maí*	**4** H3
Arney	**17** B3
Arranagh	**49** C4
Arthurstown / *Colmán*	**53** B5
Articlave / *Ard an Chléibh*	**4** E3
Artigarvan / *Ard Tí Garbháin*	**9** C1
Arvagh	**26** E2
Ashbourne / *Cill Dhéagláin*	**36** E1
Ashford / *Áth na Fuinseoige*	**46** G2
Ashhill	**51** D1
Askamore / *An Easca Mhór*	**54** E1
Askanagap	**46** E3
Askeaton / *Eas Géitine*	**49** D1
Astee / *Eas Daoi*	**48** H2
Athavallie	**23** C3
Athboy / *Baile Átha Buí*	**27** B5
Athea / *Áth an tSléibhe*	**49** B3
Athenry / *Baile Átha an Rí*	**32** F4
Athgarvan / *Áth Garbháin*	**35** C5
Athlacca / *An tÁth Leacach*	**50** F3
Athleague / *Áth Liag*	**33** A1
Athlone / *Baile Átha Luain*	**33** C2
Athnid	**43** D5
Athy / *Baile Átha Í*	**45** A2
Attanagh / *Áth Tanaí*	**44** G4
Attical / *Áth Tí Chathail*	**19** D5
Atticof fey	**33** A4
Attiregan	**32** H3
Attymass / *Áth Tí an Mheasaigh*	**14** H5
Attymon / *Áth Tiomáin*	**32** F3
Auburn	**33** D1
Aucloggeen	**31** D3
Aughacasla	**48** E5
Augher / *Eochair*	**18** E1
Aughfad	**53** D5
Aughils	**58** F1
Aughinish / *Eachinis*	**31** C5
Aughnacloy / *Achadh na Cloiche*	**18** F1
Aughnadeagh	**11** A1
Aughrim Co Clare	**41** D2
Aughrim / *Eachroim* Co Galway / *Gaillimh*	**32** H4
Aughrim / *Eachroim* Co Wicklow / *Cill Mhantáin*	**46** F3
Avoca / *Abhóca*	**46** G3

B

Baconstown — 35 B2
Baileysmill / Muileann Bhaile — 20 E1
Bailieborough / Coillan Chollaigh — 27 A2
Balbriggan / Baile Brigin — 28 G5
Balla / Balla — 23 C3
Ballaba — 42 E1
Ballady — 68 G1
Ballagh Co Galway — 33 B1
Ballagh / An Bealach — 49 C4
  Co Limerick / Luimneach
Ballagh Co Roscommon — 33 B1
Ballagh Co Roscommon — 25 B4
Ballagh Co Tipperary — 51 C2
Ballagh Co Wexford — 53 C4
Ballaghaderreen / Bealach An Doirín — 24 G2
Ballaghbehy — 49 B4
Ballaghboy — 51 D2
Ballaghkeen / An Bealach — 54 E3
Ballard — 34 F4
Ballardiggan — 42 F1
Ballare — 64 G3
Balleen — 44 F5
Ballickmoyler / Baile Mhic Mhaoilir — 45 A3
Balliggan — 12 H5
Ballilogue — 53 A3
Ballina / Béal an Átha — 14 H5
  Co Mayo / Maigh Eo
Ballina Co Tipperary — 42 H4
Ballinaboy Co Cork — 60 G5
Ballinaboy Co Galway — 29 C2
Ballinabrackey / Buaile na Bréachmhaí — 34 H2
Ballinabranagh — 45 A4
Ballinaclash / An Chlais — 46 F3
Ballinadee / Baile na Daibhche — 68 F1
Ballinafad / Béal an Átha Fada — 24 H1
Ballinagar / Béal na Glarr — 34 G4
Ballinagleragh / Baile na gCléireach — 16 G4
Ballinakill — 44 G3
Ballinalack / Béal Átha na Leac — 26 F5
Ballinalea — 46 G2
Ballinalee / Béal Átha na Lao — 26 E3
Ballinamallard / Béal Átha na Mallacht — 17 B1
Ballinameen / Béal an Átha na Min — 24 H2
Ballinamore / Béal an Átha na Móir — 17 A5
Ballinascarty / Béal na Scairte — 68 E2
Ballinasloe / Béal Átha na Sluaighe — 33 A3
Ballinaspick — 61 C2
Ballinbranagh — 45 A4
Ballinclashet — 68 G1
Ballinclay — 53 D4
Ballincollig / Baile an Chollaigh — 60 F4
Ballincor — 43 B1
Ballincrea — 53 A5
Ballincreeshig — 60 G5
Ballincurrig / Baile an Churraigh — 61 A3
Ballindaggan / Baile an Daingin — 53 C2
Ballinderreen / Baile an Doirín — 31 D5
Ballinderry / Baile an Doire — 11 C5
  Co Antrim / Aontroim
Ballinderry / Baile an Doire — 43 A2
  Co Tipperary / Tiobraid Árann
Ballindine / Baile an Daighin — 23 D5
Ballindrait / Baile an Droichid — 9 C2
Ballineanig — 57 B1
Ballineen / Béal Átha Fhínín — 67 D1
Ballingarrane / Baile an Gharráin — 49 D2

Ballingarry / Baile an Gharraí — 52 F2
  Co Tipperary / Tiobraid Árann
Ballingarry / Baile an Gharraí — 43 B2
  Co Tipperary / Tiobraid Árann
Ballingarry / Baile an Gharraí — 50 E3
  Co Limerick / Luimneach
Ballingeary / Béal Átha an Ghaorthaidh — 59 B5
Ballinglen / Baile an Gleanna — 14 F3
Ballingurteen — 67 C2
Ballinhassig / Béal Átha an Cheasaigh — 60 G5
Ballinillaun — 32 E4
Ballinkillin — 53 B1
Ballinleeny — 50 E3
Ballinloghig — 57 C1
Ballinlough / Baile an Locha — 27 A4
  Co Meath / An Mhí
Ballinlough / Baile an Locha — 24 F4
  Co Roscommon / Ros Comáin
Ballinluska — 68 H1
Ballinmuck — 25 D2
Ballinoroher — 68 E2
Ballinphonta — 40 F3
Ballinran / Baile an Raithin — 20 E5
Ballinrannig — 57 B1
Ballinree — 43 B3
Ballinrobe / Baile an Róba — 22 H5
Ballinruan / Baile an Ruáin — 42 E3
Ballinskelligs / Baile an Sceilg — 57 C5
Ballinspittle / Béal Átha an Spidéil — 68 F2
Ballintober / Baile an Tobair — 22 H4
  Co Mayo / Maigh Eo
Ballintober / Baile an Tobair — 24 H4
  Co Roscommon / Ros Comáin
Ballintogher / Baile an Tóchair — 16 E4
Ballintoy / Baile an Tuaighe — 4 H2
Ballintra / Baile an tSratha — 8 G5
Ballintubbert — 45 A2
Ballinunty / Baile an Fhantaigh — 52 E2
Ballinure / Baile an Lúir — 51 D2
Ballinurra — 52 F4
Ballinvarry — 53 A3
Ballinveny — 43 C4
Ballinvoher Co Cork — 61 A1
Ballinvoher Co Cork — 59 D5
Ballinvronig — 68 F2
Ballitore / Béal Átha an Tuair — 45 B2
Ballivor / Baile Íomhair — 35 A1
Ballon / Balana — 45 C5
Balloo — 12 F5
Balloor — 16 E1
Ballsmill / Baile na gCléireach — 19 A5
Ballure — 8 F5
Ballyadack — 60 H1
Ballyagran / Béal Átha Grean — 50 E4
Ballyallinan — 49 D3
Ballybaun — 53 B2
Ballybay / Béal Átha Beithe — 18 G4
Ballybeg Co Tipperary — 43 C4
Ballybeg / An Baile Beag — 51 D5
  Co Tipperary / Tiobraid Árann
Ballyboden / Baile Baodáin — 36 F4
Ballybofey / Bealach Feich — 9 A2
Ballyboggan — 35 A2
Ballyboghil — 36 F1
Ballybogy / Baile an Bhogaigh — 4 G3
Ballybornia — 33 D2
Ballybowler — 57 C1
Ballyboy — 34 E5

Ballybrack / An Baile Breac — 61 C3
  Co Cork / Corcaigh
Ballybrack Co Kerry — 57 D5
Ballybrack Co Kildare — 35 C3
Ballybrack Co Waterford — 61 C3
Ballybristy — 43 C5
Ballybrittas / Baile Briotais — 44 H1
Ballybrood — 50 G2
Ballybrophy / Baile Uí Bhróithe — 44 E3
Ballybroughan — 42 E5
Ballybryan — 34 H3
Ballybunnion / Baile an Bhuinneánaigh — 48 G2
Ballyburn — 45 B3
Ballycahane — 42 H5
Ballycahill / Bealach Achaille — 51 C1
Ballycallar — 52 G1
Ballycanew / Baile Uí Chonnmhaí — 54 F1
Ballycar — 42 F5
Ballycarney / Baile Uí Chearnaigh — 53 D2
Ballycarra / Baile na Cora — 22 H3
Ballycarry / Baile Cora — 12 F2
Ballycashin — 62 H1
Ballycastle / Baile an Chaistil — 5 D2
  Co Antrim / An Aontroim
Ballycastle Co Galway — 13 G3
Ballyclare / Bealach Cláir — 11 D2
Ballyclerahan / Baile Uí Chléireachain — 61 D4
Ballyclogh / Baile Cloch — 60 E1
Ballycolla / Baile Cholla — 44 F3
Ballycolman — 61 B3
Ballycommon / Baile Uí Chomáin — 43 A3
Ballycomy — 44 H4
Ballyconneely / Baile Conaola — 29 C2
Ballyconnell — 17 B5
Ballycotton / Baile Choitín — 61 B5
Ballycrossaun / Baile Crosáin — 33 A5
Ballycroy / Baile Chruaich — 13 D5
Ballycullane Co Waterford — 62 E2
Ballycullane / Baile Uí Choiléain — 53 B5
  Co Wexford / Loch Garman
Ballycullen — 46 G2
Ballycumber / Béal Átha Chomair — 34 E3
Ballycurrane — 61 D3
Ballydague — 60 G2
Ballydangan / Baile Daighean — 33 B3
Ballydavid Co Cork — 61 B5
Ballydavid Co Galway — 32 G5
Ballydavid / Baile na nGall — 57 B1
  Co Kerry / Ciarraí
Ballydavis — 44 H1
Ballydehob / Béal an Dá Chab — 66 H3
Ballydeloughy — 60 H1
Ballydesmond / Baile Deasumhan — 59 B1
Ballydonegan — 65 D2
Ballydoogan — 32 G5
Ballydoyle — 60 G1
Ballydrenid — 15 D3
Ballyduff / An Baile Dubh — 48 G3
  Co Kerry / Ciarraí
Ballyduff / An Baile Dubh — 57 D1
  Co Kerry / Ciarraí
Ballyduff / An Baile Dubh — 62 H1
  Co Waterford / Port Láirge
Ballyduff / An Baile Dubh — 61 B2
  Co Waterford / Port Láirge
Ballyduff / An Baile Dubh Co Wexford — 54 E1
Ballyea — 50 E2
Ballyeafy — 61 B1
Ballyeaston / Baile Uistín — 11 D2

Ballyeighan 43 C2
Ballyeighter 32 H4
Ballyeightragh 57 B1
Ballyfarnagh / *Bealach Fearna* 23 D3
Ballyfarnan 16 F5
Ballyfasy 53 A4
Ballyfeard / *Baile Feá Aird* 68 H1
Ballyferriter / *Baile an Fhairtéaraigh* 57 B1
Ballyfin / *An Baile Fionn* 44 F1
   Co Laois / *Laois*
Ballyfin / *An Baile Fionn* 54 F1
   Co Wexford / *Loch Garman*
Ballyforan / *Béal Átha Feorainne* 33 A2
Ballyfore 34 H3
Ballyfoyle 44 H5
Ballygalley / *Baile Geithligh* 12 E1
Ballygar / *Béal Átha Ghártha* 32 H1
Ballygarran Co Waterford 62 F2
Ballygarrett / *Baile Ghearóid* 54 F2
Ballygarries 23 C4
Ballygarvan / *Baile Garbháin* 60 G5
Ballygawley / *Baile Uí Dhálaigh* 16 E4
   Co Sligo / *Sligeach*
Ballygawley / *Baile Uí Dhálaigh* 18 F1
   Co Tyrone / *Tír Eoghain*
Ballygeana 51 A4
Ballygelly 11 D1
Ballyglass / *An Baile Glas* 24 F2
   Co Mayo / *Maigh Eo*
Ballyglass / *An Baile Glas* 14 G3
   Co Mayo / *Maigh Eo*
Ballyglass / *An Baile Glas* 23 C4
   Co Mayo / *Maigh Eo*
Ballyglass West 24 F3
Ballygorey 52 H5
Ballygortin 54 F2
Ballygowan / *Baile Mhic Gabhann* 12 F5
Ballygrady 60 E1
Ballygriffin 51 C2
Ballygub 53 A3
Ballygubba 50 F3
Ballyguyroe North 50 G5
Ballyhack 53 B5
Ballyhaght 50 F5
Ballyhahill / *Baile Dhá Thuile* 49 B2
Ballyhaise / *Béal Átha hÉis* 17 D5
Ballyhalbert / *Baile Thalbóid* 12 H5
Ballyhale / *Baile Héil* 31 C2
   Co Galway / *Gaillimh*
Ballyhale / *Baile Héil* 52 H3
   Co Kilkenny / *Cill Chainnigh*
Ballyhank 60 F5
Ballyhar / *Baile Uí Aichir* 58 H2
Ballyhaunis / *Béal Átha hAmhnais* 24 F4
Ballyhean / *Bal Átha hÉine* 22 H3
Ballyhear 31 D1
Ballyheelan / *Bealach an Chaoláin* 26 G3
Ballyheige / *Baile Uí Thaidhg* 48 F4
Ballyhenry 31 C1
Ballyhickey 42 E4
Ballyhoge / *Baile Uí Cheog* 53 D3
Ballyhomuck 52 H4
Ballyhoolahan 59 C1
Ballyhooly / *Baile Átha hUlla* 60 H2
Ballyhornan / *Baile Uí Chornáin* 20 G2
Ballyieragh 66 H4
Ballyjamesduff / *Baile Shéamais Dhuibh* 26 H2
Ballykean 34 G4
Ballykeel / *An Baile Caol* 19 D1

Ballykeeran / *Bealach Caorthainn* 33 C2
Ballykelly / *Baile Uí Cheallaigh* 3 D4
Ballykilleen 34 H4
Ballykilty 61 C4
Ballykinsella 63 B3
Ballyknockan 46 E1
Ballylanders / *Baile an Londraigh* 61 B5
   Co Cork / *Corcaigh*
Ballylanders / *Baile an Londraigh* 50 H4
   Co Limerick / *Luimneach*
Ballylaneen 62 G1
Ballylangley 68 F1
Ballyleague 25 B5
Ballyleen 62 G1
Ballyleny 19 A2
Ballylesson / *Baile na Leasán* 12 E5
Ballyliffin / *Baile Lifin* 3 A2
Ballyline 52 F2
Ballylinnen 44 H4
Ballylintagh 4 F4
Ballylongford / *Beale Átha Longfoirt* 49 A2
Ballylooby / *Beale Átha Lúbaigh* 50 H3
   Co Tipperary / *Tiobraid Árann*
Ballylooby / *Beale Átha Lúbaigh* 51 C5
   Co Tipperary / *Tiobraid Árann*
Ballylucas 54 E3
Ballylumford 12 F1
Ballylynan / *Baile Uí Laigheanáin* 45 A3
Ballymacarbry / *Baile Mhac Cairbre* 51 D5
Ballymacaw / *Baile Mhac Dháith* 63 B4
Ballymachugh 26 G3
Ballymackey / *Baile Uí Mhacai* 43 B3
Ballymacmague 62 E2
Ballymacoda / *Baile Mhac Óda* 61 C4
Ballymacurly / *Baile Mhic Thorlaigh* 25 A4
Ballymacward / *Baile Mhic an Bhaird* 32 G3
Ballymadog 61 C4
Ballymagan / *Baile Mhic Cionaoith* 3 A3
Ballymagaraghy 3 D2
Ballymagorry / *Baile Mhic Gofraidh* 9 C1
Ballymahon / *Baile Ui Mhatháin* 33 D1
Ballymakeery / *Baile Mhic Íre* 59 C4
Ballymakenny 28 E3
Ballymaquiff 42 E1
Ballymartin / *Baile Mhic Grolla Mhártain* 20 E5
Ballymartle 68 G1
Ballymena / *An Baile Meanach* 11 C1
Ballymoe / *Béal Átha Mó* 24 G4
Ballymoney / *Baile Muine* 4 G4
Ballymore / *An Baile Mór* 2 F3
   Co Donegal / *Dún na nGall*
Ballymore / *An Baile Mór* 34 E2
   Co Westmeath / *An Iarmhí*
Ballymore Eustace 35 D5
Ballymorris 62 H1
Ballymote / *Baile an Mhóta* 15 D5
Ballymount 45 C1
Ballymurphy / *Baile Uí Mhurchu* 53 B2
Ballymurragh 49 C4
Ballymurray / *Baile Uí Mhuirigh* 25 B5
Ballynabola 53 B4
Ballynabucky 32 E5
Ballynacally / *Baile na Caillí* 41 C5
Ballynacarriga / *Béal na Carraige* 67 C1
Ballynacarrigy / *Baile na Carraige* 34 F1
Ballynacarrow / *Baile na Cora* 15 D4
Ballynaclogh 43 B4
Ballynacole 61 B4
Ballynacorra 61 A4

Ballynacourty Co Waterford 62 F2
Ballynacourty Co Cork 68 G1
Ballynacree 26 H3
Ballynadrumny 35 A2
Ballynafid 26 G5
Ballynagaul Co Cork 60 H4
Ballynagaul Co Waterford 62 E3
Ballynagore / *Béal Átha na nGabhar* 34 F3
Ballynagree 59 D3
Ballynagrumoolia 60 G5
Ballynaguilkee 61 D1
Ballynahinch / *Baile na hInse* 20 E1
   Co Down / *An Dún*
Ballynahinch / *Baile na hInse* 42 H5
   Co Tipperary / *Tiobraid Árann*
Ballynahow 57 B5
Ballynahown Co Clare 40 F1
Ballynahown / *Baile na hAbhann* 30 F4
   Co Galway / *Gaillimh*
Ballynahown / *Buaile na hAbhann* 33 C3
   Co Westmeath / *An Iarmhí*
Ballynahulla 59 B1
Ballynakill Co Carlow 53 B1
Ballynakill Co Offaly 34 H4
Ballynakill Co Westmeath 33 C2
Ballynakilla 66 **F2**
Ballynamallaght 9 D2
Ballynamona / *Baile na Móna* 60 F2
   Co Cork / *Corcaigh*
Ballynamona Co Galway 33 A3
Ballynamona Co Wexford 53 C5
Ballynamuddagh 60 H2
Ballynamult / *Beal na Molt* 61 D1
Ballynana 57 B1
Ballynarry 26 G3
Ballynaskreena 48 G3
Ballynastangford / *Baile na Stanfard* 23 D4
Ballyneaner / *Baile an Aonfhir* 10 E1
Ballyneety / *Baile an Fhaoitigh* 50 G1
Ballyneill / *Baile Uí Néill* 52 F4
Ballynennan 52 F2
Ballynoe / *An Baile Nua* 61 B3
   Co Cork / *Corcaigh*
Ballynoe Co Galway 32 H4
Ballynure / *Baile an Iuir* 12 E2
Ballyorgan / *Baile Uí Argáin* 50 G5
Ballyoughter 54 F1
Ballyourane 67 A2
Ballypatrick / *Baile Phádraig* 52 E4
Ballyphilip 61 C3
Ballyporeen / *Béal Átha Póirín* 51 B5
Ballyquin Co Kerry 47 D5
Ballyquin Co Waterford 52 G5
Ballyragget / *Béal Átha Ragad* 44 G4
Ballyrashane 4 F3
Ballyre 61 B3
Ballyreagh 18 F1
Ballyregan 68 G1
Ballyroan / *Baile Átha an Róine* 44 G3
Ballyroddy 25 A3
Ballyroe 47 C5
Ballyroebuck 53 D1
Ballyronan / *Baile Uí Rónáin* 11 A3
Ballyroney / *Baile Uí Ruanai* 19 D3
Ballyroon 66 F3
Ballyryan 45 B5
Ballysadare / *Baile Easa Dara* 15 D4
Ballyshannon / *Béal Átha Seanaidh* 8 F5
Ballysheen 48 G4

Ballyshoneen	63 B3	
Ballyskeagh	11 D5	
Ballysloe	52 E1	
Ballysorrell	43 D4	
Ballysteen	49 D1	
Ballyvaghan / Baile Uí Bheacháin	40 H1	
Ballyvaldon	54 F3	
Ballyvalode	51 A2	
Ballyvaloon	60 F3	
Ballyveal	45 B5	
Ballyveera	51 C5	
Ballyvisteen	50 H5	
Ballyvoge / Baile Uí Bhuaigh	66 F4	
Ballyvoneen	32 H2	
Ballyvonnavaun	41 D4	
Ballyvorane	68 H1	
Ballyvourney / Baile Bhuirne	59 B4	
Ballyvoy / Baile Bhóidh	5 D2	
Ballywalter / Baile Bháltair	12 H5	
Ballyward / Baile Mhic an Bhaird	19 D3	
Ballywildrick	4 E3	
Ballywilliam / Baile Liam	68 F2	
Balnamore / Béal an Átha Móir	4 G4	
Balrath / Baile na Ratha	28 E5	
Balrothery	28 G5	
Balscaddan	28 F5	
Baltimore / Dún na Séad	67 A4	
Baltinglass / Bealach Conglais	45 C3	
Baltovin	48 G4	
Baltray / Baile Trá	28 F4	
Banada	15 B5	
Banagher / Beannchar	33 C5	
Banbridge / Droichead na Banna	19 C2	
Bandon / Droichead na Bandan	68 E1	
Bangor / Beannachar	12 G3	
Co Down / An Dún		
Bangor / Baingear	13 D4	
Co Mayo / Maigh Eo		
Banna	48 F4	
Bannfoot	11 A5	
Bansha Co Clare	41 C4	
Bansha / An Bháinseach	51 B3	
Co Tipperary / Tiobraid Árann		
Banteer / Bántir	59 D2	
Bantry / Beantraí	67 A2	
Baranailt	3 D5	
Barboge	67 A4	
Barefield / Gort Lomán	41 D3	
Barna / Bearna	31 C4	
Co Galway / Gaillimh		
Barna Co Limerick	50 H2	
Barna Co Offaly	43 C3	
Barnacahoge	24 E2	
Barnacrawley	24 G3	
Barnaderg / Beara Dhearg	32 F2	
Barnagowlane	67 A1	
Barnalisheen	43 D5	
Barnalyra	24 E2	
Barnmeen	19 C3	
Barnycarroll / Bearna Chearuill	23 D4	
Barrack Village	44 G5	
Barraduff	59 A2	
Barratoor	42 G1	
Barrettstown	52 H3	
Barrigone	49 C1	
Barringtonsbridge	50 G1	
Barrow	48 F5	
Barry / Barraigh	25 D5	
Bastardstown	64 E3	
Batterstown / Baile an Bhóthair	35 D2	
Baughna	34 G2	
Baulbrack	59 C5	
Baunskeha	52 H3	
Bauntlieve	40 G3	
Bawnaneel	59 C1	
Bawnboy / An Bábhún Búi	17 B5	
Co Cavan / An Cabhán		
Bawnboy Co Cork	67 A2	
Bawnfune	51 D5	
Bawnlahan	67 B4	
Beagh	32 E1	
Beal	48 G2	
Bealaclugga / Béal an Chloga	40 H1	
Bealadangan / Béal an Daingin	30 F3	
Bealaha	40 E5	
Bealin / Béal Linne	33 D2	
Bealnablath	60 E5	
Beaufort / Lios an Phúea	58 G2	
Bective	35 C1	
Beenacouma	57 B2	
Bekan / Béacán	24 E4	
Belclare / Béal Chláir	31 D2	
Belcoo / Béal Cú	16 H3	
Belderg / Béal Deirg	14 E3	
Belfast / Béal Feirste	12 E4	
Belgooly / Béal Guala	68 G1	
Bellacorick / Béal Átha Chomhraic	14 E5	
Bellagarvaun	22 E1	
Bellaghy / Baile Eachaidh	11 A2	
Bellahy	24 E1	
Bellanacargy	17 D5	
Bellanagare / Béal Átha na gCarr	24 H3	
Bellanagh	26 F2	
Bellanaleck / Bealach na Leice	17 B3	
Bellanamullia / Béal Átha na Muille	33 B2	
Bellaneeny	33 B3	
Bellanode / Béal Átha an Fhóid	18 F3	
Bellavary / Béal Átha Bhearaigh	23 C2	
Belleek / Béal Leice	19 A4	
Co Armagh / Ard Mhacha		
Belleek / Béal Leice	16 G1	
Co Fermanagh / Fear Manach		
Bellewstown / Baile an Bheileogaigh	28 E5	
Bellmount	45 C4	
Belmullet / Béal an Mhuirthead	13 C3	
Beltoy	12 F2	
Beltra Co Mayo	22 G1	
Beltra / Béal Trá	15 C3	
Co Sligo / Sligeach		
Belturbet / Béal Tairbirt	17 C5	
Benburb / An Bhinn Bhorb	18 H1	
Bendooragh / Bun Dúrai	4 G4	
Bennettsbridge / Droichead Benéid	52 H2	
Beragh / Bearach	10 E5	
Berrings / Biorainn	60 F4	
Bessbrook / An Sruthán	19 B4	
Bettystown / Baile an Bhiataigh	28 F4	
Bilboa / Biolbó	45 A4	
Birdhill / Cnocánan Éin Fhinn	42 H5	
Birr / Biorra	43 C1	
Bishops Court	20 G2	
Bishopshall	52 H5	
Black	61 B1	
Black Bull	36 E2	
Black Lion	34 E5	
Blackcastle / An Caisléan Dubh	51 D3	
Blackhall	53 D4	
Blacklion / An Blaic	16 H3	
Blackpool / An Linn Dubh	50 G4	
Blackrock / An Dúcharraig	60 H4	
Co Cork / Corcaigh		
Blackrock / An Charraig Dhubh	36 G4	
Co Dublin / Baile Átha Cliath		
Blackrock / Na Creagacha	28 E1	
Co Louth / Lú		
Blackwater / An Abhainn Dubh	54 F3	
Blackwatertown / An Port Mór	18 H1	
Blagh	4 F3	
Blanchardstown / Baile Bhlainséir	36 E3	
Blarney / An Bhlarna	60 G4	
Bleary	19 B1	
Blennerville / Cathair Uí Mhóráin	48 G5	
Blessington / Baile Coimín	35 D5	
Blue Ball / An Phailís	34 E5	
Blueford	59 C1	
Blunnick Cross	17 A3	
Boardee	68 H1	
Boardmills / An Muileann Adhmaid	20 E1	
Bodoney	9 C5	
Bodyke / Lúbám Dige	42 G3	
Boggaun	43 D4	
Boharboy	28 G1	
Boheeshil	58 F3	
Boher	50 G1	
Boheraphuca	43 D2	
Boherboy / An Bóthar Búi	59 C1	
Co Cork / Corcaigh		
Bohereen	50 G1	
Boherlahan / An Bóthar Leathan	51 C2	
Bohermeen / An Bóthar Mia	27 B5	
Bohernarnane	51 B4	
Boherquill	26 F4	
Boherroe	50 H2	
Boho / Botha	17 A2	
Bohola / Both Chomhla	23 D2	
Bolea / Both Liath	4 E4	
Boleran	4 F4	
Boley Co Laois	45 A3	
Boley Co Wicklow	45 D4	
Bolinglanna	21 D2	
Boola	61 C3	
Boolakennedy	51 B4	
Borris / An Bhuiríos	53 B1	
Borris in Ossory / Buiríos Mór Osrai	44 E3	
Borrisokane / Buiríos Uí Chéin	43 B2	
Borrisoleigh / Buiríos Ó Luigheach	43 C5	
Boston	41 D2	
Bottomstown	50 G3	
Bottomy	26 F5	
Bouladuff / An Bhuaile Dhubh	43 C5	
Bovedy	4 F5	
Bovevagh / Boith Mhéabha	3 D5	
Boyle / Mainistir na Búille	25 A1	
Brackagh	34 H4	
Bracklin	34 H1	
Brackloon	24 H3	
Bracknagh / Breacánach	35 A5	
Co Offaly / Uibh Fhaili		
Bracknagh Co Roscommon	25 B5	
Brackny	33 D5	
Brackwanshagh	14 G5	
Brahalish	66 G2	
Brandon / Cé Bhréanainn	47 D5	
Brannockstown / Baile na mBreatnach	45 C1	
Bray / Bré	36 G5	
Bready / An Bhreadaigh	9 C1	
Breaghna	67 D1	

Breaghva 48 G1
Bree / *Brí* 53 D3
Breeda 61 C3
Brickeens / *Na Broicíní* 24 E4
Brideswell / *Tobar Bride* 33 B2
Bridge End / *Ceann an Droichid* 3 A4
Bridgeland 46 E4
Bridgetown / *Baile an Droichid* 64 E2
Brigh 10 H4
Briska 62 F1
Brittas / *An Briotás* 36 E4
Britway 61 A3
Broadford / *Béal an Atha* 42 F4
　Co Clare / *An Clár*
Broadford / *Áth Leathan* 49 D4
　Co Limerick / *Luimneah*
Broadway / *Gráinseach Iúir* 64 G3
Brockagh Co Londonderry 4 E5
Brockagh Co Wicklow 46 F2
Brookeborough / *Achadh Lon* 17 C2
Brookville 51 A3
Broomfield / *Achadh an Bhrúim* 18 H5
Brosna / *Brosnach* 49 B5
　Co Kerry / *Ciarraí*
Brosna / *An Bhrosnach* 43 C2
　Co Offaly / *Uibh Fhaili*
Broughal 33 D5
Broughshane / *Bruach* 11 C1
Brownstown Co Kildare 35 B5
Brownstown Co Waterford 63 B4
Bruckana 44 E5
Bruff / *An Brú* 50 G3
Bruree / *Brú Ri* 50 F3
Bryansford / *Áth Bhriain* 20 E3
Buckna 11 D1
Bulgaden / *Builgidin* 50 G4
Bullaun 32 G4
Bunacurry 21 C1
Bunaw 58 F5
Bunbeg / *An Bun Beag* 1 D4
Bunbrosna / *Bun Brosnaí* 25 F5
Bunclody / *Bun Clóidí* 53 D1
Buncrana / *Bun Cranncha* 3 A3
Bundoran / *Bun Dobhráin* 16 F1
Bunglasha 58 E3
Bunlahy 26 E3
Bunmahon / *Bun Machan* 62 G2
Bunnafollistran 31 C1
Bunnaglass 42 F1
Bunnahown 13 C4
Bunnanaddan / *Bun an Fheadáin* 15 D5
Bunnyconnellan / *Muine Chonalláin* 15 A5
Bunratty 42 E5
Burnchurch 52 G2
Burncourt / *An Chúirt Dóite* 51 B5
Burnfoot / *Bun na hAbhann* 3 A4
Burnfort / *Ráth an Tóiteáin* 60 F2
Burren / *Boirinn* 31 C5
　Co Clare / *An Clár*
Burren / *Boirinn* 40 H5
　Co Clare / *An Clár*
Burren / *Boirinn* 19 C4
　Co Down / *An Dún*
Burren Co Mayo 22 H2
Burrenfadda 40 G5
Burtonport / *Ailt an Chorráin* 1 C5
Bushmills / *Muileann na Buaise* 4 G2
Butler's Bridge 17 D5
Butlerstown / *Baile an Bhuitléaraigh* 68 E3

Buttevant / *Cill na Mallach* 60 F1

C

Cabragh / *An Chabrach* 10 G5
Cadamstown / *Baile Mhic Ádaim* 35 A3
　Co Kildare / *Cill Dara*
Cadamstown / *Baile Mhic Ádaim* 44 E1
　Co Offaly / *Uíbh Fhailí*
Caheny 4 F5
Caher / *An Chathair* 42 F2
　Co Clare / *An Clár*
Caher Co Cork 66 F3
Caher Co Tipperary 51 C4
Caheracruttera 58 E1
Caheradrine 32 E4
Caherakillen 32 G4
Caherbarnagh / *An Chatair* 57 D5
Caherconlish / *Cathair Chinn Lis* 50 G2
Caherconnell 40 H2
Caherdaniel / *Cathair Dónall* 65 D1
Caherea 40 H5
Caherlea 31 D3
Caherlistrane / *Cathair Loistréain* 31 D2
Cahermore / *Cathair Mhor* 65 D2
　Co Cork / *Corcaigh*
Cahermore Co Galway 42 E1
Cahermuckee 67 A1
Cahermurphy 40 F5
Caherogan 40 F4
Caherphuca 32 E2
Cahersiveen / *Cathair Saidhbhín* 57 C4
Caim 53 C2
Caledon / *Cionn Aird* 18 G2
Callaghansmills 42 F4
Callan / *Callain* 52 G2
Callow / *An Caladh* 23 D1
　Co Mayo / *Maigh Eo*
Callow Co Roscommon 24 H2
Caltra / *An Chealtrach* 32 H2
Caltraghlea 32 H3
Calverstown / *Baile an Chalbhaigh* 45 C1
Camira 43 B3
Camlough / *Camloch* 19 B4
Camolin / *Cam Eolaing* 54 E1
Camp / *An Com* 58 E1
Campile / *Ceann Poill* 53 B5
Camross / *Camros* 44 E2
Canningstown / *Baile Chainin* 27 A1
Cape Castle 4 H3
Cappagh Co Cork 60 H2
Cappagh Co Limerick 49 D2
Cappagh / *An Chapóg* 10 F5
　Co Tyrone / *Tir Eoghain*
Cappagh White / *An Cheapach* 51 A2
Cappaghmore 41 D1
Cappagowlan 34 E5
Cappalinnan 44 E4
Cappamore / *An Cheapach Mhór* 50 H1
Cappataggle / *Ceapaigh an tSeagail* 32 H4
Cappeen 59 D5
Cappoquin / *Ceapach Choinn* 61 D2
Caran 24 H4
Carbury / *Cairbre* 35 A3
Carker 59 A1
Carland / *Domhnach Carr* 10 G5

Carlanstown / *Droichead Chearballáin* 27 B4
Carlingford / *Cairlinn* 19 C5
Carlow / *Ceatharlach* 45 B4
Carn Co Londonderry 10 G1
Carn Co Westmeath 34 E2
Carna / *Carna* 29 D3
Carnagh / *Carranach* 18 H4
Carnalbanagh 11 D1
Carnalbanagh Sheddings 11 D1
Carnanreagh 10 E1
Carnaross 27 A4
Carncastle 12 E1
Carndonagh / *Carn Domhnach* 3 B2
Carnew / *Carn an Bhua* 46 E5
Carney / *Fearann Uí Chearnaigh* 15 D2
　Co Sligo / *Sligeach*
Carney / *Carnaigh* 43 A2
　Co Tipperary / *Tiobraid Árann*
Carnlough / *Carnlach* 6 E5
Carnmoney / *Carn Monaidh* 12 E3
Carnoneen 31 D3
Carnteel / *Carn tSiail* 18 F1
Carracastle / *Ceathrú an Chaisil* 24 F1
Carragh / *Céarach* 35 C4
Carraghs 24 G4
Carraholly / *Ceathrú Chalaidh* 22 F3
Carran / *An Carn* 40 H2
　Co Clare / *An Clár*
Carran Co Kilkenny 52 H1
Carraroe / *An Cheathrú Rua* 30 F4
Carrawrory 33 C1
Carrick / *An Charraig* 7 C4
Carrick / *An Charraig* 53 C5
Carrick-on-Shannon / *Cora Droma Rúisc* 25 B1
Carrick-on-Suir / *Carraig na Siúire* 52 F4
Carrickaboy / *Carraigigh Bhuí* 26 G2
Carrickart / *Carraig Airt* 2 G3
Carrickashedoge 27 C2
Carrickboy / *An Charraig Bhuí* 26 E5
Carrickfergus / *Carraig Fhearghais* 12 F3
Carrickmacross / *Carraig Mhachaire* 27 C1
Carrickmines / *Carraig Mhaighin* 36 G4
Carrickmore or Termon Rock /
　An Charraig Mhór 10 F4
Carrig 43 C1
Carrigaday 48 E5
Carrigagulla 59 D3
Carrigaholt / *Carraig an Chabhaltaigh* 48 G1
Carrigahorig / *Carraig an Chomhraic* 43 B1
Carrigaline / *Carraig Uí Leighin* 60 H5
Carrigallen / *Carraig Álainn* 26 E1
Carrigan / *An Carraigín* 26 F2
Carriganimmy / *Carraig an Ime* 59 C3
Carriganroe 51 B5
Carrigans / *An Carraigin* 3 A5
Carrigatogher / *Carraig an Tóchair* 42 H4
Carriggower 46 G1
Carrigkerry 49 C3
Carrignavar / *Carraig na bhFear* 60 G3
Carrigtohill / *Carraig Thuathail* 61 A4
Carrow 51 B2
Carrowdore / *Ceathrú Dobhair* 12 G4
Carrowduff Co Clare 40 F2
Carrowduff Co Roscommon 24 H4
Carroweden 15 C4
Carrowkeel / *An Cheathrú Chaol* 2 H3
　Co Donegal / *Dún na nGall*
Carrowkeel Co Donegal 3 C3
Carrowkeel Co Galway 32 G5

Carrowkeel Co Mayo — 22 H5
Carrowkeelanahglass — 24 F5
Carrowmore Co Galway — 31 D5
Carrowmore / Ceathrú Mhór Laecan
  Co Mayo / Maigh Eo — 14 G3
Carrowmore Co Mayo — 23 C4
Carrowmore Co Sligo — 15 C5
Carrowmoreknock — 31 C2
Carrowpadeen — 15 A3
Carrowreagh — 33 A3
Carryduff / Ceathrú Aedha Dhuibh — 12 E5
Cashel Co Carlow — 53 B1
Cashel / An Caiseal
  Co Galway / Gaillimh — 24 F5
Cashel Co Laois — 44 G2
Cashel / Caiseal
  Co Tipperary / Tiobraid Árann — 51 C2
Cashelgarran / Caiseal an Ghearráin — 15 D2
Cashla — 32 E3
Cassagh — 53 B4
Castlebaldwin /
  Béal Átha na gCarraigíní — 16 E5
Castlebar / Caisleán an Bharraigh — 22 H2
Castlebellingham /
  Baile an Ghearlánaigh — 28 E2
Castleblakeney / Gallach — 32 G2
Castleblayney / Baile na Lorgan — 18 H5
Castlebridge /
  Droichead an Cháislaéain — 54 E4
Castlecat / Caiseal Cait — 4 G3
Castlecaufield / Baile Uí Dhonnaile — 10 G5
Castlecomer / Caisleán an Chomair — 44 H4
Castleconnell / Caisleán Uí Chonaill — 42 G5
Castleconor — 14 H4
Castlecor / Caisleán na Cora — 60 E1
Castlecuffe — 34 E5
Castledawson / An Seanmhullach — 11 A2
Castlederg / Caisleán na Deirge — 9 B3
Castledermot / Diseart Diarmada — 45 B3
Castledockrell — 53 D2
Castleellis — 54 E3
Castlefinn / Caisleán na Finne — 9 B2
Castlegregory / Caisleán Ghriaire — 48 E5
Castlehill / Caorthannán
  Co Mayo / Maigh Eo — 22 E1
Castlehill Co Mayo — 14 G5
Castleisland / Oileán Ciarraí — 59 A1
Castlejordan / Caisleán Shuirdáin — 34 H3
Castleknock / Caisleán Cnucha — 36 E3
Castleleiny / Caisleán Laighnigh — 43 D4
Castlelyons / Caisleán Ó Liatháin — 61 A2
Castlemaine / Caisleán na Mainge — 58 G1
Castlemartyr / Baile na Martra — 61 B4
Castleplunket / Lois Lachna — 24 H4
Castlepollard / Baile na gCros — 26 G4
Castlequin — 57 C3
Castlerahan — 26 H3
Castlerea / An Caisleánn Riabhach — 24 G3
Castlereagh — 12 E4
Castlerock / Carraig Ceasail — 4 E3
Castleshane / Caisleán an tSiáin — 18 G3
Castletown Co Clare — 40 H2
Castletown /
  Baile Chaisleáin Chinn Eich
  Co Cork / Corcaigh — 67 D1
Castletown / Baile an Chaisleáin — 44 F2
  Co Laois / Laois
Castletown / Baile an Chaisleáin — 50 E3
  Co Limerick / Luimneach

Castletown / Baile an Chaisleáin — 27 C3
  Co Meath / An Mhí
Castletown / Baile an Chaisleáin — 26 G4
  Co Westmeath / An Iarmhí
Castletown / Baile an Chaisleáin — 46 G5
  Co Wexford / Loch Garman
Castletown Bearhaven — 66 E2
Castletown Geoghegan — 34 F2
Castletownroche /
  Baile Chaisleáin an Róistigh — 60 G1
Castletownshend / Baile an Chaisleáin — 67 B3
Castleville — 23 D5
Castlewarren / Caisleán an Bhairinigh — 45 A5
Castlewellan / Caisleán Uidhilín — 20 E3
Causeway / An Tóchar — 48 G3
Cavan / An Cabhán — 26 G1
Caves — 51 B5
Ceancullig — 67 B2
Cecilstown / Baile an Bhriotaigh — 60 E1
Celbridge / Cill Droichid — 35 D3
Chanonrock — 27 D1
Chapel — 53 C3
Chapeltown / Baile an tSéipéil — 20 G2
  Co Down / An Dún
Chapeltown / An Caol — 57 B4
  Co Kerry / Ciarraí
Charlemont — 18 H1
Charlestown / Baile Cathail — 24 E1
Cheekpoint / Pointe na Síge — 53 A5
Cherryville — 35 A5
Chesney's Corner — 11 B2
Church Ballee — 20 G2
Church Cross / Cnoc na Rátha — 67 A3
Church Hill / Min an Lábáin — 2 F5
  Co Donegal / Dún na nGall
Church Hill / An Droim Meánach — 9 A4
  Co Tyrone / Tir Eoghain
Church Hill — 48 F5
Church Town / Tulaigh an Iúir — 3 A5
Churchboro Cross — 33 B1
Churchfield — 22 G5
Churchstreet — 24 H2
Churchtown / Baile an Teampaill — 50 F5
  Co Cork / Corcaigh
Churchtown / Baile an Teampaill Theas — 61 B5
  Co Cork / Corcaigh
Churchtown Co Down — 20 G2
Churchtown / Tulaigh an Iúir — 10 H3
  Co Londonderry / Doire
Churchtown Co Wexford — 64 G3
Churchtown Co Wexford — 63 C4
Clabby / Clabaigh — 17 D1
Claddaghduff / An Cladach Dubh — 29 B1
Clady Co Antrim — 11 D4
Clady Co Londonderry — 11 A1
Clady / Clóidigh — 9 B2
  Co Tyrone / Tír Eoghain
Cladymilltown / Baile an Mhuillinn — 19 A3
Claggan — 21 D1
Clane / Claonadh — 35 C4
Clara / Cióirtheach — 34 E3
Clarahill — 34 F5
Clare / An Clár — 19 B2
Clarecastle / Droichead an Chláir — 41 D4
Clareen / An Cláirin — 43 D1
Claregalway / Baile Chláir — 31 D3
Claremorris / Clár Chlainne Mhuiris — 23 D4
Clarina / Clár Aidhne — 50 F1
Clarinbridge / Droichead an Chláirin — 32 E4

Clash — 43 B3
Clash North — 49 B3
Clash South — 49 B3
Clashdrumsmith — 51 A3
Clashmore / Clais Mhór — 61 D3
Clashroe — 52 G5
Claudy / Clóidigh — 10 E1
Clawinch — 25 B5
Cleggan / An Cloigeann — 29 C1
Clenagh — 41 D5
Clerragh — 24 G3
Clifden / An Clochán — 29 C1
Clifferna / An Chliaifearna — 26 H1
Cliffony / Cliafuine — 16 E1
Clogga Co Kilkenny — 52 H5
Clogga Co Wicklow — 46 G5
Clogh / An Chloch — 4 H5
  Co Antrim / Aontriom
Clogh Co Kilkenny — 44 H4
Clogh Co Laois — 44 F3
Clogh Co Limerick — 49 D2
Clogh Co Wexford — 54 F1
Clogh Mills / Muileann na Cloiche — 4 H5
Cloghan / An Clochan — 8 H2
  Co Donegal / Dún na nGall
Cloghan Co Offaly — 33 C5
Cloghan Co Westmeath — 34 H1
Cloghane Co Cork — 66 F4
Cloghane / An Chlochan — 47 D5
  Co Kerry / Ciarraí
Cloghaun Co Clare — 40 F5
Cloghaun Co Galway — 31 C3
Cloghaun Co Galway — 31 D3
Cloghboley / Clochbhuile — 15 D2
Cloghbrack / An Chloch Bhreac — 30 G1
  Co Galway / Gaillimh
Cloghbrack Co Meath — 35 A1
Cloghcor — 9 C1
Clogheen / An Chloichín — 51 D5
  Co Tipperary / Tiobraid Árann
Clogheen Co Waterford — 51 C5
Clogher / An Clochar — 22 G3
  Co Mayo / Maigh Eo
Clogher Co Mayo — 22 H4
Clogher Co Roscommon — 25 B2
Clogher / Clochar — 18 E1
  Co Tyrone / Tir Eoghain
Cloghera — 42 F5
Clogherhead / Ceann Chlochair — 28 F3
Cloghfin — 10 F5
Cloghjordan / Cloch Shiurdáin — 43 B3
Cloghmore / An Chloich Mhoir — 21 D2
Cloghpook — 44 H5
Cloghran / Clochrán — 36 F2
Cloghroe — 60 F4
Cloghvoula — 49 B5
Cloghy / Clochaigh — 20 H1
Clohamon / Cloch Amainn — 53 D1
Clohernagh — 63 B3
Cologe — 54 E1
Clomantagh — 44 F5
Clonakenny / Cluain Uí Chionaoith — 43 D3
Clonakilty / Cloich na Coillte — 67 D2
Clonalea — 43 B4
Clonalvy / Cluain Ailbhe — 28 E5
Clonard Co Cork — 61 C4
Clonard / Cluain Ioraird — 35 A2
  Co Meath / An Mhí
Clonard Great — 54 E5

Clonascra	33 C3
Clonaslee / *Cluain na Slí*	34 F5
Clonavoe	34 H4
Clonbern / *Cluain Bheirn*	32 F1
Clonbulloge / *Cluain Bolg*	35 A4
Clonbur / *An Fhairche*	30 G1
Cloncagh / *Cluain Cath*	49 D3
Cloncrave	34 H2
Cloncreen	34 H4
Cloncullen	33 D1
Cloncully	44 E2
Clondalkin / *Cluain Dolcáin*	36 E3
Clondaw	54 E2
Clondulane	61 A2
Clonea / *Cluain Fhia*	52 F5
Clonee / *Cluain Aodha*	36 E2
Cloneen Co Offaly	34 G3
Cloneen / *An Cluainín*	52 E3
Co Tipperary / *Tiobraid Árann*	
Clonegall / *Cluain na nGall*	45 D5
Clonelly	9 A5
Clones / *Cluain Eois*	18 E4
Clonfeacle	18 H1
Clonfert / *Cluain Fearta*	33 B4
Clongeen	53 C5
Clonincurragh	44 F2
Clonkeen	44 G2
Clonkeenkerrill	32 F3
Clonlost / *Cluain Loiste*	34 H1
Clonmacnoise	33 C3
Clonmany / *Cluain Maine*	3 A2
Clonmeen	44 E4
Clonmel / *Cluain Meala*	52 E4
Clonmellon / *Ráistin*	27 A5
Clonmore / *Cluain Mhór*	45 D4
Co Carlow / *Ceatharlach*	
Clonmore Co Louth	28 F3
Clonmore Co Tipperary	43 D4
Clonmult	61 B3
Clonony	33 C4
Clonoulty / *Cluain Abhla*	51 C1
Clonroche / *Cluain an Róistigh*	53 C3
Clonsilla / *Cluain Saileach*	36 E3
Clontarf / *Cluain Tarbh*	36 F3
Clontibret / *Cluain Tiobrad*	18 G4
Clontivrin	17 D4
Clontubbrid	44 F5
Clonycavan	35 A1
Clonygowan / *Cluain na nGamham*	34 G5
Clonyquin	34 G5
Cloonacauneen	31 D4
Cloonacool / *Cluain na Cúile*	15 B5
Cloonboo	31 D3
Cloonbrennaun	24 G5
Clooncah	25 B5
Cloondara / *Cluain Dá Ráth*	25 C4
Cloone / *An Chluain*	25 D2
Cloone Grange	25 D2
Clooneagh	25 C3
Clooneen	26 F3
Cloonfad Co Roscommon	24 F4
Cloonfad / *Cluain Fada*	33 B4
Co Roscommon / *Ros Comáin*	
Cloonfallagh / *Cluain Falach*	23 D3
Cloonfeagh	40 H4
Cloonfinish	24 E1
Cloonfower	24 F3
Cloonkeelaun	15 A4
Cloonkeen Co Galway	24 G4
Cloonkeen Co Mayo	22 H3
Cloonkeen Co Roscommon	24 G5
Cloonkeevy / *Cluain Ciabhaigh*	15 D5
Cloonlara / *Cluain Lára*	42 G5
Cloonlee	23 D3
Cloonloogh / *Cluain Lua*	24 H1
Cloonlusk	51 A2
Cloonmurray	25 A4
Cloonnacat	24 F5
Cloonsheever	24 G3
Cloontia / *Na Cluainte*	24 F1
Cloontuskert	25 B4
Cloonusker	42 G3
Cloonycarney	15 A3
Cloonymorris	32 H4
Cloonyquin / *Cluain Uí Choinn*	25 A3
Closh	44 E2
Clough / *An Chloch*	20 F2
Cloyne / *Cluain*	61 B5
Coachford / *Áth an Chóiste*	60 E4
Coagh / *An Cuach*	10 H4
Coalbrook / *Glaise an Ghuail*	52 E1
Coalisland / *Oileán an Ghuail*	10 H5
Coan / *An Cuan*	44 H4
Cobh / *An Cóbh*	61 A5
Caddy	11 B2
Colbinstown / *Baile Choilbín*	45 C2
Colehill / *Cnoc na Góla*	26 E5
Coleraine / *Cúil Raithin*	4 F5
Colestown	53 D4
Collinstown / *Baile na gCailleach*	26 H5
Collon / *Collan*	27 D3
Collooney / *Cúil Mhuine*	15 D4
Colman	51 D3
Colmanstown / *Baile Uí Chlúmháin*	32 F3
Colp	28 F4
Comber / *An Comar*	12 F5
Commaun	43 B5
Commons Co Cork	60 E5
Commons / *Na Coimíní*	52 F1
Co Tipperary / *Tiobraid Árann*	
Cong / *Conga*	30 H1
Conlig / *An Choinleic*	12 G4
Conna / *Conaithe*	61 B2
Connolly / *Fioch Rua*	40 G4
Connor	11 C2
Connonagh	67 C3
Convoy / *Conmhaigh*	9 B1
Cookstown / *An Chorr Chriochach*	10 H4
Cool	61 C1
Coolagary	34 H4
Coolaney / *Cúil Áine*	15 D4
Coolanheen	61 D2
Coolattin	46 E5
Coolbaun / *An Cúl Bán*	
Co Tipperary / *Tiobraid Árann*	43 A2
Coolbaun / *An Cúl Bán*	44 H4
Coolboy / *An Cúl Buí*	46 E5
Co Wicklow / *Cill Mhantáin*	
Coolboy Co Tipperary	51 A5
Coolderry / *Cúl Doire*	43 D2
Coole / *An Chuil*	26 G4
Coole Abbey	61 A2
Coolea / *Cúil Aodha*	59 B4
Coolea	60 H2
Coolgrange	52 H1
Coolgreany / *Cúil Chréine*	46 F5
Coolgreen	60 H3
Coolinny	60 H2
Coolmaghry	10 G5
Coolmeen / *Cúil Mhín*	49 B1
Coolnafarna	24 F4
Coolnagun	26 F4
Coolock	36 F3
Coolrain / *Cúil Ruáin*	44 E2
Coolroe	54 F2
Coolross	43 B1
Coolsallagh	60 H5
Coolshaghtena	25 B5
Coomleagh	67 B1
Coonagh	50 F1
Cooneen / *An Cúinnín*	17 D2
Cooraclare / *Cuar an Chláir*	40 F5
Coorleagh	45 A5
Coosane	66 H3
Cootehall / *Uachtar Thíre*	25 B1
Cootehill / *Muinchille*	18 E5
Coralstown / *Baile Mhic Cearúill*	34 H2
Corbally Co Clare	39 D5
Corbally / *An Corrbhaile*	14 A4
Co Sligo / *Sligeach*	
Corbay Upper	26 E4
Corbet Milltown	19 C2
Corclogh	13 B3
Corcullin	14 E5
Cordal / *Cordal*	59 A1
Cordarragh	22 F4
Corduff / *An Chorr Dubh*	35 B4
Cork / *Corcaigh*	60 G4
Corkey / *Corcaigh*	4 H4
Corlea	25 C5
Corlee	23 D1
Cornafulla / *Corr na Fola*	33 B3
Cornanagh	23 C4
Corndarragh	34 F4
Corrakyle	42 G2
Corrandulla / *Cor an Dola*	31 D3
Correen	11 C1
Corrofin / *Cora Finne*	40 H3
Co Clare / *An Clár*	
Corrofin Co Galway	32 E2
Cortown / *An Baile Corr*	27 B4
Corvoley	14 F4
Costelloe / *Casla*	30 F4
Coumduff	57 D1
Countygate	61 A2
Courthoyle	53 C4
Courtmacsherry	68 F2
Courtmatrix	49 D3
Courtown	54 F1
Cousane	67 B1
Coxtown	32 H4
Craan	46 E5
Craanford / *Áth an Chorráin*	46 E5
Crafield	46 F3
Cragroe	42 E3
Craig	10 E2
Craigavad / *Creig an Bhada*	12 F3
Craigavole	4 F5
Craigavon / *Craigavon*	19 B1
Craigs / *Na Creaga*	11 B1
Cranagh / *An Chrannóg*	10 E2
Crane	54 E2
Cranford / *Creamhghort*	2 G3
Cranny / *An Chrannaigh*	40 G5
Co Clare / *An Clár*	
Cranny Co Londonderry	10 H3
Cratloe / *An Chreatalach*	42 E5

Craughwell / *Creachmhaoi* 32 F4
Crawfordsburn / *Sruth Chráfard* 12 F3
Crazy Corner 34 G1
Creagh Co Cork 67 A3
Creagh / *Créach* 17 C2
   Co Fermanagh / *Fear Manach*
Creaghanroe / *Crícheán Rua* 18 H4
Crecora / *Craobh Chomhartha* 50 F2
Creegh / *An Chrioch* 40 F5
Creeslough / *An Craoslach* 2 F3
Creevagh 14 G3
Creeves 49 D2
Cregg Co Clare 30 H5
Cregg Co Cork 67 C3
Creggan Co Offaly 33 C4
Creggan / *An Creagán* 10 F4
   Co Tyrone / *Tír Eoghain*
Cregganbaun / *An Creagán Bán* 22 E4
Creggs / *Na Creaga* 24 H5
Crilly / *Crithligh* 18 F1
Crindle 3 D4
Crinkill / *Crionchoill* 43 C1
Croaghrimbeg 22 G4
Crockets Town 14 H4
Croghan / *Cruachán* 34 G3
   Co Offaly / *Uibh Fhailí*
Croghan Co Roscommon 25 A2
Cromane / *An Cromán* 58 E2
Cromlin 17 A5
Crookedwood / *Tigh Munna* 26 G5
Crookhaven / *An Cruachán* 66 G4
Crookstown / *An Baile Gallda* 60 E5
   Co Cork / *Corcaigh*
Crookstown Co Kildare 45 B2
Croom / *Cromadh* 50 F2
Cross Barry / *Croisan Bharraigh* 60 F5
Cross Keys / *Carraig an Tobair* 26 G2
   Co Cavan / *An Cabhán*
Cross Keys Co Meath 26 H4
Cross Keys Co Meath 35 D1
Cross Mahon 68 E1
Cross Roads / *Na Croisbhealaí* 9 A2
Cross / *An Chrois* 48 F1
   Co Clare / *An Clár*
Cross Co Waterford 61 D3
Crossabeg / *Na Crosa Beaga* 54 E4
Crossakeel / *Crosa Caoil* 27 A4
Crossboyne 23 D4
Crossconnell 33 A4
Crossdoney / *Cros Domhnaigh* 26 F1
Crossea 26 E5
Crosserlough / *Crois ar Loch* 26 G2
Crossgar / *An Chrois Ghearr* 20 F1
Crossgare 4 F4
Crosshaven / *Bun an Tábhairne* 60 H5
Crosskeys / *Na hEochracha* 45 A1
Crossmaglen / *Crois Mhic Lionnáin* 19 A5
Crossmolina / *Crois Mhaoilíona* 14 G5
Crossna 25 A1
Crossooha 31 D5
Crosspatrick / *Crois Phádraig* 44 E5
   Co Kilkenny / *Cill Chainnigh*
Crosspatrick Co Wicklow 46 E5
Crosswell 24 H5
Crowbally 61 B4
Crumlin / *Cromghlinn* 11 C4
Crumpane 66 E1
Crusheen / *Croisín* 41 D3
Crutt 44 H4

Cuilkillew 22 H1
Culcavy 19 D1
Culdaff / *Cúil Dabhcha* 3 C2
Cullahill / *An Chúlchoill* 44 F4
Cullane 50 H4
Cullaville / *Baile Mhic Cullach* 18 H5
Culleen 42 E5
Culleens / *Na Coilliní* 15 A4
Cullen / *Cuillin* 59 C2
   Co Cork / *Corcaigh*
Cullen / *Cuilleann* 51 A2
   Co Tipperary / *Tiobraid Árann*
Cullenagh 50 H5
Cullenstown 63 D3
Cullin 23 D1
Cullinane 6 E5
Cullybackey / *Coill na Baice* 11 B1
Cullyhanna / *Coilleach Eanach* 19 **A4**
Culnady / *Cúil Chnáidí* 10 H1
Cultra 12 **E3**
Currabeha / *An Chorr Bheithe* 61 B2
Curracloe / *Currach Cló* 54 F4
Curraclogh 59 D5
Curragh / *An Currach* 61 D4
Curragh West / *An Currach Thiar* 24 F5
Curragha 36 E1
Curraghalicky 67 C2
Curraghboy / *An Currach Buí* 33 B2
Curraghlawn 46 E4
Curraghmore 53 A3
Curraghroe / *An Currach Rua* 25 B4
Curraglass / *Cora Chlas* 61 B2
Curragunneen / *Currach Guinín* 43 D3
Curran / *An Corrán* 10 H2
Curranavilla 30 F4
Currans 58 H1
Curreeny / *Na Coirríní* 43 B5
Currow / *Corra* 58 H1
Curry / *An Choraidh* 24 E1
Curryglass 66 F2
Cushendall / *Bun Abhann Dalla* 6 E4
Cushendun / *Bun Abhann Duinne* 6 E3
Cushina 34 H5

D

Daingean / *An Daingean* 34 G4
Dalkey 36 G4
Damastown 36 F1
Damhead 4 F4
Danesfort / *Dún Feart* 25 D4
Dangan 61 B3
Dangandargan 51 C3
Darkley / *Dearclaigh* 18 H3
Darragh / *An Darach* 40 H4
Davidstown / *Baile Dháith* 53 D3
Deerpark / *Páirc na bhFia* 31 C1
Delgany / *Deilgne* 36 G5
Delvin / *Dealbhna* 27 A5
Dernagree / *Doire na Graí* 59 C2
Derradda / *Doire Fhada* 17 A5
Derreen Co Clare 40 F3
Derreen Co Kerry 57 C4
Derreen / *An Doirín* 21 D2
   Co Mayo / *Maigh Eo*
Derreenacarrin 66 G1

Derreenard 67 A3
Derreenauliff 58 E5
Derreeny 66 F2
Derries Co Offaly 34 E4
Derries Co Offaly 35 A4
Derrineel 33 B3
Derryadd / *Doire Fhada* 11 B5
Derrybeg / *Doirí Beaga* 1 D4
Derryboy / *Doire Buí* 20 F1
Derrybrien / *Daraidh Braoin* 42 F1
Derrycanan 25 B4
Derryclogh 67 B2
Derrycon 44 F1
Derrycooly 34 E4
Derrydolney 33 D5
Derryfada 44 E5
Derryfineen 59 B4
Derrygareen 42 H5
Derrygile 44 G1
Derrygolan 34 F3
Derrygonnelly / *Doire Ó gConaíle* 17 A1
Derrygowna 25 C5
Derrygrath 51 C4
Derrygrogan 34 G4
Derrykeighan 4 G3
Derrylahan 33 B3
Derrylin / *Doire Loinn* 17 B4
Derryloughaun 30 H4
Derryloughlin 58 E5
Derrymore 48 F5
Derrynoose / *Doire Núis* 18 H3
Derryrush 30 E3
Derrywode 24 G4
Dervock / *Dearbhóg* 4 G3
Desert 61 A3
Desertmartin / *Diseart Mhártain* 10 H2
Devenish / *Daimhinis* 17 B2
Dingle / *An Daingean* 57 C1
Doagh / *Dumhach* 11 D3
Dolla / *An Doladh* 43 A4
Dollingstown 19 C1
Dollymount / *Cnocán Doirinne* 36 G3
Donabate / *Domhnach Bat* 36 G1
Donacarney 28 F4
Donadea 35 C3
Donagh 17 B3
Donaghadee / *Domhnach Daoi* 12 G4
Donaghcloney / *Domhnach Cluana* 19 C1
Donaghmore / *Domhnach Mór* 44 E3
   Co Laois / *Laois*
Donaghmore Co Meath 36 E1
Donaghmore Co Tyrone 10 G5
Donaghpatrick / *Domhnach Phádraig* 27 C4
Donard Co Wexford 53 C3
Donard / *Dún Ard* 45 D2
   Co Wicklow / *Cill Mhantáin*
Donaskeagh 51 B2
Donegal / *Dún na nGall* 8 G4
Doneraile / *Dún ar Aill* 60 F1
Donohill / *Dún Eochaille* 51 B2
Donore / *Dún Uabhair* 28 E4
Donoughmore / *Domhnach Mór* 60 E3
Dooagh / *Dumha Acha* 21 C1
Doocastle / *Caisleán an Dumha* 24 F1
Doocharry / *An Dúchoraidh* 8 F1
Dooega / *Dumha Éige* 21 C2
Dooghbeg 21 D2
Doogort 21 C1
Doohat / *Dúháite* 18 E5

Doohooma / *Dumha Thuama*   13 C5
Doolieve   68 G1
Doolin   40 F2
Doon Co Galway   32 H3
Doon / *Dún*   51 A1
  Co Limerick / *Luimneach*
Doon Co Tipperary   61 B1
Doonaha / *Dún Átha*   48 G1
Doonbeg / *An Dún Beag*   40 E5
Doonmanagh   57 D2
Doornane   52 H5
Dooyork   13 C5
Dough   66 F4
Doughiska   31 D4
Douglas / *Dúglas*   60 G5
Dovea / *Dubhfhéith*   43 C5
Dowling   52 G4
Downhill / *Dún Bó*   4 E3
Downing   60 H1
Downpatrick / *Dún Pádraig*   20 F2
Dowra / *An Damhshraith*   16 G4
Drangan / *Drongan*   52 E2
Draperstown / *Baile na Croise*   10 G2
Dreen   10 F1
Dreenagh   48 E3
Drehidasillagh   48 F5
Driminidy   67 B2
Drimmo   44 F2
Drimoleague / *Drom Dhá Liag*   67 B2
Drinagh / *Draighneagh*   67 C2
  Co Cork / *Corcaigh*
Drinagh Co Galway   29 C2
Drinagh Co Roscommon   25 C4
Drinagh Co Wexford   54 E5
Drinaghan   15 A3
Dring / *Droing*   26 F3
Dripsey / *An Druipseach*   60 E4
Drogheda / *Droichead Átha*   28 E4
Droichead Nua (Newbridge)   35 C5
Drom Co Kerry   47 D5
Drom / *An Drom*   43 C5
  Co Tipperary / *Tiobraid Árann*
Dromahair / *Droim dhá Thiar*   16 F3
Dromara / *Droim Bearach*   19 D2
Dromaragh   57 D4
Dromboy South   60 G3
Dromcolliher   49 D4
Dromcunnig   48 G4
Dromgariff   60 G3
Dromin Co Limerick   50 G3
Dromin / *Droim Ing*   28 E3
  Co Louth / *Lú*
Dromina / *Drom Aidhne*   50 E5
Dromineer / *Drom Inbhir*   43 A3
Dromiskin / *Droim Ineasclainn*   28 E2
Drommahane / *Droim Átháin*   60 F2
Dromnea   66 G3
Dromod / *Dromad*   25 C3
Dromore West / *An Droim Mór Thiar*   15 B3
Dromore / *Droim Mór*   19 D1
  Co Down / *An Dún*
Dromore / *An Droim Mór*   9 C5
  Co Tyrone / *Tír Eoghain*
Dromroe Co Waterford   61 C2
Dromtrasna   49 B4
Drum / *An Droim*   18 E5
  Co Monaghan / *Muineachán*
Drum Co Roscommon   33 B3
Drumahoe   3 B5

Drumaness / *Droim an Easa*   20 E2
Drumanure   40 H4
Drumatober   32 H5
Drumbane / *An Drom Bán*   51 C1
Drumbaun   42 H5
Drumbeg   12 E5
Drumbo   12 E5
Drumcar / *Droim Chora*   28 E2
Drumcharley   42 F3
Drumcliff Co Clare   41 D3
Drumcliff / *Droim Chliabh*   15 D2
  Co Sligo / *Sligeach*
Drumcondra / *Droim Conrach*   27 C1
Drumcree / *Droim Cria*   26 H5
Drumfin / *Droim Fionn*   16 E4
Drumfree / *Droim Fraoigh*   3 A3
Drumgriftin   31 D3
Drumkeary   42 G1
Drumkeeran / *Droim Caorthainn*   16 G4
Drumlea / *Droim Léith*   25 D1
Drumlish / *Droim Lis*   25 D3
Drumlosh   33 C3
Drummin / *An Dromainn*   40 F4
Drummullin / *Droim Ailí*   25 B3
Drumna   25 D1
Drumnagreagh Port   6 E5
Drumnakilly / *Droim na Coille*   10 E4
Drumoghill   9 B1
Drumone   26 H4
Drumquin / *Droim Caoin*   9 C4
Drumraney / *Droim Raithne*   33 D2
Drumree / *Droim Rí*   35 D1
Drumroe   61 C2
Drumshanbo / *Droim Seanbhó*   16 G5
Drumskinny / *Droim Scine*   9 A5
Drumsna / *Droim ar Snámh*   25 B2
Drumsurn / *Droim Sorn*   4 E5
Duagh / *Dubháth*   49 A3
Dually   51 D2
Dublin / *Baile Átha Cliath*   36 F3
Duggarry   33 B3
Duleek / *Damhliag*   28 E5
Dumfea   53 B1
Dunadry / *Dún Eadradh*   11 D3
Dunany / *Dún Áine*   28 F2
Dunbell   52 H1
Dunboyne / *Dún Búinne*   36 E2
Dunbyrne   35 B4
Duncannon / *Dún Canann*   63 C3
Duncormick / *Dún Chormaic*   64 E3
Dundalk / *Dún Dealgan*   28 E1
Dunderrow / *Dún Darú*   68 F1
Dunderry   27 C5
Dundian   18 F2
Dundonald / *Dún Dónaill*   12 F4
Dundoogan   32 H3
Dundrod / *Dún dTrod*   11 D4
Dundrum / *Dún Droma*   20 F3
  Co Down / *An Dún*
Dundrum Co Dublin   36 F4
Dundrum Co Tipperary   51 B2
Dunfanaghy / *Dún Fionnachaidh*   2 F3
Dungannon / *Dún Geanainn*   10 G5
Dunganstown   53 A4
Dungarvan / *Dún Garbháin*   53 A2
  Co Kilkenny / *Cill Chainnigh*
Dungarvan / *Dún Garbhán*   62 E2
  Co Waterford / *Port Láirge*
Dungiven / *Dún Geimhin*   10 F1

Dunglow / *An Clochán Liath*   1 C5
Dungourney / *Dún Guairne*   61 B4
Dunhill   62 H1
Duniry   42 H1
Dunkerrin / *Dún Cairin*   43 C3
Dunkineely / *Dún Cionnaola*   8 E4
Dunkitt   52 H5
Dunlavin / *Dún Luáim*   45 C1
Dunleer / *Dún Léire*   28 E3
Dunlewy / *Dún Lúiche*   2 E5
Dunloy / *Dún Lathaí*   4 H5
Dunmanus   66 G3
Dunmanway / *Dún Mánmhaí*   67 C1
Dunmoon   61 C3
Dunmore / *Dún Mór*   24 F5
Dunmore East / *Dún Mór*   63 B3
Dunmurry / *Dún Muirigh*   11 D5
Dunnamaggan / *Dún Iomagáin*   52 G3
Dunnamanagh / *Dún na Manach*   9 D1
Dunnamore / *Domhnach Mór*   10 F3
Dunningstown   52 G1
Dunquin / *Dún Chaoin*   57 B1
Dunseverick / *Dún Sobhairce*   4 G2
Dunshaughlin / *Dún Seachlainn*   35 D1
Durrow / *Darú*   44 G4
Durrus / *Dúras*   66 H2
Dún Laoghaire   36 G4
Dyan / *An Daighean*   18 G2
Dysart / *An Diseart*   34 F2

E

Eadestown   35 D5
Earlshill   52 E1
Easky / *Iaskaigh*   15 A3
Eden / *An tEadan*   12 F3
Edenderry / *Éadan Doire*   35 A3
Ederney / *Eadarnaidh*   9 B5
Edgeworthstown / *Meathas Troim*   26 E4
Eglinton / *An Mhagh*   3 C4
Eglish / *An Eaglais*   18 G1
Eighter / *Iochtar*   26 H3
Ellistrin / *Eileastran*   2 G5
Elphin / *Ail Finn*   25 A3
Elton / *Eiltiún*   50 G3
Emlagh Cross Roads   32 F5
Emly / *Imleach*   50 H3
Emmoo   25 B5
Emo / *Ioma*   44 H1
Emyvale / *Scairbh na gCaorach*   18 F2
Ennis / *Inis*   41 D4
Enniscorthy / *Inis Córthaidh*   53 D2
Enniskean / *Inis Céin*   67 D1
Enniskerry / *Áth an Sceire*   36 G5
Enniskillen / *Inis Ceithleann*   17 B2
Ennistimon / *Inis Diomáin*   40 G3
Erra   25 C4
Errill / *Eiréil*   44 E4
Esker / *An Eiscir*   32 F4
Esker South   25 D3
Eskragh / *Eiscreach*   18 E1
Eyeries / *Na hAorai*   66 E1
Eyrecourt / *Dún an Uchta*   33 B5

F

Faha Glen	62 F1
Fahaduff	49 A5
Fahamore	48 E5
Fahan / *Fathain*	3 A4
Co Donegal / *Dún na nGall*	
Fahan Co Kerry	57 B2
Fahanasoodry	50 H4
Fahy Co Galway	32 H4
Fahy Co Galway	33 A5
Fair Green	41 D3
Fairfield	33 D2
Fairymount / *Mullach na Sí*	24 G3
Falcarragh / *An Fál Carrach*	2 E3
Fanore	40 G1
Farahy	60 G1
Fardrum / *Fardroim*	33 C3
Farmer's Bridge	48 G5
Farnagh	33 D3
Farnaght	25 D2
Farnanes / *Na Fearnáin*	67 B1
Farnoge	53 A4
Farran / *An Fearann*	60 E5
Farranfore / *An Fearann Fuar*	58 H1
Fauna	45 D2
Feakle / *An Fhiacail*	42 F3
Fedamore / *Feadamair*	50 F2
Feeard	48 F1
Feenagh Co Clare	40 G1
Feenagh / *Fionach*	50 E4
Co Limerick / *Luimneach*	
Feeny / *Na Fineadha*	10 F1
Fenagh / *Fionnmhach*	25 D1
Fenit / *An Fhianait*	48 F5
Fennagh / *Fionnmhach*	45 B5
Fennor / *Fionnúir*	62 H1
Co Waterford / *Port Láirge*	
Fennor Co Westmeath	34 H1
Feohanagh Co Kerry	57 B1
Feohanagh / *An Fheothanach*	49 D4
Co Limerick / *Luimneach*	
Feoramore	58 G5
Ferbane / *An Féar Bán*	33 D4
Fermoy / *Mainistir Fhear Maí*	61 A2
Ferns / *Fearna*	54 E2
Ferry Bridge	50 E1
Ferrybank / *Portan Chalaidh*	46 G4
Fethard / *Fiodh Ard*	52 E3
Co Tipperary / *Tiobraid Árann*	
Fethard Co Wexford	63 C3
Fews	62 F1
Fiddane	42 H5
Fiddown / *Fiodh Dúin*	52 G4
Fieries	58 H1
Figlash	52 F4
Finavarra	31 C5
Finnea / *Fiodh an Átha*	26 G3
Finnis	19 D2
Finny / *Fionnaithe*	30 G1
Fintona / *Fionntamhnach*	9 D5
Fintown / *Baile na Finne*	8 G1
Finuge / *Fionnúig*	48 H3
Finvoy / *An Fhionnbhoith*	4 G5
Firkeel	65 D2
Firmount	61 A3
Fisherstreet	40 F2
Five Corners	11 D2

Fivealley / *An Chúirt*	33 D5
Fivemilebourne / *Abhainn an Chartúin*	16 E3
Fivemilebridge	60 G5
Fivemiletown / *Baile na Lorgan*	17 D2
Flagford	25 B2
Flagmount / *Leacain an Éadain*	42 F2
Co Clare / *An Clár*	
Flagmount Co Kilkenny	53 A1
Flatfield	11 C5
Flemingstown	58 E1
Florence Court / *Mullach na Seangán*	17 A3
Flurrybridge	19 B5
Foilnamuck	66 H3
Fontstown	45 B1
Fordstown / *Baile Forda*	27 B5
Fore / *Baile Fhobhair*	26 H4
Forkill / *Foirceal*	19 B5
Formoyle Co Clare	40 G1
Formoyle Co Mayo	21 D4
Fort Middle	50 E4
Fort William	43 B3
Forthill	33 C1
Foulkesmill / *Muileann Fúca*	53 C5
Foulkstown	51 D2
Four Mile House /	
Teach na gCeithre Mhile	25 A4
Four Roads / *Tigh Srathra*	33 A1
Fox Hill	22 G5
Foxfield / *Cnocán an Mhada Rua*	25 C1
Foxford / *Béal Easa*	23 C1
Foxhall	23 D5
Foynes / *Faing*	49 C1
Freemount / *Cillin an Chrónáin*	49 D5
Frenchpark / *Dún Gar*	24 H2
Freshford / *Achadh Úr*	44 G5
Freynestown	45 C2
Friarstown	50 F2
Frogmore	48 F5
Frosses / *Na Frosa*	8 F4
Fuerty	25 A5
Funshin More	41 D1
Furraleigh	62 F1
Furroor	40 G5
Furrow	51 A5

G

Gainestown	34 G2
Galbally / *An Gallbhaile*	50 H4
Co Limerick / *Luimneach*	
Galbally Co Wexford	53 D4
Galbertstown	51 D1
Galgorm / *Galgorm*	11 B1
Gallagh	25 B5
Galmoy / *Gabhalmhaigh*	44 E4
Galtrim	35 C1
Galway / *Gaillimh*	31 D4
Gannavane	51 A1
Garadice / *Garairis*	35 C2
Garbally	33 A3
Garlow Cross / *Crois Chearla*	27 D5
Garnavilla	51 C4
Garr	34 H3
Garrane	59 C4
Garranereagh	59 D5
Garranlahan / *An Garrán Leathan*	24 F4

Garraun Co Clare	48 H1
Garraun Co Galway	32 H5
Garraun Co Kerry	58 G1
Garravoone	52 F5
Garrettstown	45 C3
Garrison / *An Garastún*	16 G1
Garristown / *Baile Gháire*	36 E1
Garrycaheragh	61 A3
Garrycloonagh	14 G5
Garrycullen	53 C5
Garryduff	4 G4
Garryfine / *Garrai Phaghain*	50 E4
Garrymore	61 B4
Garrynafana	43 B4
Garryvoe	61 B5
Garvagh / *Garbhach*	25 C1
Co Leitrim / *Liatroim*	
Garvagh / *Garbhachadh*	4 F5
Co Londonderry / *Doire*	
Garvaghy / *Garbhachadh*	10 E5
Gattabaun / *An Geata Bán*	44 F5
Gawleys Gate / *Geata Mhic Amhlaí*	11 B5
Gaybrook / *Baile Réamainn*	34 G2
Geashill / *Géisill*	34 G4
Geevagh / *An Ghaobhach*	16 F5
Georgestown	62 G1
Gerahies	66 H2
Gilford / *Áth Mhic Giolla*	19 B2
Glanalin	66 G3
Glandart	67 A2
Glandore / *Cuan Dor*	67 C3
Glanmire / *Gleann Maghair*	60 H4
Glanoe	48 H4
Glanroon	66 F3
Glantane / *An Gleanntán*	60 E2
Glanworth / *Gleannúir*	60 H1
Glarryford / *An tÁth Glárach*	4 H5
Glashabeg	57 B1
Glashaboy East	60 G3
Glashaboy North	60 G3
Glashananoon	49 A4
Glasleck / *Glasleic*	27 A2
Glaslough / *Glasloch*	18 G2
Glassan / *Glasán*	33 C2
Glassillaun	21 D2
Glastry	12 H5
Glebe	3 D3
Glen Of Imail / *Gleann Ó Máil*	45 D2
Glen Of The Downs	36 G5
Glen / *An Gleann*	2 G3
Co Donegal / *Dún na nGall*	
Glen Co Londonderry	10 H1
Glenacroghery	61 B3
Glenade	16 E2
Glenagat	51 D4
Glenagort	22 G1
Glenahilty	43 B3
Glenamoy / *Gleann na Muaidhe*	13 D3
Glenard / *Gleann Aird*	62 E3
Glenariff or Waterfoot /	
Gleann Aireamh	6 E4
Glenarm / *Gleann Arma*	6 F5
Glenavy / *Lann Abhaidh*	11 C4
Glenbeigh	58 E2
Glenboy / *Gleann Buí*	16 G3
Glenbrien / *Gleann Bhriain*	54 E3
Glenbrohane	50 H4
Glencolumbkille / *Gleann Cholm Cille*	7 C3
Glencullen	36 F4

Glendalough Co Waterford	52 E5	
Gleneely / *Gleann Daoile*	3 C2	
Glenfarne / *Gleann Fearna*	16 H3	
Glengariff / *An Gleann Garbh*	66 H1	
Glengoura	61 B2	
Glenhead	3 D5	
Glenlara	13 B3	
Glenmore Co Clare	40 G5	
Glenmore / *An Gleann Mór*	53 A4	
Co Kilkenny / *Cill Chainnigh*		
Glennagat	51 D4	
Glennaknockane	49 B5	
Glennamaddy / *Gleann na Madach*	24 G5	
Glennascaul	31 D4	
Glenoe	12 F2	
Glenough Lower	51 B1	
Glenough Upper	51 B1	
Glenshelane	61 D1	
Glentane Co Cork	61 B3	
Glentane Co Galway	32 G2	
Glenties / *Na Gleannta*	8 F2	
Glentogher / *Gleann Tóchair*	3 B2	
Glentrasna	30 F2	
Glenvale	4 H5	
Glenvar / *Gleann Bhairr*	2 H3	
Glenville / *Gleann an Phréacháin*	60 H3	
Glin / *An Gleann*	49 B2	
Glinsk / *Glinsce*	29 D3	
Glynn / *An Gleann*	12 F2	
Co Antrim / *Aontroim*		
Glynn Co Wexford	53 B3	
Gneevgullia / *Gniomh go Leith*	59 B2	
Golden / *An Gabhailin*	51 C3	
Golden Ball	36 G4	
Goleen / *An Góilin*	66 G4	
Goold's Cross / *Crois an Ghúlaigh*	51 C2	
Goresbridge / *An Droichead Nua*	53 A1	
Gorey / *Guaire*	54 F1	
Gormanstown / *Baile Mhic Gormáin*	28 F5	
Gormanstown	51 C5	
Gort / *An Gort*	42 E1	
Gortaclady	10 F4	
Gortagowan	58 F5	
Gortahork / *Gort An Choirce*	2 E3	
Gortalough	43 C5	
Gortarevan	33 B5	
Gortaroo	61 C4	
Gorteen / *Goirtín*	32 G3	
Co Galway / *Gaillimh*		
Gorteen Co Kilkenny	44 H4	
Gorteen Co Limerick	50 E4	
Gorteen Co Sligo	24 G1	
Gorteen Co Waterford	62 E3	
Gorteens	53 A5	
Gorteeny / *Giortíní*	42 H2	
Gortgarriff	66 E1	
Gortgarrigan / *Gort Geargáin*	16 F3	
Gortglass	59 A1	
Gortin / *An Goirtín*	9 D3	
Gortleatilla	14 E3	
Gortletteragh	25 D2	
Gortmore Co Galway	30 F3	
Gortmore Co Mayo	14 G3	
Gortnadeeve	24 H5	
Gortnahaha	49 C1	
Gortnahey	3 D5	
Gortnahoo / *Gort na hUamha*	52 E1	
Gortnahoughtee	59 B5	
Gortnahurra	14 F4	
Gortnaleaha	48 G5	
Gortnamearacaun	42 E3	
Gortnasillagh	24 H3	
Gortreagh / *An Gort Riabhach*	10 G4	
Gortrelig	58 F3	
Gortskeagh	41 D1	
Gowlaun	21 D5	
Gowlin	53 B2	
Gowran / *Gabhrán*	53 A1	
Gracehill / *Baile Uí Chinnéide*	11 B1	
Graiguearush	62 F1	
Graiguenamanagh / *Gráig na Manach*	53 B2	
Granabeg	46 E1	
Granard / *Granard*	26 F3	
Graney	45 B3	
Grange / *Gráinseach Chuffe*	52 G2	
Co Kilkenny / *Cill Chainnigh*		
Grange Co Kilkenny	52 H5	
Grange Co Offaly	35 A3	
Grange / *An Ghráinseach*	15 D2	
Co Sligo / *Sligeach*		
Grange / *An Ghráinsigh*	61 D3	
Co Waterford / *Port Láirge*		
Grange Co Wexford	64 E3	
Grange Beg Co Kildare	35 B5	
Grange Beg Co Laois	44 E3	
Grange Con / *Gráinseach Choinn*	45 C2	
Grangebellew / *Gráinseach an Dísirt*	28 E3	
Grangeford / *An Ghráinseach*	45 C4	
Grangegeeth	27 D4	
Grannagh	32 E5	
Grant House	18 F1	
Granville / *An Doire Mhin*	10 G5	
Greenan / *An Grainán*	46 F3	
Greenanstown / *Baile Uí Ghrianáin*	28 F5	
Greencastle / *An Caisléan Nua*	3 D2	
Co Donegal / *Dún na nGall*		
Greencastle / *Caisleán na hOireanaí*	19 D5	
Co Down / *An Dún*		
Greencastle Co Tyrone	10 E3	
Greenisland / *Inis Glas*	12 E3	
Greenland	61 C4	
Greenore	19 D5	
Grenagh / *Grenach*	60 F3	
Greyabbey / *An Mhainistir Liath*	12 G5	
Greygrove	40 G5	
Greysteel	3 C4	
Greystone / *An Chloch Liath*	18 G1	
Greystones / *Na Clocha Liatha*	36 G5	
Griston	50 H4	
Grogan	33 D3	
Groomsport / *Port an Ghialla Chruama*	12 G3	
Gulladuff	10 H2	
Gullaun	59 B2	
Gurteen / *Goirtín*	16 F2	
Gusserane / *Ráth na gCosarán*	53 B5	
Gweedore / *Gaoth Dobhair*	1 D4	
Gweesalia / *Gaoth Sáile*	13 C5	
Gyleen	61 A5	

Harristown	52 H4	
Hays	27 D4	
Headford / *Áth Cinn*	31 C2	
Heathfield	68 G1	
Heavenstown	53 D5	
Heirhill	48 F3	
Helen's Bay / *Cuan Héilin*	12 F3	
Herbertstown / *Baile Hiobaird*	50 G2	
High Street	33 C4	
Hightown	61 A3	
Hill Of Down / *Cnoc an Dúin*	35 A2	
Hill Street	25 B2	
Hillhall	11 D5	
Hillsborough / *Cromghlinn*	19 D1	
Hilltown / *Baile Hill*	19 D4	
Co Down / *An Dún*		
Hilltown Co Wexford	54 E5	
Hilltown Co Wexford	53 C5	
Hollyford / *Áth an Chuilinn*	51 B1	
Hollyfort / *Ráth an Chuillinn*	46 F5	
Hollymount Co Galway	42 F1	
Hollymount / *Maolla*	23 C5	
Co Mayo / *Maigh Eo*		
Hollywood / *Cillín Chaoimhín*	12 F4	
Holycross / *Baile na gCailleach*	50 G3	
Co Limerick / *Luimneach*		
Holycross / *Mainstir na Croiche*	51 C1	
Co Tipperary / *Tiobraid Árann*		
Holywell	16 H3	
Holywood / *Ard Mhic Nasca*	12 F4	
Horetown	64 F2	
Horse and Jockey / *An Marcach*	51 D1	
Horseleap / *Baile Átha an Urchair*	34 E3	
Hospital / *An tOspidéal*	50 H3	
Hough	51 C1	
Howth / *Binn Éadair*	36 G3	
Hugginstown	52 H3	
Hurlers Cross	42 E5	
Hyde Park	11 D3	

I

Illaunstookagh	58 E2	
Inagh / *Eigneagh*	40 H3	
Inch Co Cork	61 A5	
Inch Co Cork	61 A5	
Inch Co Kerry	58 E1	
Inch Co Tipperary	51 B1	
Inch / *An Inis*	46 F5	
Co Wexford / *Loch Garman*		
Inchbeg	44 G5	
Inchigeelagh / *Inse Geimhleach*	59 C5	
Inchinapallas	60 H1	
Inchnamuck	51 B5	
Inishannon	68 F1	
Inishcrone / *Inis Crabhann*	14 H3	
Inishrush	11 A1	
Iniskeen / *Inis Caoin*	27 D1	
Inistioge / *Inis Tiog*	53 A3	
Innfield / *An Bóthar Buí*	35 B2	
Inveran / *Indreabhan*	30 G4	
Irishtown / *An Baile Gaelach*	24 E5	
Irvinestown / *Baile an Irbhinigh*	17 B1	

H

Hacketstown	45 D3	
Halfway House / *Tigh Leath Slí*	63 B3	
Hamiltonsbawn / *Bábhún Hamaltún*	19 A2	
Hannahstown / *Baile Haine*	11 D4	

J

Jamestown Co Laois	44 H1
Jamestown Co Leitrim	25 B2
Jerrettspass / *Bealach Sheirit*	19 B3
Johnsfort	23 D2
Johnstown / *Cill Sheanaigh*	60 H5
Co Cork / *Corcaigh*	
Johnstown Co Kildare	35 D4
Johnstown / *Baile Sheáin*	44 F5
Co Kilkenny / Cill Chainnigh	
Johnstown Co Meath	27 C5
Johnstown Co Tipperary	35 D4
Johnstown Co Wexford	53 D5
Johnstown Co Wicklow	46 G4
Johnstown Co Wicklow	46 F4
Johnstown Bridge	35 B3
Johnstownbridge	25 C3
Johnswell / *Tobar Eoin*	44 H5
Jonesborough / *Baile an Chláir*	19 B5
Julianstown / *Baile Iuiliáin*	28 F4

K

Kanturk / *Ceann Toirc*	59 D1
Katesbridge / *Droichead Cháit*	19 D2
Keadew / *Céideadh*	16 G5
Keady / *An Céide*	18 H3
Kealkill / *An Chaolchoill*	67 A1
Kealvaugh	59 B5
Keeagh	30 H3
Keel / *An Caol*	21 C1
Keelnagore	57 D4
Keeloges	24 G5
Keenagh / *Caonagh*	25 D5
Co Longford / *An Longfort*	
Keenagh Co Mayo	14 F5
Keereen	61 D2
Kells Co Kilkenny	52 G2
Kells Connor / *Na Cealla*	11 C2
Co Antrim / *Aontroim*	
Kells/Ceananas	27 B4
Kelshabeg	45 D3
Kenmare / *Neidin*	58 H4
Kentstown	27 D5
Kerloge	54 E5
Kesh / *An Cheis*	9 A5
Co Fermanagh / *Fear Manach*	
Kesh Co Sligo	16 E5
Keshcarrigan / *Ceis Charraigin*	25 C1
Kilbaha / *Cill Bheathach*	48 F2
Kilbane / *An Choill Bhán*	42 G4
Kilbarry / *Cill Barra*	52 H5
Kilbeacanty	42 E1
Kilbeg	62 G1
Kilbeggan / *Cill Bheagáin*	34 F3
Kilbegnet	24 H5
Kilbeheny / *Coill Bheithne*	51 A5
Kilberry / *Cill Bhearaigh*	45 A2
Co Kildare / *Cill Dara*	
Kilberry Co Meath	27 C4
Kilbrack	52 F5
Kilbreedy Co Limerick	50 F4
Kilbreedy Co Limerick	50 E2
Kilbreedy Co Tipperary	51 C2

Kilbrickan	30 F3
Kilbrickane	43 D5
Kilbricken / *Cill Bhriocáin*	44 F2
Kilbride Co Mayo	23 D2
Kilbride Co Meath	27 B5
Kilbride / *Cill Bhríde*	46 G3
Co Wicklow / *Cill Mhantáin*	
Kilbride Co Wicklow	36 E5
Kilbrien Co Cork	60 H2
Kilbrien Co Waterford	62 E1
Kilbrin	60 E1
Kilbrittain / *Cill Briotáin*	68 F2
Kilcaimin	31 D4
Kilcappagh	34 H5
Kilcar / *Cill Charthaigh*	7 D4
Kilcarney	45 D3
Kilcarroll	49 A1
Kilcash	52 F4
Kilcashel	33 B3
Kilcavan	34 G5
Kilchreest / *Cill Chriost*	32 F5
Kilclaran	42 F3
Kilclief	20 G2
Kilcloher	48 F2
Kilclonfert	34 G3
Kilcock / *Cill Choca*	35 C2
Kilcoe	67 A3
Kilcogy / *Cill Chóige*	26 F3
Kilcohan	63 B3
Kilcolgan / *Cill Cholgáin*	32 E5
Kilcolman Co Cork	68 E1
Kilcolman / *Cill Cholmain*	49 C2
Co Limerick / *Luimneach*	
Kilcolman Co Waterford	62 E3
Kilcomin	43 C2
Kilcommon / *Cill Chuimín*	51 C4
Co Tipperary / *Tobraid Árann*	
Kilcommon Co Tipperary	43 B5
Kilcon	14 G4
Kilconierin	32 F4
Kilconly / *Cill Chonla*	31 D1
Kilconnell / *Cill Chonaill*	32 H3
Kilconnor	50 G5
Kilcoo / *Cill Chua*	19 D3
Kilcoole / *Cill Chomhghaill*	46 G1
Kilcor	61 A2
Kilcorkan	41 D2
Kilcormac (Frankford) / *Cill Chormaic*	33 D5
Kilcornan	50 E1
Kilcorney / *Cill Coirne*	59 D2
Kilcotty / *Cill Chota*	54 E3
Kilcredan	61 C4
Kilcrohane / *Cill Chrócháin*	66 G3
Kilcronat	61 B3
Kilcullen / *Cill Chuillin*	45 C1
Kilcummin Co Kerry	58 H2
Kilcummin / *Cill Chuimín*	47 D5
Co Kerry / *Ciarraí*	
Kilcurly / *Cill Choirle*	28 E1
Kilcurry / *Cill an Churraigh*	19 B5
Kilcusnaun	49 A5
Kildalkey / *Cill Dealga*	35 B1
Kildangan / *Cill Daingin*	45 A1
Kildanoge	51 C5
Kildare / *Cill Dara*	35 B5
Kildavin / *Cill Damhain*	53 C1
Kildermody	52 G5
Kildorrery / *Cill Dairbhre*	50 H5
Kildress	10 G4

Kilduffahoo	50 H1
Kildurrihy	57 B1
Kilfeakle	51 B3
Kilfearagh	48 G1
Kilfenora / *Cill Fhionnúrach*	40 G2
Kilfinnane / *Cill Fhíonáin*	50 G4
Kilfinny	50 E2
Kilflynn / *Cill Flainn*	48 G4
Kilgarvan / *Cill Gharbháin*	59 A4
Kilglass Co Galway	32 H2
Kilglass / *Cill Ghlais*	33 B1
Co Roscommon / *Ros Comáin*	
Kilglass / *Cill Ghlas*	15 A3
Co Sligo / *Sligeach*	
Kilgobnet / *Cill Ghobnait*	58 G2
Co Kerry / *Ciarraí*	
Kilgobnet Co Waterford	62 E2
Kilgowan	45 C1
Kilgrogan	50 E2
Kilkea	45 B3
Kilkeasy	52 H3
Kilkee / *Cill Chaoi*	39 D5
Kilkeel / *Cill Chaoil*	20 E5
Kilkelly / *Cill Cheallaigh*	24 E2
Kilkenny / *Cill Chainnigh*	52 G1
Kilkenny West	33 D2
Kilkerran	68 F2
Kilkerrin / *Cill Choirín*	32 G1
Kilkieran / *Cill Chiaráin*	30 E3
Kilkilleen	67 A3
Kilkinlea	49 B4
Kilkishen / *Cill Chisín*	42 E4
Kill / *An Chill*	26 H1
Co Cavan / *An Cabhán*	
Kill Co Kildare	35 D4
Kill Co Waterford	62 G1
Killachonna	33 D2
Killaclug	50 H5
Killacolla	50 E4
Killadeas / *Cill Chéile Dé*	17 B1
Killaderry	32 H2
Killadoon / *Coill an Dúin*	21 D4
Killadysert / *Cill an Disirt*	49 C1
Killafeen	42 E2
Killag	64 E3
Killahaly	61 C2
Killala / *Cill Ala*	14 H3
Killallon	27 A4
Killaloe	42 G4
Killaloo	10 E1
Killamery	52 F3
Killane	35 A3
Killanena	42 F2
Killann / *Cill Anna*	53 C2
Killard	40 E5
Killare	34 E2
Killarga / *Cill Fhearga*	16 F3
Killarney / *Cill Airne*	58 H2
Killarone	30 H2
Killaroo	34 E2
Killashandra / *Cill na Seanrátha*	26 F1
Killashee / *Cill na Sí*	25 C4
Killasser / *Cill Lasrach*	23 D1
Killaun	43 D1
Killavally / *Coill an Bhaile*	22 G5
Killavilly	61 A2
Killavarrig	60 G3
Killavil / *Cill Fhábhail*	15 D5
Killavoher	32 F1

Killavullen / Cill an Mhuilinn 60 G2
Killea Co Donegal 3 A5
Killea Co Leitrim 16 G2
Killea / Cill Shléibhe 43 C4
   Co Tipperary / Tiobraid Árann
Killea Co Waterford 63 B3
Killead / Cill Éad 11 C4
Killeagh / Cill Ia 61 C4
Killeany 39 D1
Killeary 39 D1
Killedmond 53 B1
Killeedy 49 C4
Killeen Co Galway 42 E2
Killeen Co Tipperary 43 C1
Killeen Co Tyrone 10 H5
Killeenaran 31 D5
Killeenasteena 51 C3
Killeenavarra 31 D5
Killeeneenmore 32 E5
Killeenleagh 67 A2
Killeens Cross 60 G4
Killeevan 18 E4
Killeglan 33 A2
Killeigh / Cill Aichidh 34 F5
Killen / Cillin 9 B3
Killenagh 54 F1
Killenaule / Cill Náile 43 C1
   Co Tipperary / Tiobraid Árann
Killenaule Co Tipperary 52 E2
Killeshil 34 G3
Killeter / Coill Iochtair 9 B4
Killimer 49 A1
Killimor / Cill Iomair 33 A5
Killinaboy / Cill Inine Baoith 40 H2
Killinardrish / Cill an Ard-dorais 60 E4
Killinaspick 52 H4
Killinchy / Cill Dhuinsí 12 G5
Killincooly 54 F3
Killiney / Cill Iníon Léinin 36 G4
   Co Dublin / Baile Átha Cliath
Killiney Co Kerry 48 E5
Killinick / Cill Fhionnóg 54 E5
Killinierin / Cill an Iarainn 46 F5
Killinkere / Cillin Chéir 27 A2
Killinny 41 D1
Killinthomas 35 A4
Killiskey 46 G1
Killmacahill 61 B5
Kilmore Co Armagh 19 A1
Kilmore Co Down 20 F1
Kilmore Co Clare 42 F5
Kilmore Upper 25 C4
Killogeary 14 G3
Killogeenaghan 33 D3
Killaghteen 49 C3
Killoluaig 57 C4
Killomoran 41 D1
Killoneen 34 G4
Killoran / Cill Odhráin 32 H4
Killorglin / Cill Orglan 58 F2
Killoscobe 32 G2
Killough / Cill Locha 20 G3
Killsallaghan 36 F2
Killucan / Cill Liúcainne 34 H1
Killukin 25 B2
Killurin / Cill Liúráin 53 D4
Killurly 57 C5
Killusty 52 E3
Killybegs Co Antrim 11 B2

Killybegs / Na Cealla Beaga 8 E4
   Co Donegal / Dún na nGall
Killyclogher 9 D4
Killygar 26 E1
Killygordon / Cúil na gCuiridín 9 B2
Killykergan / Coill Uí Chiaragain 4 F5
Killylea / Coillidh Léith 18 G2
Killyleagh / Cill Ó Laoch 20 G1
Killyneill / Coill Uí Néill 18 G3
Killyon 43 D1
Killyrover 17 B3
Kilmacanoge / Cill Mocheanóg 36 G5
Kilmacow / Cill Mhic Bhúith 52 H5
Kilmacrenan / Cill Mhic Réanáin 2 G4
Kilmacthomas / Coill Mhic Thomáisín 62 F1
Kilmactranny / Cill Mhic Treana 16 F5
Kilmaganny / Cill Mogeanna 52 G3
Kilmaine / Cill Mheáin 31 C1
Kilmainham Wood / Cill Maighneann 27 B3
Kilmalady 34 E3
Kilmaley / Cill Mháille 40 H4
Kilmalin 36 G5
Kilmallock / Cill Mocheallóg 50 G4
Kilmanagh / Cill Mhanach 52 F1
Kilmaniheen 49 A4
Kilmeadan / Cill Mhíodháin 52 H5
Kilmeage / Cill Maodhog 35 B4
Kilmeedy / Cill Mide 49 D4
Kilmessan / Cill Mheasáin 35 C1
Kilmichael / Cill Mhichil 59 C5
Kilmihil / Cill Mhichil 40 G5
Kilmona 60 G3
Kilmoon 67 A4
Kilmore / An Chill Mhór 19 A1
   Co Armagh / Ard Mhaca
Kilmore Co Cavan 26 F1
Kilmore Co Clare 42 F5
Kilmore Co Down 20 F1
Kilmore Co Mayo 23 C1
Kilmore / Cill Mhór 25 B2
   Co Roscommon / Ros Comáin
Kilmore / An Chill Mhór 64 E3
   Co Wexford / Loch Garman
Kilmore Quay / Cé na Cille Móire 64 E3
Kilmorna / Cill Mhaonaigh 49 A3
Kilmorony 45 A3
Kilmovee 24 F2
Kilmuckridge / Cill Mhucraise 54 F2
Kilmurrin 62 G2
Kilmurry Co Clare 42 E4
Kilmurry / Cill Mhuire 40 F4
   Co Clare / An Clár
Kilmurry / Cil Mhuire 59 D5
   Co Cork / Corcaigh
Kilmurry Co Limerick 50 E4
Kilmurry Co Limerick 50 H2
Kilmurry Co Wicklow 45 C3
Kilmurry McMahon / 49 B1
   Cill Mhuire Mhic Mhathúna
Kilmurvy / Cill Mhuirbhigh 30 E5
Kilmyshall 53 D1
Kilnacarriga 61 C2
Kilnacreagh 42 F5
Kilnagross / Coill na gCros 25 C1
Kilnahown 32 H4
Kilnaleck / Cill na Leice 26 G2
Kilnamanagh / Cill na Manach 54 F2
Kilnamartyra 59 C4
Kilnamona / Cill na Móna 40 H3

Kilntown 19 C1
Kilpatrick 68 F1
Kilpedder 46 G1
Kilquane 57 B1
Kilquiggin 45 D4
Kilraghts / Cill Reachtais 4 H4
Kilrane / Cill Ruáin 54 F5
Kilrea / Cill Ria 4 G5
Kilrean Cill Riáin 8 E2
Kilreekill Cill Rícill 32 H4
Kilroghter 31 C3
Kilronan / Cill Rónáin 39 D1
Kilross / Cill Ros 51 A3
Kilrush / Cill Rois 48 H1
Kilsallagh Coill Salach 24 G5
   Co Galway / Gaillimh
Kilsallagh / Coil Salach 22 E3
   Co Mayo / Maigh Eo
Kilsaran 28 E2
Kilshanchoe 35 B3
Kilshannig 48 E5
Kilshanny / Cill Seanaigh 40 G2
Kilsheelan 52 E4
Kilshinahan 68 E2
Kilskeer / Cill Scire 27 A4
Kilskeery / Cill Scire 17 B1
Kiltamagh 23 D3
Kiltarsaghaun 22 G4
Kiltartan 42 E1
Kiltealy / Cill Téile 53 C2
Kilteel 35 D4
Kilteely / Cill Tíle 50 H2
Kiltegan 45 D3
Kiltiernan / Cill Tiarnáin 36 G4
   Co Dublin / Baile Átha Cliath
Kiltiernan Co Galway 32 E5
Kiltober 34 F3
Kiltoom / Cill Tuama 33 B2
   Co Roscommon / Ros Camáin
Kiltoom Co Westmeath 26 G5
Kiltormer / Cill Tormóir 33 A4
Kiltullagh / Cill Tulach 32 F4
Kiltyclogher / Coilte Clochair 16 G2
Kilvemnon 52 F3
Kilvine 24 E5
Kilwatermoy 61 C3
Kilwaughter / Cill Uachtair 12 E1
Kilwoghan 35 D3
Kilworth / Cill Uird 61 A1
Kilworth Camp 61 A1
Kinard 49 B2
Kinawley / Cill Náile 17 B3
Kingarrow 8 G1
Kingscourt / Dún an Rí 27 B2
Kingsland 24 H2
Kingsmill 10 H4
Kingsmills 19 B3
Kinlough / Cionn Locha 16 F1
Kinnegad / Cionn Átha Gad 34 H2
Kinnitty / Cionn Eitigh 43 D1
Kinsale / Cionn tSáile 68 G1
Kinsalebeg / Baile an Phoill 61 D3
Kinsaley 36 G2
Kinvarra Co Galway 30 F3
Kinvarra / Cinn Mhara 31 D5
   Co Galway / Gaillimh
Kircubbin / Cill Ghobáin 12 G5
Kirkhills 4 G4
Kirkistown 20 H1

Kishkeam / Coiscéim na Caillí 59 C1
Knights Town 57 C4
Knock / An Cnoc 49 A1
  Co Clare / An Clár
Knock Co Mayo 23 D3
Knock Co Tipperary 44 E3
Knockacaurhin 40 H3
Knockaderry / Cnoc an Doire 49 D3
Knockagurraun 30 H4
Knockaholet / Cnoc an Chollait 4 H4
Knockainy / Cnoc Áine 50 G3
Knockalafalla 52 F5
Knockalaghta 24 H4
Knockalough / Cnoc an Locha 40 G5
Knockalunkard 40 H3
Knockananna / Cnoc an Eanaigh 46 E3
Knockanarra 24 E4
Knockane 59 D5
Knockanevin / Cnocán Aobhainn 50 H5
Knockanure 49 A3
Knockaroe 44 E3
Knockaun 32 H5
Knockaunarast 61 C1
Knockaunbrack 49 A4
Knockaunnaglashy 58 F2
Knockaunroe 58 E2
Knockayrogeen 57 C1
Knockboy / An Cnoc Buí 62 E1
Knockbrack Co Clare 42 F4
Knockbrack / An Cno Breac 9 B1
  Co Donegal / Dún na nGall
Knockbrack Co Kerry 48 G4
Knockbride 27 A1
Knockbridge / Droichead an Cnoic 27 D1
Knockbrit / Cnoc an Bhriotaigh 51 D3
Knockbrown 68 E2
Knockburden 60 F5
Knockcloghrim / Cnoc Clochdhroma 10 H2
Knockcroghery / Cnoc an Chrochaire 33 B1
Knockdarnan 50 F3
Knockdrislagh 60 F2
Knockeenadallane 59 B1
Knockeencreen 49 A5
Knocklofty 51 D4
Knocklong / Cnoc Loinge 50 H3
Knockmael 42 E2
Knockmore / An Cnoc Mór 23 C1
Knockmourne 61 B2
Knocknaboley 40 G4
Knocknacurra 68 F1
Knocknagashel / Cnoc na gCais 49 A4
Knocknageeha 66 H3
Knocknagower 42 G3
Knocknagree 59 B2
Knocknahaha 48 G5
Knocknahila 40 F4
Knocknahilan 60 E5
Knocknalina 13 C3
Knocknalower 13 D3
Knocknaskagh 61 B4
Knockraha / Cnoc Rátha 60 H4
Knockroe Co Cork 67 A3
Knockroe Co Kerry 57 D4
Knockroe Co Waterford 62 E2
Knocks Co Cork 67 D2
Knocks Co Laois 44 F2
Knockskagh 67 D2
Knockskavane 49 D5
Knocktopher / Cnoc an Tóchair 52 H3

Knuttery 60 G2
Kyle 44 H2
Kyleballyhue 45 B4
Kylebrack / An Choill Bhreac 32 G5
Kylegarve 51 A1

L

Labasheeda / Leaba Shíoda 49 B1
Labby 10 G2
Laban 32 E5
Lack / An Leac 9 B5
Lackagh 35 A5
Lackamore / An Leac Mhór 42 H4
Lackan Cross 33 A1
Lackan Co Carlow 45 A5
Lackan Co Westmeath 26 F5
Lackan / An Leacain 36 E5
  Co Wicklow / Cill Mhantáin
Lackareagh 59 D5
Lackbrooder 49 A5
Lacken / Leacain 53 B4
Lackendarragh North 60 H2
Lackey 43 D2
Ladysbridge / Droichead na Scuab 61 B4
Lagavara 4 H2
Lagganstown 51 C3
Laghey Corner 10 H5
Laghy / An Lathaigh 8 G4
Lahardaun 22 H1
Lakyle 49 B1
Lambeg / Lann Bheag 11 D5
Lamoge 52 G3
Lanesborough / Béal Átha Liag 25 C5
Lannaght 42 F2
Laracor 35 C1
Laragh Co Kildare 35 C3
Laragh Co Wicklow 46 F2
Largan Co Mayo 14 E4
Largan Co Roscommon 25 B3
Largan Co Sligo 15 A5
Largy 7 D4
Larne / Latharna 12 F1
Lattin / Laitean 51 A3
Lauragh 66 F1
Laurelvale / Tamhnaigh Bhealtaine 19 B2
Laurencetown / An Baile Mór 33 A4
Lavagh / Leamhach 15 C5
Lawrencetown / Baile Labhráis 19 B2
Laytown / An Inse 28 F4
Leamlara / Léim Lára 61 A4
Leap / An Léim 67 C3
Lecarrow / An Leithcheathrú 33 B1
Leckemy / Leic Éime 3 C2
Leenaun / An Líonán 22 E5
Legan or Lenamore 26 E5
Leggah 26 E2
Legoniel / Lag an Aoil 11 D4
Lehinch / An Leacht 40 F3
Leighlinbridge / Leithghlinn an Droichid 45 A5
Leitrim Co Clare 40 F5
Leitrim Co Down 20 E3
Leitrim Co Leitrim 25 B1
Leitrim East 49 A2
Leixlip / Léim an Bhradáin 36 E3
Lemanaghan 33 D4

Lemybrien / Léim Uí Bhriain 62 F1
Leperstown 63 B3
Lerrig 48 G4
Letterbreen / Leitir Bhruín 17 A2
Letterfrack / Leitir Fraic 29 D1
Letterkelly 40 G4
Letterkenny / Leitir Ceanainn 2 G5
Letterloan 4 F4
Lettermacaward / Leitir Mhic an Bhaird 8 E1
Lettermullan / Leitir Mealláin 30 E4
Lettermore 30 E4
Levally / An Leathbhaile 32 F1
  Co Galway / Gaillimh
Levally Co Mayo 23 C5
Licketstown 52 H5
Lifford 9 C2
Limavady / Léim an Mhadaidh 3 D4
Limerick / Luimneach 50 F1
Limerick Junction / Gabhal Luimnigh 51 A3
Lisbellaw / Líos Béal Átha 17 C2
Lisburn / Lios na gCearrbhach 11 D5
Liscananaun 31 D3
Liscannor / Lios Ceannúir 40 F3
Liscarney / Lios Cearnaigh 22 F4
Liscarroll / Lios Cearúill 50 E5
Liscasey / Lios Uí Chathasaigh 40 H5
Liscloon / Lios Claon 9 D1
Liscrona 48 G1
Lisdargan 57 D1
Lisdoart / Lios Dubhairt 18 F1
Lisdoonvarna / Lios Dúin Bhearna 40 G2
Lisdowney 44 G4
Lisduff / An Lios Dubh 27 A3
  Co Cavan / An Cabhán
Lisduff Co Cork 60 G3
Lisduff Co Offaly 33 D5
Lisgarode 43 B3
Lisgoold 61 A3
Lisheen 41 D5
Lisheenaguile 33 A5
Liskeagh 24 H1
Lislea / Lios Liath 19 B4
Lisnacaffry 26 F4
Lismore / Lios Mór 61 C2
Lismoyle 33 B1
Lisnacree / Lios na Crí 19 D5
Lisnadill / Lios na Daille 18 H3
Lisnageer / Lios na gCaor 18 E5
Lisnagry / Lios na Graí 50 G1
Lisnakill Cross 62 H1
Lisnamuck / Lios na Muc 10 H2
Lisnarrick / Lios na nDaróg 17 A1
Lisnaskea / Lios na Scéithe 17 C3
Lispatrick 68 G2
Lispole / Lios Póil 57 D1
Lisroe 40 H4
Lisronagh / Lios Ruanach 52 E4
Lisryan 26 F4
Lissaha 51 D2
Lissalway / Lios Sealbhaigh 24 H4
Lissanacody 33 A5
Lissananny 24 G3
Lissarnona 66 H4
Lisselton / Lios Eiltin 48 H3
Lissycasey / Lios Uí Chathasaigh 40 H5
Listellick 48 G5
Listerlin 53 A4
Listooder 20 F1
Listowel / Lios Tuathail 48 H3

Lisvarrinane / *Lios Fearnáin* 51 A4
Littleton / *An Baile Beag* 51 D1
Lixnaw / *Leic Snámha* 48 G4
Loanends / *Carn Mhéabha* 11 D3
Lobinstown / *Baile Lóibín* 27 C3
Loch Gowna 26 F2
Loghill / *Leamhchoill* 49 B2
  Co Limerick / *Luimneach*
Loghill / Co Limerick 49 D3
Logleagh 61 B1
Lombardstown / *Baile Limbaird* 60 E2
Londonderry / *Doire* 3 B5
Longford / *An Longfort* 25 D4
  Co Longford / *An Longfort*
Longford Co Offaly 43 D1
Longwood / *Maigh Dearmahaí* 35 B2
Lorrha / *Lothra* 43 B1
Lorum 53 B1
Loskeran 62 E3
Loughaclerybeg 32 G3
Loughacutteen 51 C4
Loughanaboll 15 B4
Loughanavally 34 F2
Loughbrickland / *Loch Bricleann* 19 C2
Lougher 58 E1
Loughgall / *Loch gCál* 19 A1
Loughglinn / *Loch Glinne* 24 G3
Loughguile / *Loch gCaol* 4 H4
Loughinisland / *Loch an Oileánn* 20 F2
Loughmoe / *Luachma* 43 D5
Loughmorne / *Loch Morn* 18 G5
Loughrea / *Baile Loch Riach* 32 G5
Loughshinny 36 G1
Louisburgh / *Cluain Cearbán* 22 E3
Louth / *Lú* 27 D1
Lowertown 66 G3
Lowtown 19 D2
Lucan / *Leamhcán* 36 E3
Lugdoon 15 B3
Luggacurren / *Log an Churraigh* 44 H3
Lukeswell 52 H4
Lullymore 35 B4
Lurgan / *An Lorgain* 19 B1
  Co Armagh / *Ard Mhaca*
Lurgan Co Offaly 33 D3
Lurgan Co Roscommon 24 H2
Lurganboy Co Donegal 2 H3
Lurganboy Co Leitrim 16 F2
Lusk / *Lusca* 36 G1
Lyracrumpane / *Ladhar an Chrompáin* 48 H4
Lyradane 60 F3
Lyre /
  Ladhar an Chrompáin or An Ladhar 60 E2
  Co Cork / *Corcaigh*
Lyre Co Kerry 49 A5
Lyre Co Waterford 61 B3
Lyrenaglogh 61 B1

M

Maam Cross 30 F2
Maas 8 E2
Mace 22 G3
Mackan / *Macan* 17 B3
Macosquin / *Maigh Choscáin* 4 F4
Macroney 61 A1

Macroom / *Maigh Chromtha* 59 D4
Maddockstown / *Baile Mhadóg* 52 H1
Maganey / *Maigh Geine* 45 B3
Maghaberry 11 C5
Maghera Co Down 20 E3
Maghera / *Machaire Rátha* 10 H1
  Co Londonderry / *Doire*
Maghera Cross 42 E3
Magherafelt / *Machaire Fíolta* 10 H2
Magheralin / *Machaire Lainne* 19 C1
Magheramason 3 B5
Magheramorne / *Machaire Morna* 12 F2
Magheraveely / *Machaire Mhílie* 17 D4
Maghery / *An Machaire*
  Co Donegal / *Dún na nGall* 8 E1
Maghery Co Armagh 11 A5
Magilligan / *Aird Mhic Giollagain* 3 D3
Maguiresbridge / *Droichead Mhig Uidir* 17 B3
Mahoonagh 49 D3
Mainham 35 C3
Malahide / *Mullach Íde* 36 G2
Malin / *Málainn* 3 B1
Malin Beg / *Málainn Bhig* 7 B3
Mallaranny / *An Mhala Raiothní* 22 E2
Mallow / *Mala* 60 F2
Mallusk / *Maigh Bhloisce* 11 D3
Manorcunningham /
  Mainéar Uí Chuinneagáin 2 H5
Manorhamilton / *Cluainín* 16 F3
Manselstown 43 D5
Mansfieldstown 28 E2
Mantua / *An Mointeach* 25 A3
Manulla 23 C3
Marble Arch 17 A3
Mardyke 52 E2
Margymonaghan 3 D3
Markethill / *Cnoc an Mhargaidh* 19 A3
Markhamstown 51 D4
Marlfield 51 D4
Marshalstown / *Baile Mharascail* 53 D2
Martinstown / *Baile Uí Mháirtín* 5 D5
Marty 27 B4
Masterstown 51 C3
Matehy 60 F4
Maulatrahane 67 B3
Maulavanig 67 A1
Maulawaddra 66 G3
Maum / *An Mám* 30 F1
Mauricesmills / *Muilte Mhuiris* 40 H3
Mayglass 53 D5
Maynooth / *Maigh Naud* 35 D3
Mayo / *Maigh Eo* 23 C4
Mayobridge / *Droichead Mhaigh Eo* 19 C4
Mazetown 11 D5
McGaffins Corner 19 C3
McGregor's Corner 5 D5
McLaughlins Corner 4 G5
Meanus / *Méanos* 50 F2
Meelick 33 B5
Meelin / *An Mhaoilinn* 49 C5
Meenaclady 1 D3
Meenbannivane 49 A5
Meenglass 9 A2
Meennaraheeny 49 B5
Meigh 19 B4
Menlough Co Galway 32 G2
Menlough / *Mionlach* 31 C4
  Co Galway / *Gaillimh*
Middlequarter 61 D1

Middletown / *Coillidh Chanannain* 18 G3
Midfield / *An Trian Láir* 23 D2
Midleton / *Mainistir na Corann* 61 A4
Milehouse / *Teach an Mhíle* 53 D2
Milemill 45 C1
Milestone / *Cloch an Mhile* 51 B1
Milford / *Áth an Mhuilinn* 18 H2
  Co Armagh / *Ard Mhacha*
Milford / *Áth na Muilte* 50 E4
  Co Cork / *Corcaigh*
Mill Brook 17 D4
Mill Town / *Baile an Mhuilinn* 11 C3
Millbrook / *Sruthán an Mhuilinn* 12 E1
Millford / *Baile na nGallóglach* 2 G4
Millisle / *Oilean an Mhuilinn* 12 H4
Millstreet / *Sráid an Mhuilinn* 61 A1
  Co Cork / *Corcaigh*
Millstreet Co Cork 59 C2
Millstreet Co Waterford 61 D1
Milltown Co Armagh 18 G3
Milltown Co Armagh 19 A2
Milltown / *Baile an Mhuilinn* 17 C5
  Co Cavan / *An Cabhán*
Milltown Co Donegal 8 F4
Milltown Co Down 19 C4
Milltown Co Down 19 C3
Milltown Co Dublin 36 E3
Milltown Co Galway 32 G1
Milltown Co Galway 24 E5
Milltown Co Kerry 57 C1
Milltown Co Kerry 58 G1
Milltown Co Kildare 35 B5
Milltown Co Kilkenny 52 H4
Milltown Co Londonderry 4 E3
Milltown Co Londonderry 4 F4
Milltown Co Tyrone 10 E4
Milltown Co Westmeath 34 F1
Milltown Malbay / *Sráid na Cathrach* 40 F4
Milltownpass /
  Bealach Bhaile an Mhuilinn 34 H2
Minane Bridge /
  Droichead an Mhionnáin 68 H1
Minerstown / *Baile na Mianadóirí* 20 F3
Minorstown 52 E4
Minterburn / *Muintir Bhirn* 18 G1
Mitchelstown / *Baile Mhistéale* 51 A5
Moanmore Co Clare 48 H1
Moanmore Co Tipperary 50 H3
Moate / *An Móta* 33 D3
Modelligo 61 D2
Modreeny 43 B3
Mogeely / *Maigh Dhíle* 61 B4
Mohil 44 H5
Mohill / *Maothail* 25 C2
Moira / *Maigh Rath* 11 C5
Monaghan / *Muineachán* 18 F3
Monagoun 61 B2
Monaincha Bog 43 D3
Monalour 61 C1
Monamolin / *Muine Moling* 54 F2
Monamraher 62 E3
Monard Co Tipperary 51 A3
Monard Co Waterford 61 C1
Monaseed / *Móin na Saighead* 46 E5
Monaster / *An Mhainistir* 50 F2
Monasteraden / *Mainistir Réadáin* 24 G2
Monasterevin / *Mainistir Eimhín* 35 A5
Monea / *Maigh Niadh* 17 A2
Moneen Co Clare 48 F2

Moneen Co Galway 31 D2
Monettia Beg 34 F5
Moneycusker 59 C5
Moneydig / Muine Dige 4 F5
Moneygall / Muine Gall 43 C3
Moneyglass / An Muine Glas 11 B2
Moneymore / Muine Mór 10 H3
Moneyneany / Món na nIonadh 10 G2
Moneyslane 19 D3
Moneyreagh / Monadh Riabhach 12 F5
Monilea / An Muine Liath 34 G1
Monivea / Muine Mhéa 32 F3
Monkstown / Baile na Manach
  Co Antrim / Aontroim 12 E3
Monkstown / Baile na Mhanach
  Co Cork / Corcaigh 60 H5
Montpelier 42 G5
Mooncoin / Móin Choinn 52 H5
Moone / Maoin 45 B2
Montpelier 42 G5
Moord 61 D4
Moorfields / Páirc an tSléibhe 11 C2
Morenane 50 E3
Mornington / Baile Uí Mhornáin 28 F4
Moroe / Maigh Rua 50 H1
Mortlestown 50 G4
Moskeagh 60 E5
Mosney Camp 28 F5
Moss-side / Mas Saide 4 H3
Mossley / Maslaí 12 E3
Mothel 52 F5
Mountbellew / An Creagán 32 G2
Mount Nugent / Droichead Uí Dhálaigh 26 G3
Mount Stewart 12 G5
Mount Talbot / Mun Talbóid 33 A1
Mount Temple / An Grianan 33 D2
Mount Uniacke / Cúil O gCorra 61 B3
Mountallen 16 G5
Mountbolus / Cnocán Bhólais 34 E5
Mountcatherine 60 H3
Mountcharles / Moin Searlas 8 F4
Mountcollins / Cnoc Uí Choileáin 49 B5
Mountfield / Achadh Ard 10 E4
Mountjoy / Muinseo 9 D4
Mountmellick / Móinteach Milíe 44 G1
Mountnorris / Achadh na Cranncha 19 A3
Mountrath / Maiglean Rátha 44 F2
Mountshannon / Baile Uí Bhealáin 42 H3
Moveen 48 G1
Moville / Bun an Phobail 3 D3
Moy Co Galway 41 D1
Moy / An Maigh
  Co Tyrone / Tir Eoghain 18 H1
Moyard / Maigh Ard 29 C1
Moyasta / Maigh Sheasta 48 H1
Moycarky 51 D1
Moycullen / Maigh Cuilinn 31 C3
Moydow / Maigh Dumha 25 D5
Moygashel / Maigh gCaisil 10 G5
Moyglass / Maigh Ghlas 51 D2
Moyle 45 B4
Moylisha 45 D5
Moylough / Maigh Locha
  Co Galway / Gaillimh 32 G2
Moylough Co Sligo 24 F1
Moymore 42 E4
Moynalty / Maigh Locha 27 B3
Moynalvy 35 C2
Moyne 46 E3

Moyne / An Mhaighean
  Co Roscommon / Ros Comáin 24 G3
Moyne Co Tipperary 43 D5
Moyrahan 13 C3
Moyreen 49 B2
Moyrus 29 D3
Moys 3 D5
Moyvally / Maigh Bhealaigh 35 B2
Moyvane / Maigh Mheain 49 A3
Moyvore / Maigh Mhórdha 34 E1
Moyvoughly / Maig Bhachla 33 D2
Mt.Melleray Monastery 61 C1
Muckamore / Maigh Chomair 11 C3
Mucklon 35 B3
Muckross 58 H3
Muckrush 31 C3
Muff / Magh 3 B4
Muine Bheag (Bagnalstown) 45 B5
Muinganear 49 A5
Muingaphuca 58 F2
Muingwee 49 A4
Muingydowda 57 C4
Mulhuddart / Mullach Eadrad 36 E3
Mullafarry 14 G4
Mullagh / An Mullach 27 A3
  Co Cavan / An Cabhán
Mullagh / Mullach 40 F4
  Co Clare / An Clár
Mullagh Co Galway 32 H5
Mullagh Co Mayo 22 E4
Mullagh Co Meath 35 D2
Mullaghbane 19 A5
Mullaghmacormick 25 B3
Mullaghmore / An Mullach Mór 16 E1
Mullaghroe 24 G1
Mullan Head 4 G5
Mullan Co Londonderry 4 F4
Mullan / An Muileann 18 G2
  Co Monaghan / Muineachán
Mullany's Cross 15 B5
Mullartown 20 E4
Mullen 24 H3
Mullenaboree 60 G2
Mullennaglogh 52 F3
Mullennakill 53 A3
Mullinacuff / Muileann Mhic Dhuibh 45 D4
Mullinahone / Muileann na hUamhan 52 F2
Mullinavat / Muileann an Bhata 52 H4
Mullingar / An Muileann gCear 34 G1
Multyfarnham / Muilte Farannáin 26 G5
Mungret / Mungairit 50 F1
Murher 49 A3
Murntown / Baile Mhúráin 54 E5
Murreagh 57 B1
Murrisk / Muraisc 22 F3
Murroogh 40 G1
Mweennalaa 48 H5
Myross 67 C3
Myshall / Miseal 45 C5

N

Naas / An Nás 35 C5
Nad 60 E2
Nahana 34 H5
Naran 8 E2

Narraghmore / An Fhorrach Mhór 45 B1
Naul / An Aill 28 F5
Navan / An Uaimh 27 C5
Neale / An Éill 30 H1
Nealstown 44 E2
Nedanone 58 E5
Nenagh / An tAonach 43 A4
New Birmingham / Gleann an Ghuail 52 E1
New Buildings / An Baile Nua 3 B5
New Chapel Cross 57 D5
New Inn / An Dromainn 26 H2
  Co Cavan / An Cabhán
New Inn / An Cnoc Breac 32 G4
  Co Galway / Gaillimh
New Inn Co Laois 44 H1
New Kildimo 50 E1
New Ross / Ros Mhic Thriúin 53 B4
New Twopothouse Village /
  Tigh Nua an Dá Phota 60 F1
Newbawn / An Bábhún Nua 53 C4
Newbliss / Cúil Darach 18 E4
Newbridge / An Droichead Nua 32 H1
  Co Galway / Gaillimh
Newbridge Co Limerick 49 D2
Newcastle / An Caisléan Nua 20 E3
  Co Down / An Dún
Newcastle Co Dublin 35 D4
Newcastle Co Galway 32 F3
Newcastle Co Tipperary 51 D5
Newcastle Co Wicklow 46 G1
Newcastle West / An Caisléan Nua 49 C3
Newcestown / Baile Níos 67 D1
Newchapel 51 D4
Newferry 11 A2
Newinn / Loch Ceann 51 C3
Newmarket / Áth Trasna 59 D1
  Co Cork / Corcaigh
Newmarket Co Kilkenny 52 H3
Newmarket On Fergus / Cora Chaitlín 41 D5
Newmills Co Cork 67 D3
Newmills / An Muileann Úr 9 A1
  Co Donegal / Dún na nGall
Newmills / An Muileann Nua 10 H5
  Co Tyrone / Tir Eoghain
Newport / Baile Uí Fhiacháin 22 F2
  Co Mayo / Maigh Eo
Newport / An Port Nua 42 H5
  Co Tipperary / Tiobraid Árann
Newry / An tIur 19 B4
Newtown Co Galway 32 G4
Newtown Co Kildare 35 C3
Newtown Co Kilkenny 52 F1
Newtown Co Laois 45 A4
Newtown Co Limerick 50 G3
Newtown Co Mayo 22 H3
Newtown Co Meath 27 D3
Newtown Co Offaly 33 B5
Newtown Co Roscommon 33 A3
Newtown Co Roscommon 24 H4
Newtown Co Tipperary 51 A3
Newtown Co Tipperary 43 D3
Newtown Co Waterford 62 E2
Newtown Co Waterford 61 D3
Newtown Co Wexford 64 E3
Newtown Co Wexford 63 D4
Newtown Cashel / Baile Nua an Chaisil 33 C1
Newtown Cloghans / An Baile Ur 14 H5
Newtown Cunningham / An Baile Nua 3 A5
Newtown Forbes / An Lois Breac 25 B4

Newtown Gore / *An Dúcharraig* 17 B5
Newtown-Crommelin /
  Baile Nua Chromlain 5 D5
Newtownabbey / *Baile na Mainstreach* 12 E3
Newtownadam 51 C4
Newtownards / *Baile Nua na hArda* 12 G4
Newtownbutler / *An Baile Nua* 17 D4
Newtownhamilton / *Baile Úr* 19 A4
Newtownlow 34 F3
Newtownlynch 31 D5
Newtown Mt.kennedy /
  Baile an Chinnéidigh 46 G1
Newtownshandrum /
  Baile Nua Sheandroma 50 E4
Newtownstewart / *An Baile Nua* 9 D3
Nicholastown 53 A5
Ninemilehouse / *Tigh na Naoi Mile* 52 F3
Nobber / *An Obair* 27 C3
Nohaval / *Nuach a Bháil* 68 H1
North Ring 68 E2
Northlands / *An Táchairt Thuaidh* 27 B1
Noughaval Co Clare 41 D4
Noughaval Co Clare 41 D4
Nurney / *An Urnaí* 45 B5
  Co Carlow / *Ceatharlach*
Nurney Co Kildare 45 B1
Nutts Corner / *Coirnéal Nutt* 11 C4

O

Oaghley 48 H3
Oatfield 42 F5
O'Briensbridge 42 G5
Oghill 33 A4
Ogonnelloe / *Tuath Ó gConáile* 42 G3
Oilgate / *Maolán na nGabhar* 53 D3
Old Head 68 G2
Old Kilcullen 45 C1
Old Kildimo 50 E1
Old Ross 53 B4
Old Town Co Laois 44 G3
Old Town / *An Seanbhaile* 33 B4
  Co Roscommon / *Ros Comair*
Old Town Co Wexford 53 C2
Oldcastle / *An Seanchaisleán* 26 H3
Oldgrange 51 D5
Oldleagh 45 A3
Oldleighlin / *Seanleithghlinn* 45 A5
Oldtown Co Dublin 36 F1
Oldtown Co Roscommon 33 C3
Omagh / *An Ómaigh* 9 D4
Omeath / *Ó Meith* 19 C5
Onaght 30 E5
Oola / *Úlla* 51 A2
Oranmore / *Órán Mór* 31 D4
Oristown 27 B4
Orritor / *Na Coracha Beaga* 10 G4
Oughtdarra 40 F1
Oughter 34 E4
Oughterard / *Uachtar Ard* 30 H2
Oulart / *An tAbhallort* 54 E2
Outeragh 51 C4
Ovens / *Na hUamhanna* 60 F4
Owenbeg / *An Abhainn Bheag* 15 A3
Owenbristy 32 E5
Owning / *Ónainn* 52 G4

P

Palace / *An Phailís* 53 B3
Palatine 45 B4
Palatine Street 50 H2
Pallas Co Galway 32 H3
Pallas Co Laois 44 G2
Pallas Green / *An tSeanphailís* 50 H2
Pallas Green (New) / *Pailís Ghréine* 50 H2
Pallasboy 34 G3
Pallaskenry / *Pailís Chaonraí* 50 E1
Pallis 46 F5
Palmerston / *Baile Phámar* 36 E3
Park 64 E3
Parkacunna 60 H1
Parkbane 68 E1
Parkgate 11 D3
Parkmore / *An Phairc Mhór* 31 D5
Parknasilla 58 E5
Parteen 42 F5
Partry / *Partraí* 22 H4
Passage 32 H1
Passage East 63 B3
Passage West / *An Pasáiste* 60 H5
Patrickswell / *Tobar Phádraig* 50 F2
Paulstown 53 A1
Peak 32 G4
Peterswell / *Tobar Pheadair* 42 F1
Pettigo / *Paiteagó* 9 A5
Pharis / *Fáras* 4 H4
Piercetown Co Cork 60 G4
Piercetown Co Wexford 54 E5
Pike 43 B1
Pike Corner 35 C1
Pike of Rush Hall / *An Paidhc* 44 F3
Piltown / *Baile an Phoill* 52 G4
Pluck 2 H5
Plumbridge / *Droichead an Phlum* 9 D2
Pollagh Co Galway 31 D5
Pollagh / *Pollach* 33 D4
  Co Offaly / *Uíbh Fhailí*
Pollatlugga 32 H4
Pollboy 33 A4
Pollshask 24 G5
Pomeroy / *Pomeroy* 10 F4
Pontoon 23 C1
Port 28 F3
Port Laoise 44 G2
Portacloy 13 D2
Portadown / *Port an Dúnáin* 19 B1
Portaferry / *Port an Pheire* 20 G1
Portaleen 3 C1
Portarlington / *Cúil an tSúdaire* 34 H5
Portavogie / *Port an Bhogaigh* 20 H1
Portballintrae / *Port Bhaile an Trá* 4 G2
Portglenone / *Port Ghluain Eoghain* 11 A1
Portland 43 A1
Portlaw / *Port Lach* 52 G5
Portmagee / *An Caladh* 57 B4
Portmarnock / *Port Mearnóg* 36 G2
Portmuck 12 F1
Portnablaghy / *Port na Bláiche* 2 F3
Portnashangan 26 G5
Portnoo / *Port Nua* 7 D2
Portraine 36 G1
Portroe / *An Port Rua* 42 H3
Portrush / *Port Rois* 4 F3
Portsalon / *Port an tSalainn* 2 H2

Portstewart / *Port Stiobhaird* 4 F3
Portumna / *Port Omna* 43 A1
Pottore 16 H5
Poulnamucky 51 D4
Power's Cross / *Crois an Phaoraigh* 42 H1
Poyntz Pass / *Pas an Phointe* 19 B3
Priest Town 61 D1
Priesthaggard 53 B5
Prosperous / *An Chorrchoill* 35 C4
Puckaun / *Pocán* 43 A3

Q

Quarrytown 11 C1
Querrin / *An Cuibhreann* 48 H1
Quilty / *Coilte* 40 F4
Quin / *Cuinche* 42 E4

R

Radestown 44 H5
Raffrey / *Rafraidh* 20 F1
Rahan / *Raithean* 34 E4
Raharney / *Ráth Fhearne* 35 A1
Raheen Co Carlow 45 D4
Raheen Co Cork 60 F5
Raheen Co Kerry 59 A2
Raheen Co Kilkenny 52 G4
Raheen Co Tipperary 51 C4
Raheen Co Westmeath 34 E2
Raheen / *An Ráithin* 53 C4
  Co Wexford / *Loch Garman*
Raheenlusk 54 F2
Rake Street 14 F5
Ramsgrange / *An Ghráinseach* 53 B5
Ranamackan 32 H5
Randalstown / *Baile Raghnaill* 11 B2
Rapemills 43 C1
Raphoe / *Ráth Bhoth* 9 B1
Rascalstreet 59 C1
Rasharkin / *Ros Earcáin* 4 G5
Rashedoge 2 G5
Rathcormack / *Ráth Chormaic* 61 A2
Rath 43 D1
Ráth Luirc (Charleville) 50 F4
Rathangan / *Rath Iomgháin* 35 A5
Rathanny 48 H5
Rathaspick 25 E5
Rathbrit 51 D3
Rathcabban / *Ráth Cabáin* 43 B1
Rathconor 25 A4
Rathconrath / *Ráth Conarta* 34 F1
Rathcoole 36 E4
Rathcore / *Ráth Cuair* 35 B2
Rathcrony 40 H4
Rathdangan / *Ráth Daingin* 45 D3
Rathdowney / *Ráth Domhnaigh* 44 E4
Rathdrum / *Ráth Droma* 46 F3
Rathduff 26 E5
Ratheenroe 66 H3
Rathernan 35 B4
Rathfeigh / *Ráth Faiche* 28 E5
Rathfilode 60 H3

Rathfriland / *Ráth Fraoileann* — 19 D3
Rathfylane — 53 C3
Rathgarry — 44 H4
Rathgormuck / *Ráth Ó gCormaic* — 52 F5
Rathgranagher — 23 C5
Rathkeale / *Ráth Caola* — 49 D2
Rathkeevin — 51 D4
Rathkenny / *Ráth Cheannaigh* — 27 C4
Rathkeva — 25 A3
Rathkineely — 24 H3
Rathlackan — 14 G3
Rathlee / *Ráth Lao* — 15 A3
Rathlyon — 45 C4
Rathmaiden — 62 F1
Rathmelton / *Ráth Mealtain* — 2 H4
Rathmore / *An Ráth Mhór* Co Kerry / *Ciarraí* — 59 B2
Rathmore / *An Ráth Mhór* Co Kildare / *Cill Dara* — 35 D5
Rathmoylan Co Waterford — 63 B4
Rathmoylon Co Meath — 35 B2
Rathmullan / *Ráth Maoláin* — 2 H4
Rathnew / *Ráth Naoi* — 46 G2
Rathnure / *Ráth an Iúir* — 53 C3
Rathoma — 14 G4
Rathorgan — 61 A3
Rathowen — 26 F5
Rathroeen — 14 H4
Rathruane — 66 H3
Rathvilly / *Ráth Bhile* — 45 C3
Rathwire — 34 H1
Ratoath / *Ráth Tó* — 36 E1
Ratooragh — 66 G3
Ravensdale / *Gleann na bhFiach* — 19 B5
Ravernet / *Ráth Bhearnait* — 11 D5
Ray / *An Ráith* — 2 H4
Reaghstown — 27 D2
Reanaclogheen — 62 E3
Reanascreena / *Rae na Scríne* — 67 C2
Rear Cross / *Crois na Rae* — 51 A1
Recess / *Sraith Salach* — 30 E2
Reclain — 10 F5
Redcross / *Chrois Dhearg* — 46 G3
Redgate — 54 E3
Redhills / *An Croc Rua* — 17 D5
Redwood — 43 B1
Renvyle — 21 C5
Rerrin / *Raerainn* — 66 F2
Revallagh — 4 G3
Rhode / *Ród* — 34 H3
Richill / *Log an Choire* — 19 A2
Riesk — 61 A3
Ring / *An Rinn* — 64 G3
Ringaskiddy / *Rinn an Seidídh* — 60 H5
Ringsend / *Droichead an Carraige* — 4 E4
Ringstown — 44 F2
Ringville / *An Rinn* — 62 E3
Rinneen Co Clare — 40 F3
Rinneen Co Cork — 67 B3
Rinville — 31 D4
Riverchapel — 54 F1
Riverstick / *Áth an Mhaide* — 68 G1
Riverstown Co Cork — 60 H4
Riverstown / *Baile Idir dha Abhainn* Co Sligo / *Sligeach* — 16 E4
Riverstown / *Baile Uí Lachnáin* Co Tipperary / *Tiobraid Árann* — 43 C1
Roadford — 40 F2
Robertstown / *Baile Riobaird* — 35 B4

Robinstown / *Baile Riobín* Co Meath / *An Mhí* — 27 C5
Robinstown Co Wexford — 53 D5
Rochestown Co Kilkenny — 52 H4
Rochestown Co Kilkenny — 53 A5
Rochestown Co Tipperary — 51 C5
Rochfortbridge / *Droichead Chaisleán Loiste* — 34 G2
Rockchapel / *Séipéal na Carraige* — 49 C5
Rockcorry / *Búiochar* — 18 F5
Rockhill — 50 F3
Rockmills — 60 H1
Rockstown — 46 G3
Rodeen — 25 B2
Roevehagh — 32 E5
Rooaun — 33 B5
Roonah Quay — 21 D3
Roosky Co Mayo — 24 F1
Roosky / *Rúscaigh* Co Roscommon / *Ros Comáin* — 25 C3
Rooty Cross — 33 B3
Rosapenna — 2 G3
Rosbercon — 53 A4
Roscat — 45 C4
Roscommon / *Ros Comáin* — 25 A5
Roscrea / *Ros Cré* — 43 D3
Rosegreen / *Faiche Ró* — 51 D3
Rosenallis / *Ros Fhionnghlaise* — 44 F1
Rosmuck / *Ros Muc* — 30 F3
Rosmult — 51 C1
Rosnakill / *Ros na Cille* — 2 G3
Ross Behy — 58 E2
Ross Carbery — 67 C3
Ross Port / *Ros Dumhach* — 13 D3
Ross / *An Ros* Co Meath / *An Mhi* — 26 G3
Rossadrehid / *Ros an Droichead* — 51 B4
Rossanean — 58 H1
Rossaveel — 30 F4
Rossbrin — 66 H3
Rosscahill / *Ros Cathail* — 30 H3
Rosses Point / *An Ros* — 15 D2
Rossinver / *Ros Inbhir* — 16 G2
Rosslare / *Ros Láir* — 54 E5
Rosslare Harbour — 54 F5
Rosslea / *Ros Liath* — 18 E3
Rossmore Co Cork — 67 D2
Rossmore / *An Ros Mór* Co Cork / *Corcaigh* — 59 C5
Rossmore Co Laois — 45 A4
Rossmore Co Monaghan — 18 F3
Rossnowlagh / *Ros Neamhlach* — 8 F5
Rostellan / *Ros Tialláin* — 61 A5
Rostrevor / *Ros Treabhair* — 19 C5
Rosturk — 22 E2
Roundfort — 23 C5
Roundstone / *Cloch na Rón* — 29 D2
Roundwood / *An Tóchar* — 46 F1
Rousky — 10 E3
Ruan / *An Ruán* — 41 D3
Rubane / *Rú Bán* — 12 H5
Rush / *An Ros* — 36 G1
Rusheeny — 30 G2
Russellstown — 61 D5
Ryehill — 32 F3
Rylane Cross — 60 E3

S

Saggart / *Teach Sagard* — 36 E4
Saint Johnstown — 9 C1
Saintfield / *Tamhnaigh Naomh* — 20 F1
Sallahig — 57 D4
Sallins / *Na Solláin* — 35 C4
Sallybrook — 60 H4
Sallypark — 43 B4
Salthill — 31 C4
Saltmills / *Muileann an tSáile* — 63 C3
Sandholes / *Glais an Ghainimh* — 10 G4
Sandyford / *Áth an Ghainimh* — 36 F4
Santry / *Seantrabh* — 36 F2
Saul — 20 G2
Scardaun Co Mayo — 23 D5
Scardaun Co Roscommon — 33 A1
Scarriff / *An Scairbh* — 42 G3
Scartaglin — 59 A1
Scarva / *Scarbhach* — 19 B2
Scotch Corner — 18 G4
Scotch Street / *Sráid na hAlbanach* — 19 A1
Scotshouse / *Teach an Scotaigh* — 17 D5
Scotstowm / *Baile an Scotaigh* — 18 F3
Scrahan — 48 F5
Scrahanfadda — 59 A2
Scramoge / *Scramóg* — 25 B4
Scrarour — 60 H1
Screen / *An Scrín* — 54 E3
Screggan / *An Screagán* — 34 E4
Scriggan — 3 D5
Scurlockstown — 27 A4
Seaforde / *Baile Forda* — 20 F2
Seapatrick — 19 C2
Seskin — 52 E4
Seskinore / *Seisceann Odhar* — 9 D5
Sess Kilgreen / *Seis Chill Ghrianna* — 18 F1
Shanagarry / *An Seangharraí* — 61 B5
Shanaglish — 42 E2
Shanagolden / *Seanghualainn* — 49 C2
Shanahoe / *Seanchua* — 44 F3
Shanballard — 32 G3
Shanbally / *An Seanbhaile* Co Cork / *Corcaigh* — 60 H5
Shanbally Co Galway — 32 G1
Shanbally Co Waterford — 62 F2
Shanballyedmond — 51 A1
Shanballymore / *An Seanbhaile Mór* — 60 G1
Shanecrane — 67 B1
Shangarry — 32 H5
Shankill / *Seanchill* — 36 G4
Shanlaragh / *Seanlárach* — 67 C1
Shannakea / *Seanachae* — 49 C1
Shannon — 42 E5
Shannon Harbour / *Caladh na Sionainne* — 33 C5
Shannonbridge / *Droichead na Sionainne* — 33 B4
Shannonville — 42 H3
Shanragh — 45 B3
Shanrahan — 51 B5
Shanrath — 49 D4
Shantonagh / *Seantonnach* — 18 G5
Shanavogh — 40 G4
Sharavogue / *Searbhóg* — 43 C2
Shercock / *Searcóg* — 27 B1
Sheskin — 14 E4
Shevry — 43 B5

Shillelagh / Síol Ealaigh — 45 D5
Shinrone / Suían Róin — 43 C2
Shrigley — 20 G1
Shrone — 48 H2
Shronell — 51 A3
Shronowen / Srón Abhann — 48 H2
Shrule / Sruthair — 31 C1
Sillahertane — 67 B1
Silver Bridge / Béal Átha an Airgid — 19 A5
Silver Stream — 18 F3
Silvermines / Béal Átha Gabhann — 43 A4
Sion Mills / Muileann an tSiáin — 9 C2
Six Crosses — 48 H3
Six Road Ends — 12 G4
Sixmilebridge / Droichead Abhann — 42 E5
Sixmilecross / Na Coracha Móra — 10 E5
Skahanagh — 67 A1
Skahanagh North — 60 H3
Skahanagh South — 60 H3
Skeagh Co Cork — 67 A3
Skeagh Co Westmeath — 34 E1
Skehanagh Co Galway — 32 F2
Skehanagh Co Galway — 42 E1
Skeheen — 51 A5
Skerries / Na Sceirí — 28 G5
Skibbereen / An Sciobairin — 67 B3
Skreen Co Meath — 27 D5
Skreen / An Scrín
  Co Sligo / Sligeach — 15 C3
Skull / An Scoil — 66 H3
Slane / Baile Shlaine — 27 D4
Slieveroe / Sliabh Rua — 53 A5
Sligo / Sligeach — 15 D3
Smithborough / Na Mullaí — 18 E3
Smithstown — 44 H4
Sneem / An tSnaidhm — 58 E5
Spa / An Spá — 48 F5
Spanish Point / Rinn na Spáinneach — 66 G4
Sperrin — 10 F2
Spiddle — 30 H4
Spink — 44 H3
Spittaltown — 34 E3
Spring Town — 3 B5
Springfield / Achadh an Fhuaráin — 17 A2
Sraghmore — 46 F1
Srah — 13 C4
Srahanboy — 44 E2
Sraheens / Na Sraithíní — 23 C2
Srahmore / An Srath Mór — 13 D4
Sruh — 61 C1
St Margaret's — 36 F2
Stabannan — 28 E2
Stackallan / Stigh Colláin — 27 D4
Staffordstown / Baile Stafard — 11 B3
Stamullin — 28 F5
Staplestown — 35 C3
Steen's Corner — 11 C2
Stepaside — 36 F4
Stewartstown / An Chraobh — 10 H4
Stickstown — 60 E5
Stillorgan — 36 G4
Stone Bridge — 18 E4
Stonepark — 50 G2
Stonyford Co Antrim — 11 D4
Stonyford / Áth Stúin
  Co Kilkenny / Cill Chainnigh — 52 H2
Stormont — 12 F4
Strabane / An Strath Bán — 9 C2
Stradbally Co Waterford — 62 F2

Stradbally / An tSraidbhaile — 44 H2
Stradone / Sraith an Domhain — 26 H1
Straffan / Teach Srafáin — 35 D4
Strahart / Sraith Airt — 53 D1
Straid / An tSraid — 12 E2
Strand / An Trá — 49 C4
Strandhill / An Leathros — 15 D3
Strangford / Baile Loch Cuan — 20 G2
Stranocum / Sraith Nócam — 4 H3
Stranorlar / Srath an Urláir — 9 A2
Stratford / Áth na Sráiole — 45 C3
Streamstown Co Galway — 29 C1
Streamstown / Baile an tSruthain
  Co Westmeath / An Iarmhí — 34 E2
Street / An tSráid — 26 F4
Strokestown / Béal na mBuillí — 25 B3
Summer Cove — 68 G1
Summerhill / Cnoc an Linsigh — 35 C2
Suncroft / Crochta na Gréine — 45 B1
Swan — 44 H3
Swanlinbar / An Muilcann Iarainn — 17 A4
Swatragh / An Suaitreach — 10 H1
Swinford / Béal Átha na Muice — 23 D2
Swords / Sord — 36 F2

T

Taghmon / Teach Munna — 53 D5
Taghshinny — 26 E5
Tagoat / Teach Gót — 54 E5
Tallaght / Tamhlacht — 36 E4
Tallanstown / Baile an Tallúnaigh — 27 D2
Tallow / Tulach an Iarainn — 61 B2
Tallowbridge — 61 B2
Tamlaght / Tamhlacht
  Co Fermanagh / Fear Manach — 17 B2
Tamlaght O'Crilly — 11 A1
Tamnamore / An Tamhnach Mhór — 10 H5
Tandragee / Tóin re Gaoith — 19 B2
Tang / An Teanga — 33 D1
Tankardstown — 50 F4
Tara / Teamhair — 34 E3
Tarbert / Tairbeart — 49 A2
Tarmon / An Tearmann — 49 A1
Tassagh / An Tasach — 18 H3
Taur — 59 C1
Tawny / An Tamhnaigh — 2 G3
Tawnyinah — 24 E2
Tedagh — 66 H2
Tedavnet / Tigh Damhnata — 18 F3
Tedd — 9 B5
Teemore — 17 C4
Teer — 47 D5
Teeranearagh — 57 C4
Teeravane — 57 B1
Teerelton / Tír Eiltín — 59 D5
Teermaclane / Tír Mhic Calláin — 41 D4
Teevurcher / Taobh Urchair — 27 B2
Templeboy / Teampall Baoith — 15 B3
Templederry / Teampall Doire — 43 B5
Templeetney — 52 E4
Templemartin / Teampall Mártan — 60 E5
Templemore / An Teampall Mór — 43 D4
Templenoe — 58 G5
Templeoran — 34 G3
Templepark — 43 C3

Templepatrick / Teampall Phádraig — 11 D3
Templeshanbo / Teampall Seanbhoth — 53 C2
Templetouhy / Teampall Tuaithe — 43 D4
Templetown — 63 C3
Templeusque — 60 H4
Tempo / An tIompú Deiseal — 17 C2
Termonbarry — 25 C4
Termonfeckin / Tearmann Feichin — 28 F3
Terryglass / Tír Dhá Ghlas — 43 A1
Tevrin — 34 H1
The Bush — 28 F1
The Butts — 45 A5
The Cock — 20 F1
The Cross / An Chrois — 3 B5
The Cross Keys — 18 H3
The Curragh / An Currach — 35 B5
The Diamond / An Diamant
  Co Antrim / Aontroim — 11 C4
The Diamond Co Tyrone — 11 A4
The Downs / Na Dúnta — 34 H1
The Drones — 4 H4
The Dry Arch — 4 H3
The Five Roads — 36 F1
The Harrow — 54 E2
The Leap — 53 C4
The Loup / An Lúb — 11 A3
The Pigeons / Na Colúir — 33 D1
The Pike Co Tipperary — 43 B2
The Pike Co Waterford — 62 F2
The Pike Co Waterford — 61 C3
The Quarter — 4 F5
The Rock / An Charraig — 10 G4
The Rosses — 1 C5
The Rower / An Robhar — 53 B3
The Sheddings — 11 D1
The Spa / An Spá — 20 E2
The Sweep — 52 G4
The Temple / An Teampall — 12 E5
Thomastown / Baile Mhic Andáin
  Co Kilkenny / Cill Chainnigh — 52 H2
Thomastown Co Limerick — 50 H4
Thomastown Co Meath — 27 B3
Thomastown Co Tipperary — 51 B3
Thornton — 45 C1
Three Wells — 46 F3
Thurles / Durlas — 51 D1
Tibohine / Tigh Baoithán — 24 G2
Tiduff — 48 E3
Tikincor — 52 E4
Timahoe Co Kildare — 35 B3
Timahoe / Tigh Mochua
  Co Laois / Laois — 44 H2
Tim Aoleague / Tigh Molaige — 68 E2
Timolin — 45 B2
Tinahely / Tigh na hÉille — 46 E4
Tinmuck — 33 D3
Tinnakilla — 53 D4
Tipperary / Tiobraid Árann — 51 A3
Tirkane / Tír Chiana — 10 H1
Tirnaneill — 18 F3
Tirneevin — 42 E1
Toames / Tuaim — 59 D5
Tober Co Cavan — 16 G4
Tober Co Offaly — 34 E3
Toberbeg — 45 C2
Tobercurry / Tobar an Choire — 15 C5
Toberelatan — 32 F5
Tobermore / An Tobar Mór — 10 H2
Tobernadarry — 31 C1

Toberscanavan	15 D4
Toem / Tuaim	51 A2
Togher Co Cork	67 C1
Togher Co Louth	28 F3
Togher Co Meath	35 B2
Togher Co Offaly	34 H3
Togher Co Wicklow	45 D1
Togherbane	48 F4
Tomhaggard / Teach Moshagard	64 F3
Tonabrocky	31 C4
Tonlegee	22 G4
Tonyduff / An Tonnaigh Dhubh	27 A1
Toom / Tuaim	67 C1
Toomaghera	40 G2
Toomard / Tuaim Ard	32 G1
Toombegla	29 D2
Toombeola	29 D2
Toome / Droichead Thuama	11 A2
Toomyvara / Tuaim Uí Mheára	43 B4
Toor / An Tuar	43 A5
Tooraneena	61 D1
Tooraree	49 B2
Tooreen / Tuairín	60 G2
Tooreencahill	59 B1
Tooreendermot	49 C5
Toorgarriff	60 G2
Toormakeady / Tuar Mhic Éadaigh	22 G5
Toormore / An Tuar Mór	66 G3
Torque	34 F3
Towergare	62 H1
Trabolgan	61 A5
Tracton	68 H1
Tralee / Trá Lí	48 G5
Tramore / Trá Mór	62 H1
Trasternagh	32 F2
Trawlebane	67 A2
Trean	22 G5
Treantagh / Na Treantachta	2 G5
Trien / An Trian	24 G4
Trillick / Trileac	17 C1
Trim / Baile Átha Troim	35 C1
Trust	32 H3
Tuam / Tuaim	32 E1
Tuamgraney / Tuaim Gréine	42 G3
Tubber / An Tobar	42 E2
Tubbrid Co Kilkenny	44 F5
Tubbrid Co Tipperary	51 C5
Tulla / An Tulach Co Clare / An Clár	42 E3
Tulla Co Clare	41 D1
Tullagh	59 B5
Tullaghaboy	40 G4
Tullaghan / An Tulachán	16 E1
Tullagher / Tulachar	53 A3
Tullaghought	52 G4
Tullaherin	52 H2
Tullamore Co Kerry	48 H3
Tullamore / Tulach Mhór Co Offaly / Uíbh Fhailí	34 F4
Tullaree	48 E5
Tullaroan / Tulach Ruáin	52 F1
Tullassa	40 H4
Tullig Co Clare	48 F1
Tullig Co Kerry	48 H4
Tullig Co Kerry	58 F2
Tullow / An Tulch	45 C4
Tullyallen / Tulaigh Álainn	28 E4
Tullycanna	53 D5
Tully Cross	21 D5
Tullyhogue / Tulaigh Óg	10 H4
Tullylease	49 D5
Tullyroar Corner	18 H1
Tullyvin / Tulaigh Bhinn	18 E5
Tulrohaun / Tulach Shrutháin	24 E4
Tulsk / Tuilsce	25 A3
Tuosist / Tuath Ó Siosta	58 F5
Turlough Co Clare	40 H1
Turlough / Turlach Co Mayo / Maigh Eo	23 C2
Turloughmore / An Turlach Mór	32 E3
Turnaspidogy	59 B5
Turnpike Cross	60 G1
Turreen	25 C5
Twomileborris / Buiríos Léith	51 D1
Tylas	35 D1
Tynagh / Tíne	32 H5
Tynan / Tuíneán	18 G2
Tyrella	20 F3
Tyrrellspass / Bealach an Tirialaigh	34 G3

U

Unionhall / Breéantrá	67 C3
Upperchurch / An Teampall Uachtarach	43 B5
Upperlands / Áth an Phortáin	10 H1
Upton / Garraí Thancaird	68 F1
Urlaur / Urlár	24 F2
Urlingford / Áth na nUrlainn	44 E5

V

Valleymount / An Chrois	45 D1
Ventry / Ceann Trá	57 B1
Vicarstown / Baile an Bhoicáire	45 A1
Victoria Bridge / Droichead Victoria	9 C2
Villierstown / An Baile Nua	61 D2
Virginia / Achadh an Iuir	27 A3

W

Walshtown	61 A3
Walterstown	27 D5
Ward / An Barda	36 F2
Waringsford / Áth an Bhairínigh	19 D2
Waringstown / Baile an Bhairínigh	19 C1
Warrenpoint / An Pointe	19 C5
Watch House Cross Roads	35 D5
Watch House Village	45 D5
Waterfall / Tobar an Iarla	60 G5
Waterford / Port Láirge	52 H5
Watergrasshill / Cnocán na Biolraí	60 H3
Waterloo	60 F4
Waterville / An Coireánn	57 C5
Wellingtonbridge / Droichead Eoin	53 C5
Westport / Cathair na Mart	22 G3
Westport Quay	22 F3
Westtown	62 H2
Wexford / Loch Garman	54 E4
Wheelam Cross Roads	35 B5
White Gate Cross Roads	58 F1
White's Cross / Crois an Fhaoitigh	60 G4
Whiteabbey / An Mhainistir Fhionn	12 E3
Whitechurch / An Teampall Geal Co Cork / Corcaigh	60 G3
Whitechurch Co Waterford	61 D2
Whitechurch Co Wexford	53 A5
Whitecross / Corr Leacht	19 A3
Whitegate / An Geata Bán Co Clare / An Clár	42 H3
Whitegate / An Geata Bán Co Cork / Corcaigh	61 A5
Whitehall or Paulstown	53 A1
Whitehall / An Baile Nua Co Roscommon / Ros Comáin	25 C4
Whitehall Co Westmeath	26 G5
Whitehead / An Cionn Bán	12 F2
Whites Town	28 G1
Whitesides Corner / An Phrochlais	11 B2
Wicklow / Cill Mhantáin	46 H2
Wilkinstown / Baile Uilcín	27 C4
Willbrook	40 H3
Williamstown / Baile Liam Co Galway / Gaillimh	24 G4
Williamstown / Baile Liam Co Westmeath / An Iarmhí	33 C2
Windgap / Bearna na Gaoithe	52 G3
Wolfhill / Cnocán na Mactíre	44 H3
Woodburn / Sruth na Coille	12 E3
Woodenbridge	46 F4
Woodford / An Ghráin	42 H1
Woodgreen	11 C2
Woodstown	63 B3

Y

Yellow Furze	27 D4
Youghal / Eochaill Co Cork / Corcaigh	61 C4
Youghal Co Tipperary	42 H3